Biella

Novara ○

Vercelli ○

Turin
○

Alessandria
Asti ○   ○

Mombaruzzo
d'Asti

Fossano
○   ○
Dogliani

Cuneo
○

PIEDMONT

SOFT SOIL, BLACK GRAPES

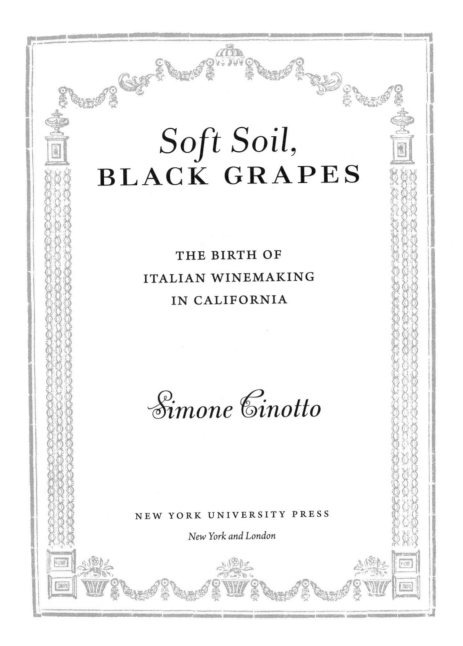

Soft Soil,
BLACK GRAPES

THE BIRTH OF
ITALIAN WINEMAKING
IN CALIFORNIA

Simone Cinotto

NEW YORK UNIVERSITY PRESS

New York and London

NEW YORK UNIVERSITY PRESS
New York and London
www.nyupress.org

Chapters 1–10 translated by Michelle Tarnopoloski.
Endpaper map of California wine counties from *A History of Wine in America*,
by Thomas Pinney, Berkeley, 2005

References to Internet Websites (URLs) were accurate at the time of writing.
Neither the author nor New York University Press is responsible for URLs that
may have expired or changed since the manuscript was prepared.

LIBRARY OF CONGRESS CATALOGING-IN-PUBLICATION DATA
Cinotto, Simone.
[Terra soffice uva nera. English]
Soft soil, black grapes : the birth of Italian winemaking in California / Simone Cinotto ; translated from the
Italian by Michelle Tarnopolski.
p. cm.
Includes bibliographical references and index.
ISBN 978-0-8147-1738-7 (cloth : acid-free paper)
ISBN 978-0-8147-1739-4 (ebook)
ISBN 978-0-8147-9031-1 (ebook)
1. Wine and wine making—California—History. 2. Wine and wine making—Social aspects—California—
History. 3. Viticulture—California—History. 4. Italians—California—History. 5. Italian Americans—
California—History. 6. Vintners—California—History. 7. Vintners—Italy—Piedmont—History. 8. Wine
and wine making—Italy—Piedmont—History. 9. California—Ethnic relations—History. 10. California—
Economic conditions. I. Title.
TP557.C515513 2012
641.2'2—dc23   2012016870

New York University Press books are printed on acid-free paper,
and their binding materials are chosen for strength and durability.
We strive to use environmentally responsible suppliers and materials
to the greatest extent possible in publishing our books.

Manufactured in the United States of America
10 9 8 7 6 5 4 3 2 1

Contents

Acknowledgments

The fact that this book was first written and published in Italian and then, thoroughly revised, in English, means it has kept me busy for quite a long time. But it also means that I have had the great fortune of enjoying twice the amount of help that one could normally expect.

Some of this support has been financial, and for this I am very thankful to the Regione Piemonte, which funded both of my research trips to California, assisted in organizing a book tour to San Francisco and the Bay Area for the presentation of the Italian book, and provided a translation grant. None of this would have been possible without the help of the Commissioner for Emigration and "Piemontesi nel Mondo" Fabrizio Bruno, who believed in the project from the very start and supported it enthusiastically to the end.

The idea for this book developed many years ago, when I was working on my first book on food and the social production of ethnicity in the Italian American community of New York City during the interwar years (now also being published in a new English edition). Donna Gabaccia encouraged me to pursue the idea and pointed me in the direction of some of the most important sources at UC Berkeley, the San Francisco Wine Institute, and elsewhere that I eventually used for this work. Maurizio Rosso was also instrumental in putting me to work by kindly sharing two full boxes of rare material he had collected for his own book on Piedmontese immigration to California. My mentor Maurizio Vaudagna generously offered his time to discuss the historical issues that cropped up in the research process. Carole Counihan was also incredibly supportive. She invited me to present my research at Millersville University, where I received intelligent feedback, and later was crucial in recommending my manuscript to NYU Press. Alberto Capatti, Allen Grieco, and Angelo Torre were insightful discussants at the presentation of the Italian book at the University of Turin. I have tried to incorporate their suggestions in this new version of the book. I am also very thankful to Gerald J. Meyer and Robert Oppedisano for their reading of and comments on the introduction.

In California, the past and present presidents of the Piemontesi nel Mondo Association of Northern California, Kathy Rogers and Andrew Canepa, were both very helpful. Kathy worked with the Italian Cultural Institute of San Francisco for my book presentation and put me in touch with Dianne Rossi Andrews, who kindly opened for me the doors of both the Italian Swiss Colony and the home of her ancestor Pietro Carlo Rossi in Asti, and E. & J. Gallo Winery's head winemaker, Marcello Monticelli. Andrew provided friendship and important source material on the Italian community of San Francisco. In San Francisco, Paola Sensi-Isolani was of great help, spending much of her valuable time with me while also preparing to open an exhibit at the Museo Italo-Americano. Another prominent scholar of the Italian experience in California, Laura Ruberto, was so gracious to invite me to talk about "Italian immigration to California and the Risorgimento" as part of the celebrations for the 150th anniversary of Italy's unification, again at the Italian Cultural Institute of San Francisco.

Up and down the state of California, I have been assisted by some of the finest library staff members a historian could possibly expect to meet—at the Viticulture and Enology section of the Shields Library at the University of California, Davis; the Bancroft Library at University of California, Berkeley; the San Francisco History Center at the San Francisco Public Library; the Sonoma County Wine Library in Healdsburg; and the Cal Poly Pomona Special Collections and University Archives (with a special thanks to curator Danette Cook Adamson).

Michelle Tarnopolsky is a competent, efficient, caring, and tireless translator. It has been a real pleasure to work with her, and I am very grateful for the extra effort she has put into this project. My editors at NYU Press, Eric Zimmer and Ciara McLaughlin, have been supportive and helpful throughout. They arranged for two rounds of comments from their anonymous readers—first on the Italian book, then on the English manuscript—so I had the distinctive pleasure of receiving critical comments from four different scholars. I want to thank them all for their useful remarks.

A small textual note: throughout the text, any uncredited translations of source material from Italian to English are my own.

Finally, I want to thank my family with all my heart for their patience regarding all the weekends, dinners, soccer games, and school parties I have had to miss out on and the many times they have had to talk to me via computer screen. I love you very much Valeria, Pier Ferdinando, and Cristina.

Introduction

Italians have played a major role in shaping the California wine industry, as is clear by the profusion of vowel-ending names among the
state's wineries. In fact, many of the Italian American wineries that
now dot the map of California's wine regions are third-generation
immigrant operations whose heritage goes back to men and women
who left Italy for the Golden State at the turn of the twentieth century. Italian grape growers and winemakers have not been alone in
making California wine a quintessentially immigrant industry: when
they first started arriving in the 1880s, they joined already established
German, French, and Scandinavian immigrant winemaking ventures.
In the century that spanned from the 1880s to the 1980s, however,
Italians almost single-handedly transformed the American wine market from a reserve of immigrant groups and urban Europhile elites
into the mass national market it remains today.

Soft Soil, Black Grapes explores why, of all the many ethnic and
immigrant groups in turn-of-the-twentieth-century California, Italians were the ones who came to dominate one of the state's most

important agricultural industries; why a small minority of recent immigrants (in 1900, at the peak of immigration, Italians in California numbered 14,495 out of a population of 1,485,053) had the vision and the resources to accomplish such a task. In so doing, it illuminates some of the dynamics that have shaped ethnic entrepreneurship in the United States and the relative success of different immigrant groups at different times in different economic sectors.

Soft Soil, Black Grapes argues that the single most defining factor in the experience of Italian immigrant entrepreneurs and workers in California winemaking was race—something scholars on ethnic entrepreneurship have traditionally understood as an invariable attribute that predetermines human relations and the social mobility of ethnic groups. *Soft Soil, Black Grapes*, on the other hand, takes race as a changing, modular, and heavily contextual process that influences, in different and often unpredictable ways, everything from the social status of ethnic entrepreneurs and workers to power relations within the ethnic group to the reception of the commodities produced by ethnic businesses in the marketplace at large.[1] From this perspective, Italians established such a strong presence in the California wine industry because they were able to make sense of the complicated ethnic mosaic in which they were immersed from the time of their arrival in the late nineteenth century. Within California's articulated ethno-racial structure—which included Asians, Latinos and Latinas, other European immigrants, and whites of Anglo-Saxon heritage—a group of Northern Italians managed to actively transform their middle-ground racial status into a crucial factor for the development of an ethnic niche. From the long-standing image of wine as a foreign beverage; to Anglo winemakers' discrimination against Italian workers; to the presence of a vast workforce of disenfranchised Asian and Mexican laborers; to Northern Italian immigrants' own prejudicial attitude toward immigrants from Southern Italy, race decisively shaped Italian winemaking in California.

Even immigrant entrepreneurs' choice to enter winemaking in the first place depended largely on racial dynamics. With the rise of the temperance movement at the turn of the twentieth century, race combined with morality and business to make wine an especially promising field for Italian immigrants in California. While entrepreneurs from other ethnic backgrounds were deterred by wine's increasing stigma as a foreign vice in the United States, Italian winemakers, who were latecomers to the trade, turned this ghettoization to their advantage. By the time Prohibition came along, their ethnic specialization was well established and they profited from the loophole allowing for the yearly domestic production of two hundred gallons of wine per household by turning into grape growers and purveyors of a product that often verged on the illegal. Accepting the risks and drawbacks of such an informal market proved rewarding: at the time of the repeal, a few Italian wineries emerged from Prohibition as undisputed market leaders.

The social and cultural capital that stemmed from the racial identity of these ethnic entrepreneurs allowed them to attract a nationwide Italian American consumer base and develop their commercial networks. Even more important, it helped them to secure the low-cost labor, expertise, and allegiance of the Italian labor migrants who tended their vineyards, crushed their grapes, and operated their wineries. In Italian wineries, ethnicity often prevailed over class: anti-Italian prejudices pushed immigrant workers into providing their labor to fellow ethnic winemakers for lower wages, and anti-Asian and anti-Mexican prejudices entitled Italian laborers in Italian wineries to special rights and benefits purely on the basis of their race. As race made the formation of a wine niche market a bargain for both Italian winemakers and workers, minimal labor conflict ensued. Within the Italian community, regionalism—yet another form of ethno-racial identification—was also important. For immigrant entrepreneurs from the single Italian region of Piedmont, regional solidarity functioned as social capital by giving them a competitive edge over entrepreneurs from other regions of Italy, and as cultural capital by helping to establish a narrative of the "Piedmontese as skilled wine-maker," which would become a commercial asset.

Soft Soil, Black Grapes deals with three companies in particular. These three wineries were founded and run by first- and second-generation Italian immigrants who eventually succeeded in expanding California winemaking into a mass-market operation and turning wine into a national beverage. Decades before middle-class Americans developed their taste for quality wine and California wines began competing on equal footing with the world's most prestigious wines, the Italian Swiss Colony, the Italian Vineyard Company, and the E. & J. Gallo Winery had already developed large-scale systems of production and nationwide marketing and distribution.

The Italian Swiss Colony winery of Asti in Sonoma County was established in 1881 as a grape-growing estate by a group of Italian immigrant businessmen from San Francisco. By 1900 it was producing more than two million gallons of wine from fourteen thousand tons of grapes. Its storing capacity amounted to more than three million gallons. By statute, the winery reserved jobs for Italian immigrants: fifty of them worked at the winery year-round, but at harvest time and other peak periods a full two hundred were employed. Years before the Panama Canal was opened in 1914, the Colony shipped thousands of gallons of wine each year from its warehouses in San Francisco to cities along the east coast of the United States, as well as to international markets like South America, China, and Japan. While the Colony's most important consumer bases were the large Italian communities of cities like New York, Chicago, and Boston, the winery also had licensed distributors in Denver, Kansas City, Cincinnati, St. Louis, Memphis, New Orleans, London, Liverpool, Germany, and Switzerland.[2] The Colony's director, an Italian-born former pharmacist named Pietro Carlo Rossi (1855–1911), was widely considered responsible for these successes and one of the brightest minds in the California wine industry. When he died suddenly in a horse accident in 1911, his children inherited the management of the winery. They ran it for three more decades, helping it survive Prohibition (1920–1933) and emerge as one of the three largest winemaking companies in the nation. In 1942 the Italian Swiss Colony was sold to National Distillers Corporation for a substantial sum.

Secondo Guasti (1859–1927) started his own winemaking business five hundred miles south of Asti, in Cucamonga, a former Mexican rancho east of Los Angeles in the San Bernardino Valley. In 1900, with the small amount of capital he had managed to collect from a few Italian immigrant investors, he founded the Italian Vineyard Company. Ten years later, Guasti's company could claim to possess the largest vineyards in the world, comprising five thousand acres of grapevines. The winery harvested more than twenty thousand tons of grapes each fall and, to contain all the wine it produced, its storage capacity was 3.5 million gallons. During the crushing season, 300 Japanese pickers accompanied the 250 mostly Italian permanent workers. While the Italian Swiss Colony's forte was dry wine with a high tannin content, the Italian Vineyard Company specialized in sweet white wines, which better suited the warm climate of Southern California. Like the Italian Swiss Colony up north, Guasti also boasted a vast national market for his wines and branches in New York, Chicago, and New Orleans. Under the Volstead Act, he decreed that "no vines will be removed until it is certain that the wine industry can no longer survive commercially because of Prohibition," and successfully converted the Italian Vineyard Company into a wine grape–growing and grape juice–making operation. He never lived to see the repeal of Prohibition, however, and the premature death of his son Secondo Jr. inaugurated a series of property transfers that by the end of the 1940s had transferred control of the Italian Vineyard Company from immigrant hands into those of financial corporations.[3]

Notwithstanding the dominant position they had achieved in the U.S. wine industry by the 1940s, the thirteen-year hiatus of Prohibition frustrated the efforts of the Italian Swiss Colony and the Italian Vineyard Company to break out of the secure but limited immigrant market and reach a truly interethnic mass market. The ultimate success these two companies achieved was the fact that major corporations bought them out. Right after the repeal of Prohibition in 1933, however, second-generation immigrants Ernest (1909–2007) and Julio Gallo (1910–1993) took on the dreams of Rossi and Guasti to create a national market for wine and be accepted as full-fledged American entrepreneurs. The winery they established in Modesto, in the Central Valley, with negligible capital and hardly any winemaking skills, would become the leading American wine company after World War II. The Gallos arguably contributed more to the creation of a mass wine market in postwar America than anyone else by selling branded, standardized, and inexpensive wines to consumer segments that had never been reached before, well beyond the largely ethnic market dominated by the Italian Swiss Colony and the Italian Vineyard Company. (Ironically, for many years the Gallos' vital source of profit was yet another "race market"—the African American drinkers of cheap fortified wines who lived in inner-city ghettoes—and their success could not be complete until the cultural revolution of the 1960s began to give wine full American citizenship.)[4] By the early 1980s, the two brothers had finally accomplished the task envisioned by the preceding generation of immigrant winemakers by turning California wine into a national beverage and, in the process, creating an empire. By 1985, the E. & J. Gallo Winery was selling 140 million gallons of wine, or a 26.1 percent share of the U.S. wine market, including imports (their closest competitor, Seagram, came in a distant second at 8.3 percent), and employing more than three thousand workers in Modesto alone. In the 1990s, the Gallos began responding to the increasingly discriminating demand of consumers by expanding their production of quality wines and acquiring thousands of acres of vineyards in the prestigious Sonoma Valley. They succeeded in this new direction as well, and without departing from their ethnic roots. Despite its dramatic growth—today it is the single largest exporter of California wine and one of the world's largest wineries—the E. & J. Gallo Winery has never gone public. The family-run winery remains in the hands of Ernest and Julio's many children, grandchildren, great-grandchildren, and in-laws.[5]

The immigrant status of Rossi, Guasti, and the Gallos forms a connecting thread between the stories of these three wineries. Their founders all set out from two small neighboring provinces in the Northern Italian region of Piedmont: Langhe and Monferrato. Rossi, Guasti, and the father of Ernest and Julio Gallo all came from rural towns in the area, a characteristically hilly land bordering with the Alps and France to the west and Liguria and the sea to the south. Rossi left his native Dogliani in 1881 as a young pharmacology graduate, perhaps to break away from his family, who owned some land and properties. In San Francisco he joined his uncle, who was one of only two pharmacists in the city at the time. Guasti grew up in a family of bakers in Mombaruzzo d'Asti. He was on the road to becoming a merchant when he decided to sail to Mexico, moving on to Arizona and finally arriving in Los Angeles in 1883. Joe Gallo was born into a family of butchers and tavern keepers in Fossano. In 1900, he immigrated to Venezuela and later to Pennsylvania, where relatives had preceded him, before heading to the West Coast after hearing of opportunities in the mining towns of Northern California. Many of the workers that Rossi, Guasti, and the Gallos would later employ in their wineries in California also came from the same areas of Piedmont.

The fact that the Italian hegemony in California winemaking was mostly born out of the agency of a few immigrant petty capitalists and a few hundred workers from a single small section of Northern Italy not only adds to the value of these stories but also helps us better understand the dynamics of ethnic entrepreneurship in the United States. Why did men like Rossi, Guasti, and the Gallos reach such a dominant position in California wine, to the point that they even managed to create the conditions for developing a national market for this product (a process only briefly interrupted by Prohibition) and eventually succeeded in transforming one of the country's most important agricultural sectors? Why did Italians in particular embark on such an undertaking and why were the most successful of these a handful of immigrants from a poor, mountainous backcountry of Piedmont?

PIEDMONT ON THE PACIFIC: POPULAR AND HISTORICAL MYTHS ABOUT ITALIAN WINEMAKING IN CALIFORNIA

Soft Soil, Black Grapes focuses on the history of a few specific ethnic businesses because it is only by moving away from general theories and toward the actual historical experience of immigration that the many different and interrelated variables at work in the production of an ethnic economic niche can be perceived. Analyzing the life stories of ethnic businessmen and the contexts in which they made their decisions helps to dispel the stereotypes that too often mar any explanation of the relative success of one ethnic group in a particular economic field. As Werner Sollors has noted, "It is not any a priori cultural difference that makes ethnicity. 'The Chinese laundryman does not learn his trade in China; there are no laundries in China.' . . . One can hardly explain the prevalence of Chinese American laundries by going back to Chinese history proper. It is always the specificity of power relations at a given historical moment and in a particular place that triggers off a strategy of pseudo-historical explanations that camouflage the inventive act itself."[6]

Chapter 1 shows how traditional explanations for the success of Rossi, Guasti, and the Gallos have indeed been laden with stereotypes in addition to being essentialist and determinist. Conventional wisdom in both historiography and popular culture has credited the achievements of Piedmontese winemakers to the striking similarities in landscape, ecology, and climate between California and Italy. Such geographical affinities allegedly functioned as the basis for the successful transplantation of Old World wine culture and expertise from Langhe and Monferrato to the west coast of the United States.

As chapter 2 demonstrates, however, the "striking similarity" between California and Italy was a cultural construct of nineteenth-century travel and commercial literature that sought to provide an Anglo-Protestant reading public with a California landscape (the sun, the sea, the hills, and then the vineyards, the olive groves, and the citrus fruit orchards) that resembled the geographical imagery of relaxation, pleasure, and fantasy that Northern Europeans had for centuries perceived in the Mediterranean, and Italy in particular.[7] In his account of his expedition to Northern California (1843–1844), John Charles Frémont was the first to depict the soon-to-be state as an "Italy on the Pacific."[8] By 1875, the San Francisco–born real estate developer Charles Victor Hall published *California: The Ideal Italy of the World: An Outline Mirror of the State for Health, Happiness, and*

Delightful Homes, codifying an imaginary spatial connection that anticipated many later writings equating the hills of Sonoma County to those of the Langhe.[9] Immigrants themselves absorbed and reinforced this connective discourse in their accounts of the American Far West, raising the issue of "striking similarity" when, for various reasons, they wanted to attract further immigration from their own *paesi* (hometowns) to California. In 1882, the Emigration Commissioner of Genoa wrote, "Although geographically distant, San Francisco is the destination of many emigrants from this province. Emigration agents have been presenting San Francisco and the surrounding territory as a duplicate of our province, and returnees seem to agree."[10]

Chapters 3 and 4 deconstruct this discourse and the agendas that shaped it to dispel the geographical determinism that obfuscates the historical explanation. Constrained as they were by their often-minimal starting capital, Italian immigrant grape growers ended up cultivating *whatever* land was available to them. Lacking money, the would-be winemakers typically purchased poor or marginal tracts of land that scarcely resembled the idyllic hillsides of their native Piedmont. Intensive immigrant labor is what first transformed those lands into "winescapes."[11] The other stereotype to be dispelled is that of the technical winemaking know-how that Piedmontese immigrants supposedly transplanted to their new homes in California. A reconstruction of the biographies of the most successful Italian winemakers— Rossi, Guasti, and the Gallos—reveals that none of these children of professionals and merchants had any serious winemaking experience before emigration, let alone the training and skills required to build a modern wine industry. The very limited role that traditional Piedmontese grape varieties played in the immigrant winemakers' world provides another clue of the inventive nature of Piedmontese winemaking in California. For example, Nebbiolo, perhaps the most

important varietal in Piedmont, was hardly ever planted in California; even the more common Barbera was only ever produced in limited quantities.

As was the case for the Chinese laundryman, purported traditional skills or Italian history per se cannot be credited with causing
a successful economic niche to emerge. The success stories of Rossi,
Guasti, and the Gallos show that ethnicity, when applied to business,
is best understood as a productive source of symbols, meanings, soli-
darities, and power, rather than as a resilient legacy in the face of the
homogenizing forces of the capitalist market and commodification.
The establishment and eventual success of a Piedmontese niche in
California winemaking was not predetermined by geography, environment, and traditions. Rather, it was the result of the agency, social
capital, and cultural invention used by these immigrants as they
negotiated their relations with the many others they encountered in
California.

WINE INTO BLOOD: RACE AND LABOR
IN THE EXPERIENCE OF ITALIAN
WINEMAKERS IN CALIFORNIA

Chapters 5 through 8 illustrate how, in the complicated ethnic scenario of the West Coast, race determined many of the circumstances
in which immigrant winemakers and wine workers operated. The
different racial structures and social circumstances that turn-of-the-
twentieth-century Italian immigrants met in the agricultural West
make for a perfect example of the contextuality of race in U.S. history, and of the different opportunities that such contextuality provided for ethnic groups in different times and places in the United
States. For their part, Northern and Southern Italian immigrants

had already been classified as two distinct races by Italian scientific racism, and they thought about themselves in this way upon their arrival. The immigrants' racialized self-identification was only reinforced by the different degrees of racist discrimination they had to suffer in different parts of the United States. In California before 1900, the mostly Northern Italian immigrants from Liguria, Tuscany, and Piedmont encountered other European immigrants who had been there for only a short time, as well as large minorities of Chinese, Mexicans, and Japanese who were categorized as non-European and nonwhite. As the Italian newcomers soon understood, racialization crisscrossed the social division of work. In post-1850 California, large industrial farms would begin to displace small family farms. California was admitted to the United States as a free state, which implied the recruitment of large numbers of proletarian wageworkers. Large-scale farmers preferred to hire migrants—predominantly Mexicans and Asians, but also Europeans, Canadians, and "Okies"—because their status as alien or transient workers made them more easily exploitable. Employers could also take advantage of ethnic and racial divisions to segment and control agricultural labor forces. But this scenario had no place in the republican agrarian ideal of the family farm as the foundation of economic security and individual freedom. At the same time that it came to represent the bulk of farm labor, agricultural wage work was stigmatized as undesirable, fit only for workers with no other options, and, because of the historical association between dependent work and slavery, racially degraded. As a result, whiteness became the main means of moving out of wage labor in the fields to skilled agricultural jobs or into independent farming or nonagricultural occupations, and social mobility and whiteness thus became interconnected.[12]

In New York, Boston, Philadelphia, and the other industrial cities of the East, where mostly Southern Italian immigrants from

Campania, Sicily, Calabria, and Basilicata settled, "nonwhite" minorities were smaller or nonexistent. African Americans were a relatively minor presence in the large cities of the North before World War I, which significantly "darkened" already racially suspect Southern Italians. In the East, the positions of Southern Italian immigrants at the lowest levels of the racial hierarchy also matched the menial jobs in construction work and the garment industry that were open to them. By contrast, in the economically and racially more diverse California, Northern Italian immigrants had comparatively better prospects to ascend to whiteness, which they understood as especially dependent on their ability to distance themselves from their darker Southern cousins as well as from Asians and Latinos. This explains the determination of the Northerners to appear in the eyes of Anglos as dynamic, hardworking, and law-abiding new Americans, unlike the irrational, hot-blooded, and insular Southerners.[13]

Further, unlike what happened in the East, the early Italian business leaders of California (mostly Ligurian merchants who had migrated from Peru to join the Gold Rush of 1848–1849 as miners' suppliers and investors) had participated from the very start in the construction of a white society in the territory the United States had taken from Mexico. Indeed, a relatively solid, mostly Northern Italian business and financial community had already been established by the time the great wave of Northern and Southern Italian immigrants hit California after 1900. This meant that recent immigrants could take advantage of an ethnic leadership that was more influential and dynamic than back east. Of special importance were the greater opportunities to work for other Italians in Italian businesses—in olive oil, pasta, and chocolate factories, fisheries, canneries, and dairies, as well as in fields, groves, and vineyards.[14] This condition resembled that often enjoyed in Eastern cities by Jewish immigrants—a group that, because of similarities in time of arrival, number, and place of residence in the United States, has frequently been compared to underperforming Italians to prove the existence of a direct correspondence between ethnicity and social mobility.[15]

Italian and in particular Piedmontese immigrant workers in California thus navigated a complex landscape of racially structured labor markets and regional economies. They constantly tested the boundaries of their racial identities within a social system that had largely preestablished different chances for upward mobility for different groups. Their social identity as Piedmontese was constantly being created and recreated in relation to some other social group. Being non–Southern Italian qualified them as workers familiar with viticulture and other specialized agricultural tasks, seen as relatively disciplined and culturally adaptable to American life. But this status was not enough for them to find occupations in the higher-paid tiers of the agricultural job market. The racial division of labor caused all Italians in California to be placed in what the historians David Roediger and James Barrett have called "inbetween jobs": unskilled, low-paid occupations in agriculture destined for immigrants from Southern and Eastern Europe whose racial identity was disputed.[16] In its 1911 survey on "The Wine-Making Industry of California," the Immigration Commission of the U.S. Congress differentiated between white, Japanese, Chinese, Mexican, and Italian winery workers. Italians and Japanese were among the lowest-paid workers in the trade.[17]

Northern Italian immigrants settled for work at Piedmontese wineries like the Italian Swiss Colony and the Italian Vineyard Company, where jobs were available at any level and fluency in English was unimportant. For these Italians, being non-Chinese, non-Japanese, and non-Mexican was a basic, if mutable, part of their personal identity and sense of self from the day they arrived in California. It was a crucial asset that ensured them minimal competition (at the Italian Swiss Colony nonwhite labor was explicitly banned) or landed them the most desirable jobs in the trade (at the Italian Vineyard Company, the seasonal, menial, and most demanding tasks like picking were performed by Asians and Mexicans). Italians had access to privileges because they were never at the very bottom of a racially determined social hierarchy, one sanctioned by legalized inequalities in the areas of immigration, naturalization, intermarriage, and the right to property. Being entitled to rights from which Asian immigrants were legally deprived, such as naturalization and landowning, and that were de facto denied to Mexicans by virtue of their colonized status, Italian migrant workers could envision a path of mobility to independent occupations as farmers and winemakers—a social condition so deeply entrenched with the notions of freedom and whiteness in the United States.[18]

But this was only one part of the racially sanctioned deal on which the development of a Piedmontese winemaking trade niche so necessarily relied. Their fellow Piedmontese employers, who were busy making themselves known as fierce supporters of free white labor and gaining credit as diasporic nationalist leaders, resorted vigorously to paternalism, nonmonetary benefits, and open discrimination against nonwhite workers in order to secure the loyal cooperation of Italian employees. Rossi and Guasti provided their Italian workers with respectable working-class housing, Italian schools, Italian churches, and other amenities in close-knit communities. They always took advantage of the problematic racial status of Italian workers by championing "free white labor" and marking the distance between Italian workers and nonwhite temporary laborers. The Japanese and Mexican pickers of the Italian Vineyard Company (much less so at the Italian Swiss Colony) worked in labor gangs organized and subcontracted to the Italian employer by Japanese and Mexican middlemen (padroni).[19] Italian workers were hired individually for year-round contracts, as free wageworkers who received nonmonetary benefits and the prospect to turn their labor into skilled wage work. In exchange, however, Rossi and Guasti asked their Northern Italian laborers to work long hours for low wages—as the Immigration Commission noticed—and to cease unionization and class conflict. Above all, for Piedmontese immigrant wine workers, not being Chinese, Japanese, or Mexican meant accepting this bargain, and, through it, letting their whiteness define everything from their jobs, wages, social status, and everyday life conditions to their dreams of upward mobility, sense of place, and view of the world.

As ethnic entrepreneurs and cultural mediators, the Rossis, Guastis, and Gallos also managed complex identities and walked a fine racial line in their relationships with counterparts as diverse as Anglo economic and political stakeholders and the Italian government, which saw them as prominent representatives of an Italian "colony" abroad and potential commercial partners.[20] They had to meet the everyday needs of self-identified Italian diasporic consumers and create new markets among other Americans. They played a complex ethnic card with Piedmontese and other Italian workers in order to both foster productivity and discourage unionization. At the same time, they needed to manage relations with Chinese, Japanese, and Mexican workers who served as a necessary transient and cheap labor force and as a threat to Italian workers.

Piedmontese immigrant winemakers acted to both profit from and resist the very real structure of race in California and the United States. They recalled their nationality in order to claim a heritage of high culture and good taste, rooted in an alleged ancient civilization of the grape. They used their *italianità* not only to motivate immigrant consumers and control immigrant workers, but to support further immigration of select "best elements" (Northern Italians) as an alternative to despised Asian and Mexican laborers. At the same time, being aware of the deep suspicion that middle-class Protestant

Americans had toward their tradition of winemaking and the extra lengths they had to go to be accepted in California's elite economic and political circles, they proclaimed their staunch Americanism as true believers of the gospel of capitalism, technological progress, and the racial hierarchies of U.S. society. Ultimately, Piedmontese winemakers in California were authors of their ethnicity: they carefully constructed an ethnic labor and consumer market by navigating racial margins, creating value by exploiting their transnational culture, and inventing, narrating, and profiting from cultural difference.

A DIFFERENT INFLECTION OF AMERICAN RACE: ITALIAN REGIONALISM

As chapter 9 details, race was also an important factor in determining the success of Piedmontese winemakers over other competing Italians. The histories of the Italian Swiss Colony, the Italian Vineyard Company, and the E. & J. Gallo Winery show how it was in late nineteenth-century California that Italian immigrant regionalism, or the affiliation with a single region of Italy, grew out of the local, village-centered identities that linked labor migrants to their native paesi, and established itself as an alternative to nationalism. Diasporic regionalism arose out of the concentration of different and competing groups of immigrants from several neighboring villages in Italy in particular occupational niches—a Californian development that was only strengthened by the racism internal to the Italian immigrant community. Piedmontese immigrants benefited from this new regional identity to establish and secure their hegemony over wine well into the twentieth century.

The Italian regions that sent most immigrants to California before 1900 had long been autonomous political entities. Piedmont was the leading region of the Kingdom of Sardinia, the state ruled by the House of Savoy that, through a sequence of wars, uprisings, and annexations known as the Italian Risorgimento, unified Italy in 1861. Liguria, the region from which most early Italian immigrants to California came, had been a republic for eight centuries when it was annexed to the Kingdom of Sardinia in 1815. The regions of Tuscany (especially the province of Lucca) and Sicily also sent many immigrants to California early on, and both had long been independent states. The former was a Grand Duchy from 1569 to 1859 and the latter was part of the Kingdom of the Two Sicilies until 1860. However, because of the very limited participation of the population at large in the public affairs of these regional states, the latter did not provide their migrants with any sense of affiliation. Mobile Italian workers of the preunification era felt an almost exclusive loyalty to their families and communities based in their native hometowns. Long after Italy had become a nation-state, Italian migrant workers continued to be village-minded and hold on to their local cultures.[21]

Regional identities coalesced around the control of economic niches and a common understanding of racial differences, not politics. In California—unlike elsewhere in the United States—Northern Italians from Piedmont, Liguria, and Tuscany were more numerous than were Southern Italians from areas like Naples, Calabria, and Sicily, and the racially defined differences between North and South were often invoked in the struggles among these different groups over the control of specific trades. Local identities expanded to a larger spatial scale of identification (the region) out of practices of economic and social competition with other immigrant Italians, which racist assumptions encouraged and bolstered. The violent struggles between Ligurians and Sicilians for control of the fishing industry in San Francisco, for example, fueled such racist prejudices. In other cases, however, the high concentration of certain Italian groups in certain occupations helped peacefully allocate the market along regional lines. Following conflicts over control of the produce market in San Francisco, Ligurians retained control of truck gardening and farming while Lucchesi specialized in peddling Ligurian produce in the city's markets. Many Lucchesi later became grocers and restaurateurs.[22]

The Piedmontese grip on winemaking emerged within the same relational system of group economic interests and racial prejudices. Their early takeover of the wine trade provided the Piedmontese with a dramatic competitive advantage over later migrants, and the case of the Italian Swiss Colony was pivotal in the process. The Colony was founded in 1881 by the Ligurian merchant and real estate developer Andrea Sbarboro (1839–1923) as a grape-growing cooperative venture uniting the wealthiest Ligurian businessmen of San Francisco. Sbarboro ostensibly included the term "Swiss" in the name of the company to expand the opportunity to join the new venture to the small San Francisco Italian-speaking community from the Ticino Canton in Switzerland, but the most significant effect of (and perhaps reason for) his choice was to characterize the new grape-growing operation as a *Northern* Italian–only operation.[23] The company was supposed to thrive on a spectacular rise in the price of grapes that proved short-lived; after a few years, the organization was downright floundering. This was when Rossi came into the picture, called to the rescue by a desperate Sbarboro, and saved the Colony by transforming it into a winemaking operation. In the following years, the Piedmontese directorship of the Colony attracted a chain migration of workers from a number of Piedmontese villages, some of whom later opened their own wineries around Sonoma County and other developing wine regions. These social networks first created a Piedmontese identity and then helped associate that identity with winemaking in both Northern and Southern California. The Piedmontese in turn transformed their dominant position into the cultural capital so often seen in the

"Piedmontese as skilled winemaker" narrative. (Ironically, the historiography of Italian immigration to California has subsequently accepted this narrative as the *explanation* rather than the result of the success of the Piedmontese in the California wine business.) Once the identity was established, the practices of a Piedmontese specialization in winemaking further connected winemakers, workers, distributors, and consumers within a thicker network of trade relationships that from the outside became an ethnic trademark.

TURNING THE STIGMA OF A FOREIGN DRINK INTO AN ECONOMIC OPPORTUNITY: TEMPERANCE, PROHIBITION, AND THE CREATION OF AN ITALIAN WINEMAKING NICHE

Even the determination of Rossi, Guasti, and the Gallos to enter the winemaking business in the first place was influenced by the complicated ethnic scenario they encountered on the West Coast. In fact, the making and selling of wine in late nineteenth- and early twentieth-century America was fashioned out of a crossroads between issues of race, culture, and business, which helps to explain why these Piedmont natives chose a trade for which they had no specific skills or hands-on experience.

Chapter 10 discusses how the stigma of foreignness that the temperance movement and its political supporters attached to the production, commerce, and consumption of wine—which culminated in the national Prohibition of 1920–1933—was a vital factor in the concentration of Piedmontese immigrants in the trade, not to mention, paradoxically, their ensuing success.

When Italian immigrants joined the wine industry of California in the late nineteenth century, wine had never been a drink of choice for more than a minority of Americans. Despite the fact that a market for wine existed in the United States and attempts had already been made to establish domestic viticulture from the eighteenth century onward, most Anglo-Saxon Protestant Americans considered wine an exotic beverage with roots in the Roman Catholic liturgy, Southern European traditions, and Mediterranean foodways. Wine's foreign image was reinforced by the temperance movement, which mounted during the nineteenth century and conjoined religious, social, and political initiatives. As the United States was transforming into an urban and industrial society, reformers targeted the consumption of wine and liquors as an evil force that jeopardized the morality and soundness of the family, the communities, and American democratic polity as a whole. In response, American-born entrepreneurs and investors increasingly shunned the wine trade as dangerous and inconvenient, leaving the field open to the near monopoly of immigrants. In California, even before the Italians had arrived, Northern European immigrants had already begun developing modern viticulture after having taken over from the earlier experiments of Spanish colonial Franciscan friars.[24]

Protestant and Republican America's century-long reform efforts against wine and other alcoholic beverages finally culminated in the early twentieth century by merging with the fear of a white (Anglo-Saxon) "race suicide" and the upsurge of nativist sentiments in the face of the massive influx of poor, prolific, and culturally diverse people from Southern and Eastern Europe. It was widely assumed that immigrant men were blowing their paychecks at saloons, devastating their families, failing as workers and citizens, and becoming easy prey to party machine bosses or, worse, radical agitators. Reform lobbying had already led roughly two-thirds of the United States to ban alcohol by the time the United States entered World War I. During the war, rural and Protestant America's battle for temperance became the final battle against anything that reeked of un-Americanism—modern urban culture, Catholicism, radicalism, and immigrants' alleged wartime disloyalty. The common association of wine and other alcoholic beverages with "alien forces" in American society, not incidentally concurrent with the racist Immigration Acts of 1921–1924 that excluded Italians and other Southern and Eastern European national groups, led to the National Prohibition Act of 1919.[25]

In a context in which competition was relatively low and waning, then, Rossi, Guasti, and the Gallos were encouraged to enter an idiosyncratic market like winemaking, even as incompetent latecomers, because of their status as immigrants. As new as they were to the trade, Rossi and Guasti were able to cater successfully to the overwhelmingly immigrant consumers of their wines on the East Coast because their names proved they had the cultural capital necessary to know the tastes and needs of other immigrant Italians. Indeed, they came from a place that had been known as the cradle of viticulture for centuries, with only the French to rival them in terms of winemaking traditions, skills, and producers. But what truly created opportunities for ethnic entrepreneurs like Rossi, Guasti, and the Gallos was the stigma attached to wine as a foreign alcoholic beverage as well as its wavering legal status. Not only could these Italians assume the extra risks involved in the trade, but they were *racialized* as being fit to operate in a largely informal economy.

The Eighteenth Amendment was passed in December 1917 as a wartime measure to ensure that grains were used for feeding GIs rather than destined for distilleries. This was easily read as patriotic for how hard it hit German Americans, the leading ethnic group in the brewing industry at the time. Prohibition was finally effected on January 17, 1920. By scaring away German Americans and other important ethnic competitors, Prohibition essentially helped Italians take over the wine industry—as shattered as it was by then—and consolidate a distinctive Italian niche in viticulture.[26] Because the act allowed the domestic production of wine for private consumption, Piedmontese winemakers turned into grape growers and shippers and relied on a wide commercial network of ethnic distributors to flood the markets of immigrant consumers in the Eastern cities. Much of the wine produced from the grapes they shipped eventually entered the illegal market. The high prices Italians in the East would pay for grapes that could be made into illegal commercial wine allowed Piedmontese growers not only to survive Prohibition, but also to gain even more shares of the market. By the time Prohibition was repealed in 1933, they had emerged as the top players in the wine business.

Italian immigrant winemakers' experience of Prohibition shows how the Italian taste and talent for winemaking was far from effortlessly transplanted to the ideal environment of California's "soft soil." On the contrary, it was largely a product of the social and economic conditions these immigrant entrepreneurs encountered on the Pacific Coast. The stories of Rossi, Guasti, the Gallos, and their winemaking companies, which span a hundred years and several historical turning points, allow us to ground theories of race and culture about the relative success of ethnic entrepreneurship and ethnic economies in the United States in the living experience of the immigrant actors themselves, both the entrepreneurs and the workers, as well as the settings in which they made their decisions. Compared to the more widely known stories of Southern Italian immigrants in the industrial East, the stories of Rossi, Guasti, and the Gallos illuminate the contextual power of race in determining the relative success of American ethnic and immigrant groups. These Piedmontese stories show how such power is also multidimensional, working in many interacting terrains—the labor market, the workplace, the marketplace, business and financial operations, and even the transnational narratives about the quality and value of goods and products.

CHAPTER ONE

The Success *of* Italian Winemakers *in* California *and the* "Pavesian Myth"

THE ITALIAN SWISS COLONY, THE ITALIAN VINEYARD COMPANY, AND THE E. & J. GALLO WINERY

March 12, 1881, provides a convenient and definitive start date for the history of the Piedmontese immigrant presence in the California wine industry. On that day, the Italian Swiss Colony was incorporated in San Francisco, with its premises to be established on the gently sloping hills of the Russian River Valley, eighty-five miles north of the city. The idea for the enterprise had been hatched among the Italian immigrant merchant elite of San Francisco as an ethnic utopia; a community-bred company that could both provi3de jobs to Italian immigrant workers with experience in viticulture and reward its ethnic financial backers with a decent return on their investment. The original promoter of the enterprise was Andrea Sbarboro, a merchant and banker who had immigrated to San Francisco from a village in western Liguria as a boy. Using a modest amount of capital provided by the circle of northern Italian businessmen with whom he mingled in the city, Sbarboro acquired fifteen thousand acres of land in Sonoma County, just south of Cloverdale. He then brought in a handful of northern Italian immigrant laborers and renamed the site Asti in honor of the Piedmontese town famous for its wines. The substantial and steady growth of grape prices on the San Francisco market during the 1870s had inspired Sbarboro to focus his enterprise on grape growing. However, not only did grape prices proceed to plummet during the following decade, but the company's first crops were a considerable disappointment. The only reason the Italian Swiss Colony even survived these early years was thanks to additional injections of money from the Italian financiers in San Francisco.

Andrea Sbarboro inspects Italian Swiss Colony's vineyards at Asti, ca. 1890. Courtesy Alfreda Cullinan/San Francisco Museum and Historical Society.

Pietro Carlo Rossi, ca. 1900. Courtesy Center for Migration Studies, Staten Island, New York.

The turning point for the Italian Swiss Colony's success was when Pietro Carlo Rossi, a native of Dogliani (in the Langhe) and a pharmacological graduate from the University of Turin, took over the reins in 1888. Rossi wisely decided to transform the company into a winery as a way to cope with the fluctuations of the grape market. Shortly thereafter, he began to experiment with innovative wine-making techniques and made the fateful decision to produce bulk wine and ship it to the vast urban immigrant markets in the Eastern United States. By the end of the century, the Italian Swiss Colony had become the largest winery in California in terms of vineyard acreage, production capacity, distribution network, and market reach. Asti had grown from a plot of land to the size of a small town, complete with Italian school and church. Rossi's colonial house and Sbarboro's neoclassical villa, which hosted parties for visiting politicians, diplomats, and royalty, symbolized the settlement's prosperity.[1]

Rossi's sons Robert and Edmund took over the company after their father's sudden death in 1911 and continued to employ prevalently

Piedmont-born immigrants as both laborers and winemakers. Some of these employees, like Edoardo Seghesio, went on to found their own independent wineries; others, like Joe Vercelli, pursued careers as highly skilled winemakers.[2] Prohibition was naturally a major shock when it came to the company's prospects for growth, inaugurating a more complicated period in its history. In 1920, a few months after total Prohibition came into effect, a four-way partnership was formed by the two Rossi brothers, the then-superintendent Enrico Prati, and Edoardo Seghesio, under the name Asti Grape Products (the Dogliani-born Seghesio, who was a relative of the Rossis and Prati's father-in-law, dropped out of the partnership just one year later). The company survived this period remarkably well by selling grapes, grape juice, and grape concentrate to its already-consolidated market for domestic wine production and use (permitted as an exception to the Eighteenth Amendment in the amount of two hundred gallons per family per year), and it resumed its old name of Italian Swiss Colony at the repeal of Prohibition in 1933. After relaunching the company as a leading U.S. winery following the repeal of Prohibition, Robert and Edmund Rossi ceded control to the National Distillers Corporation in 1942.[3] The company went back into family hands in 1953 when it was sold to another conglomerate, the United Vintners Company, and Pietro Carlo Rossi's grandson, Edmund A. Rossi Jr., took over as vice president and director of quality control.[4]

The Italian Vineyard Company would get its start nearly twenty years later and some six hundred miles further south on flat, sandy, barren land in the San Bernardino Valley, a hundred miles northeast of Los Angeles. Despite such different environmental and climatic conditions, the winery would come to have much in common with its Asti-based rival. In 1881, the same fateful year the Italian Swiss Colony was founded, future Italian Vineyard Company founder Secondo Guasti emigrated from his birthplace of Mombaruzzo d'Asti, leaving

Italy on a ship headed for Panama. In 1883, after brief and discouraging stays in San Francisco, Mexico, and Arizona, Guasti arrived in Los Angeles, where he found work as a cook in an Italian-owned hotel–restaurant. After marrying the owner's fifteen-year-old daughter, Louisa Amillo (1872–1937), he began working as a wine merchant.[5] In 1900, Guasti, like Sbarboro before him, used capital provided by predominantly Piedmontese immigrant investors to buy a vast plot of land split off from a former Mexican rancho in South Cucamonga, where tracks for the Southern Pacific Railroad were just being laid.[6] By the end of the decade, Guasti's grapevines had expanded so far as to garner the distinction of forming the "largest vineyard in the world." Like Asti in Sonoma County, Guasti's property had expanded to the size of a small town. Indeed, Guasti was so proud of his accomplishments that he renamed the township after himself.[7] It, too, became a company town assembled around the winery, a church, a

Secondo Guasti, ca. 1910. Collection of the author.

school, and the house of the founding father, where receptions were held for local dignitaries and visiting Europeans. Some of Guasti's Piedmontese employees likewise went on to open their own wineries. Giacomo and Giovanni Vai, natives of San Mauro Torinese, acquired the North Cucamonga Winery, where they made tonics, sacramental wine, and other products that managed to pass through the legal net of Prohibition. Giovanni De Matteis of Viale d'Asti, one of the Italian Vineyard Company's first shareholders, also ran the Italian American Vineyard of San Gabriel during the 1920s and 1930s.[8] Finally, most of the Italian Vineyard Company's early laborers were also Piedmontese immigrants whom Guasti had specifically called to Los Angeles. Unlike what happened at the Italian Swiss Colony, however, where Sbarboro made the strategic and ideological choice to employ a strictly "white" workforce, much of the seasonal field labor at the Italian Vineyard Company was performed by Japanese, and later Mexican, migrants.

Secondo Guasti Sr. died without witnessing the repeal of Prohibition that he had long hoped for, and management of the company passed to his son, Secondo Guasti Jr. Upon the latter's premature death in 1933, the Italian Vineyard Company entered a phase in which it repeatedly changed hands. In 1957 it came under the control of the Brookside Winery owned by Franco American Philo Biane and Piedmont native Joe Aime. The company was eventually absorbed by a series of large financial corporations in the wine and food sector, while the area of Cucamonga gradually declined as a region for extensive grape cultivation. Today, only a few relics remain of Guasti's winery and the once largest vineyards in the world.[9]

The E. & J. Gallo Winery, founded by the brothers Ernest and Julio Gallo, started right where Rossi's and Guasti's efforts had been forced to leave off—the hiatus of Prohibition. Reaping the fruits of these pioneering attempts to build a national wine market in the United States,

Ernest Gallo with collaborators, ca. 2005. Courtesy Associated Press.

the Gallo Winery went on to achieve extraordinary results. Today, the company is a winemaking colossus that employs more than five thousand people worldwide, owns more than fifteen thousand acres of vineyards across the state of California, and sells seventy-five million cases of wine per year in the United States and ninety other countries, for a total yearly revenue of $1.5 billion. The winery's roots can be traced back to 1900, when Giuseppe Gallo (1882–1933), one of seven children born into a family of butchers, horse traders, and tavern keepers, left the his native rural town of Fossano, Piedmont, for the United States. Giuseppe (who by then went by the name of Joe) eventually arrived in California after spending time in Venezuela and Philadelphia. He spent his early years in the United States working various pick-and-shovel jobs before entering the petty commerce of wine with his younger brother Michele (Mike) (1885–196?) and becoming a saloon keeper in various boomtowns on the California mining frontier. In 1908, Joe married Assunta (Susie) Bianco (1889–1933), the daughter of an immigrant farmer from Agliano d'Asti. With the substantial help of his young wife, Joe ran a number of different saloons and boardinghouses (informal hotels for single migrants) up and down Northern and Central California before Prohibition forced him out of the trade. Joe had just started his own grape-growing business when Ernest and Julio were born a year apart in the town of Jackson, at the foot of the Sierra Nevada, and he began training them as vineyard workers at a very young age.

Ernest and Julio's life was to be indelibly marked by their parents' dramatic death, which was ruled as a murder–suicide. In June 1933, Joe Gallo apparently fatally shot his wife before turning the gun on himself. Just weeks later, the two brothers founded their winery in Modesto. While the Eighteenth Amendment had just been repealed, as promised by newly elected President Franklin Delano Roosevelt, the market for wine had shrunk significantly since the pre-Prohibition era. The Gallos made it their mission to expand and dominate that market through the vertical organization of their company's departments, large-scale production, and mass marketing. The first of their products to become vastly popular were sweet, sparkling, and fortified wines whose main consumers were poor minorities in decaying inner cities. But substantial acquisitions of vineyards in California's Central Valley and the renowned wine regions of Sonoma and Napa; innovative quality research originally overseen by Julio; and aggressive marketing strategies masterminded by Ernest gradually transformed the Modesto-based winery into a brand that met the tastes of more discriminating consumers while still holding mass-market appeal. Over the years, the E. & J. Gallo Winery has become renowned for remaining in family hands despite its massive growth. Indeed, by the time Ernest Gallo died in 2007, the company's brands and divisions were being run by as many as sixteen different family members spanning three generations.[10]

Julio Gallo inspects a vineyard of the E. & J. Gallo Winery, 1992. Courtesy Corbis.

WHERE THEY CAME FROM:
PIEDMONT, ITALY

The successes of Piedmontese winemakers and their placement within California's racial and socioeconomic hierarchies must be understood within the historical context of Piedmontese migration to the United States and elsewhere. Despite hailing from the comparatively richer Northern section of the Italian peninsula, Rossi, Guasti, and the Gallos came from a place where *la miseria*—extreme poverty—was almost as prevalent as in the parts of Southern Italy that have been most often the subject of the histories of Italian immigration to the United States. In the rural surroundings from which they departed, migration was a common experience that touched the daily and emotional lives of those who left as well as those who stayed.

Piedmont, the northwestern part of Italy, derives its name from its location at the foot (*pied*) of the Alps, the chain of mountains that separates it from nearby France. The geography of the region is varied, with the mountains in the west sloping down toward the plain of the Po Valley in the east, and the rolling hills of Langhe and Monferrato in the south bordering on the coastal region of Liguria. Most of the recorded history of Piedmont coincides with the House of Savoy, which ruled over the land from 1046 until 1861, when King Victor Emmanuel II became the first King of Italy, thus unifying the country as an independent state. Since 1720, when the Treaty of The Hague handed Sardinia to the Kingdom of Savoy, the state became the Kingdom of Sardinia with the city of Turin as its capital. The political history of the Kingdom of Sardinia, and Piedmont therein, was especially influenced by its proximity to France. Even the dialects spoken in the region derive from French and are more similar to it than to Italian. In 1798, the Napoleonic invasion extended legal reform to Piedmont that provided for the end of the remnants of feudalism and the seizure of lands from the Church. In 1848, King Charles Albert introduced a Constitution (Statuto), inspired by the bourgeois revolutions occurring on the other side of the Alps, which would become the supreme law of the Kingdom of Italy after 1861. On the eve of Italian unification under the Savoy crown (a process in which the military role of the French was also crucial), Piedmont was one of the country's more developed areas. It boasted industrial districts in Biella and Turin (the Italian capital between 1861 and 1865, home to a population of 175,000), an advanced irrigation system that supported the capitalist agriculture of the Eastern plains, more than one-third of Italy's railroads, and rates of literacy that widely surpassed the rest of Italy.[11]

But the economic and social development of the region was far from continuous or homogeneous, and this was particularly true for the struggling Southern part of Piedmont where Rossi, Guasti, and the Gallos were born—Langhe and Monferrato. Today this section of Piedmont is one of the richest in all of Italy and is renowned for its food and wine. Langhe and Monferrato have become the destinations of choice for upscale international tourists interested in exciting local cuisine and sought-after wines—Barolo, Barbaresco, Nebbiolo, Grignolino, Barbera, Dolcetto, Freisa, Arneis, and Moscato. Until globalization, deindustrialization, and economic restructuring changed its social and human landscape, however, Southern Piedmont was long one of the poorest areas in Northern Italy. The mostly hilly provinces of Langhe and Monferrato lie halfway between Turin and Genoa and for centuries endured the dearth and excessive fragmentation of arable plots. Bypassed by industrialization, which did not reach them until after World War II, Langhe and Monferrato suffered from their marginal position in relation to nearby centers of economic activity.

During the eighteenth and early nineteenth centuries, Langhe and Monferrato provided large numbers of seasonal migrants to other parts of Piedmont and especially across the Alps in France. For some time each year, local peasants—both men and women—became construction workers, chimney sweeps, silk spinners, wet nurses, street performers, beggars, or rural laborers abroad. They used their income from migrant work to bolster their extremely fragile family economies.

By the mid-nineteenth century, the consolidation of an Italian market for wine, the early industrialization of winemaking, and the damaging effects of the phylloxera blight on competing French vineyards encouraged the intensive development of grape cultivation, consequently converting the local rural subsistence economy into market-oriented crop agriculture. For a while, the introduction of large-scale viticulture seemed to provide hope for the region. By the 1880s, however, many critical factors converged to transform traditional short-range seasonal migrations into a mass exodus to destinations both near and far. In the last quarter of the nineteenth century, the population of the area grew at an unprecedented rate. The high taxes levied by the new Italian state—to check its national debt and the tariff war it waged against France—worsened the effects of the agrarian crisis caused by the arrival on European markets of cheap grains from Russia and the United States. In Southern Piedmont, the crisis was made even more acute by the spread of the phylloxera epidemic on Italy's side of the Alps. Against the backdrop of these ongoing problems, the wide availability of jobs elsewhere and the transport revolution, which made even transoceanic travel cheaper and shorter, opened up unprecedented opportunities for mobile, rural Piedmont natives. Migration went from being a short-term economic resource that was needed to survive and stay on the land, to offering the chance to imagine a different way of life.[12] As a result, until 1900 Piedmont was ahead of nearly all other regions in Italy in terms of emigration rates. In the period 1876–1900, Piedmont ranked second only to the Veneto for its number of emigrants, with 709,076 of its men and women leaving for destinations abroad (13.5 percent of the total Italian emigrant population). Even after the turn of the century, when the sources of Italian emigration shifted to the Southern regions, Piedmontese mobility remained strong: 831,088 emigrants were registered in the period of 1901–1915, which accounted for 9.5 percent of all Italian emigrants.[13]

Migrants from Langhe and Monferrato followed the routes paved by earlier immigrants. The vast majority chose France, traditionally the most favored destination, or Argentina, where a contingent of Piedmontese contractors and businessmen had immigrated in the wake of the War of Independence (1810–1818). While in France many Piedmontese entered construction work, in Argentina they concentrated themselves in the rural areas around Santa Fe and Mendoza, seeking opportunities in independent farming.[14] Only one in ten turn-of-the-twentieth-century Piedmontese migrants chose the United States as their destination. Of those who did, some settled

in New York, where many found work in the restaurant business. A
sizable Piedmontese community survived on Manhattan's West Side
around 23rd Street through the 1920s.[15] Others moved on to the mining frontier between the Midwest and the West and found work in
soft coal, iron, copper, and gold mines in Southern Illinois, Nevada,
Colorado, Montana, Idaho, and California.[16]

Overall, an estimated ten thousand Piedmontese immigrants traveled to the Pacific Coast, with an unknown number eventually returning to Italy. The regional diaspora reached its peak before the opening
of the Panama Canal in 1914, when California remained a costly destination for European newcomers and only certain kinds of jobs and
migration projects offered benefits. In fact, many Piedmontese immigrants were penniless peasants who left Langhe and Monferrato with
the intention to work, save money, return home, and buy property.
Many of them ended up working in the wineries run by their fellow
Piedmont natives. Others, mostly men but also women, possessed
some skills and money and did not necessarily regard migration as
temporary. The martyr and icon of labor internationalism Bartolomeo
Vanzetti (1888–1927) was part of this massive human movement, having left his native Villafalletto in 1908 as a modest pastry maker seeking fortune in the United States. Similarly, Rossi, Guasti, and Gallo Sr.
departed their small hometowns as a trained pharmacist, a baker–merchant, and a butcher–tavern keeper, respectively, with a small amount
of capital in their pockets and the determination to "make America."

THE PAVESIAN MYTH: ITALIAN WINEMAKING
IN CALIFORNIA AND THE HISTORIANS

The deprivation that plagued late nineteenth-century Southern
Piedmont and the concurrent belief that human mobility offered

the best opportunity for escape helps to explain why such an optimistic narrative of the immigrant experience in California developed in both popular memory and historiography. Back in the rural towns where the entrepreneurial and labor "wine diaspora" originated, the outstanding achievements of Rossi, Guasti, the Gallos, and other "sons of Piedmont" fostered a popular mythology of California as a Piedmontese promised land, a view that easily overlooked class differences and all-too-common failures. Moreover, this celebratory migration narrative developed and thrived largely due to the fact that these immigrants succeeded in an area of human activity so deeply entrenched in Piedmontese native culture—that of winemaking and wine drinking.

This myth of a "Piedmont on the Pacific"—a triumphant public memory of Piedmontese immigration to California that incorporates all the verbal and nonverbal "texts" that have accumulated about that experience since the late nineteenth century, in California and transnationally—has gained further currency since the 1950s through its inclusion in the writing of Cesare Pavese (1908–1950). Pavese is arguably the most accomplished Piedmontese novelist and one of the most important Italian writers of the twentieth century. A pioneering translator and critic of modern American literature (despite never having actually visited the United States), Pavese did more to create a hegemonic literary image of Piedmont than did any other writer. The cafés, streets, and courtyards of Turin and the hilly landscape of his native rural Langhe during the war-torn 1940s are the vivid canvases on which Pavese deployed his personal, poetic dramas of love, despair, existential angst, and loneliness. For the protagonist of his last novel, *The Moon and the Bonfires*, published posthumously after his suicide in 1950, Pavese chose a migrant who has returned to the Langhe after World War II and undergoes the painful process of acknowledging the merciless work of time. His experience of migration and the hybridizing effect it has had on his identity have alienated him from his childhood friends. The estranged returnee, known only by his nickname "Eel," now measures his once familiar surroundings against another place that is bound in memory—his personal America: "From station to station [I] had reached California, and, seeing those long hills under the sun, had said: 'I'm at home.' Even America ended in the sea, and this time there was no sense in shipping out again, so I stayed there among the pine trees and the vineyards. 'Me, with a hoe in my hands,' I thought, 'How they'd laugh at home.' But you don't hoe in California. It's more like being a gardener with us."[17]

This passage ably condenses the image of nineteenth- and twentieth-century Piedmontese immigration to California as it is preserved in memory, narrated in letters and photographs, and written about in history books. According to this popular discourse, now over a century in the making, turn-of-the-twentieth-century California was just like the hills of Southern Piedmont, except that its bountiful soil hardly even required effort to extract the fruits of human labor. This legendary California provided a familiar landscape and climate, not to mention abundant career opportunities. Though not the worker's paradise described by the shipping-line agents who traversed the Italian countryside at the turn of the twentieth century ("How they'd laugh at home to see me with a hoe in my hands," remarks Eel), this Piedmontese California is the dreamed-of "Merica" that delivers what it has promised to those courageous enough to make the journey. "Everyone here seems to think that I've come back to buy myself a house," Eel continues. "They call me 'the American,' and show me their daughters. For a man who left without so much as a surname I ought to be pleased, and in fact I am."[18] As Pavese's character conveys, Piedmontese immigration to California is a success story, a narrative of continuity and transplantation to a familiar physical and cultural–economic environment whose central theme is found in the symbols of the hoe and the vineyards. This discourse, originated in popular memory and consolidated in its literary transposition, can be called the "Pavesian myth" of Piedmontese winemaking success in California.

The extent to which the Pavesian myth has influenced the historical interpretation and narration of the role of Piedmontese immigrants in California winemaking has been significant to say the least. Perhaps unsurprisingly, among the considerably diverse works published on both sides of the Atlantic documenting that history, Italian/Piedmontese local historians have written the most enthusiastic accounts. Maurizio Rosso's *Piemontesi nel Far West: Studi e testimonianze sull'emigrazione piemontese in California* (Piedmontese in the Far West: Studies and Testimonies on Piedmontese Immigration to California) is the most comprehensive and well-crafted of these quasi-scholarly contributions, which tend to be analytically naive, occasionally digressing into impressionism and the biographical celebration of a group of "illustrious men" and their impressive accomplishments.[19] The celebratory tone of such regional heritage–oriented histories is largely due to an uncritical reading of the primary sources available. In fact, many of these sources consist of documents that were either produced by the same wineries being studied—printed publicity material, pamphlets, autobiographies, and interviews—or published by circles of Italian American potentates to which the Piedmontese wine entrepreneurs belonged—biographical collections, almanacs on the Italian "colonies" of California, and official narratives by Italian consuls in San Francisco and Los Angeles. It should come as no surprise, then, when such sources concentrate on the "marvelous achievements and destinies" of the major winemakers and their companies, limiting themselves to a few, brief passages that disclose the power relations—in terms of class, gender, and race—implicit in their work.

The scholarship published in the United States, on the other hand, belongs to two major fields: the history of wine in the United States—mostly written by non–Italian American agricultural and wine historians—and the history of Italian immigration to California—mainly written by Italian American historians. While both groups of scholars have shown far less interest in the regional background of Piedmontese immigrant winemakers, often addressing them generically as "Italians," they have also taken the Pavesian myth for granted when dealing with the Italian Swiss Colony, the Italian Vineyard Company, and the E. & J. Gallo Winery, thus reinforcing the myth with an academic patina. The rich historiography of California wine has understandably focused on the technical and commercial aspects of winemaking, and wine historians have underscored the extensive practical knowledge and cultivation methods introduced by Italian immigrant winemakers, most of whom happened to be Piedmontese. Their insistence has been on the wide-ranging reverberation of an "Italian" legacy on California wine.[20] Immigration historians, for their part, have widely discussed winemaking as one of the industries that best characterized Italian immigration to California between the late nineteenth and early twentieth centuries. The overall experience of Italian immigrants in California was in fact substantially different from that of their far more populous counterparts in the urban enclaves of the East and the Midwest, whose history has been studied more extensively. California's peculiar history, with its early specialization in agriculture, its delayed industrialization, and its unique ethnic and racial composition (especially the large numbers of Asian and Mexican/Chicano minorities) influenced the conditions of its Italian immigrants to a significant extent. Contrary to what occurred in New York, Chicago, Boston, and Philadelphia, where Italians concentrated themselves in low-skilled construction and industrial jobs, many Italian Californians pursued the path of agriculture. In 1900, 32.1 percent of them had rural occupations, as opposed to 5.3 percent in

New York State, 5.5 percent in New Jersey, 2.4 percent in Pennsylvania, and 1.9 percent in Massachusetts.[21] They also arrived in California with more starting capital and a better education, they came from more economically developed regions of Italy, and they were more predisposed to permanent immigration. Not only did these immigrants therefore occupy a higher social position upon their arrival, but their interest in agriculture also allowed them to assimilate and climb the social ladder more quickly than their counterparts in the rest of the United States.[22]

A decisively optimistic vision of this collective experience was central to its historiography from the start, inaugurated as it was in the pioneering work on Italian immigration to California, Andrew Rolle's *The Immigrant Upraised: Italian Adventurers and Colonists in an Expanding America*, published in 1968. Though later revisited and rendered more complex, Rolle's sanguine perspective has never been radically contested by later generations of Italian American historians.[23] As for the specific case of Italian immigrant winemakers in California, the historian Sebastian Fichera has noted how such entrepreneurs enjoyed privileged access to credit thanks to the cooperative instincts and financial aggregation skills of the Northern Italian business community in San Francisco, which was already in place before the full-blown mass immigration of Italians to California in the early twentieth century. According to Fichera, the main reason the Italian community in San Francisco and its rural surroundings was so much more successful than its sister communities in Eastern U.S. cities was because its members were uniquely prepared to create social capital and develop autonomous financial institutions.[24] The immigration and food historian Donna Gabaccia has also emphasized the importance of a vast national ethnic market of fellow Italian Americans poised to consume the products of these new California winemakers.[25]

Despite making rare mention of the predominantly Piedmontese origins of these immigrant winemakers, and dealing with Rossi,

Guasti, and the Gallos under a national rather than regional rubric, two paradigms come up repeatedly in wine and immigration histories that perpetuate the Pavesian myth. According to the first, California's ecology, environment, and climate all greatly resembled those of the land that Italian immigrants had left behind. The supposedly striking resemblance between the hills around Oakland and those of his native Langhe is precisely what caused the protagonist of Cesare Pavese's *The Moon and the Bonfires* to exclaim, "I'm at home!" Therefore, a less traumatic transition can hardly be imagined for these immigrants than what they experienced moving from Piedmont to California. The second paradigm insists that the mostly Northern Italian immigrants arrived in California well-equipped with the skills required to cultivate grapevines and obtain wine of marketable quality, since they came from what was, and still is, a widely known Italian wine region. It was thus *natural* for them to find an occupational niche in grapes and wine in California, which in turn guaranteed them social and financial success.

The optimistic determinism of the Pavesian myth is a powerful discourse that has worked effectively, since its late nineteenth-century inception, as an *agent of history*. A century ago, it helped immigrant winemakers and padrones recruit laborers from their distant diasporic homes by luring them with the prospect of work and security in a familiar, if more fertile, land overseas. Up to this day, the myth has suggested a direct lineage, bound by blood as well as craft, between the wines of California and Europe; a narrative framed within the larger discourse about California as an American Mediterranean, which has been part of the national mystique of the American West and advertised as such to generations of U.S. consumers.[26] As a historical explanation, however, the determinist Pavesian narrative is extremely shallow, if not utterly misleading. First, it underestimates the importance of the dense networks of social relations both inside and outside the Piedmontese community that were crucial in helping immigrants develop their careers and life goals as wine entrepreneurs and laborers. It also precludes asking important questions about the complex connection between Piedmontese migration to California and the unique economic development of the state of California, as mentioned above. For example, what specific jobs were actually open to immigrant workers and middle-class immigrants from Piedmont? What roles did they perform in the local labor market? And what kinds of independent occupations were available to them as gateways to upward mobility?

Second, the determinist explanation of the Piedmontese success in California winemaking neglects to sufficiently consider the multiracial and multiethnic nature of Californian society at the turn of the twentieth century (see table 1). When Piedmontese immigrants began to arrive in large numbers during the late nineteenth century, California seemed like an open frontier between Asia, Europe, and Latin America. Piedmontese immigrants' own village-based diasporas intersected with many other migration flows from elsewhere in the Western Hemisphere and across the Pacific.[27] As the focus of numerous internal and international migrations, California was also the stage for much of the contemporary debate over how to build the American nation, who belonged and who did not, who was desirable and who was not, and what role each race should play in the division of labor required to develop the country.[28] The related perception of Northern and Southern Italians as irreconcilably different racial groups was especially potent in that environment. More than just the kind of fragmentation that can arise from Italian *campanilismo*, or civic pride, this unequivocal notion of racial difference was stoked by the widespread racism of early twentieth-century America.

In texts dealing with the experience of Piedmontese winemakers in California, there is an overall tendency to ignore the fact that

Table 1

NATIONAL ORIGIN OF IMMIGRANTS (FOREIGN BORN) IN CALIFORNIA, 1850–1920

	1850	1860	1870	1880	1890	1900	1910	1920
Chinese	660	34,935	48,790	74,548	71,066	40,262	36,248	28,812
English	3,050	12,227	19,202	24,657	35,457	35,746	48,667	58,572
French	1,546	8,462	8,063	9,550	11,855	12,256	17,390	20,387
Germans	2,926	21,646	29,699	42,532	61,472	72,449	76,305	67,180
Irish	2,452	33,147	54,421	62,962	63,138	44,476	52,475	45,308
Italians	228	2,805	4,660	7,537	15,495	22,777	63,601	88,502
Japanese	32	133	1,224	10,264	41,356	71,952		
Mexicans	6,454	9,150	8,978	8,648	7,164	8,068	33,444	86,610
Portuguese	109	1,459	2,495	4,705	9,859	12,068	22,427	24,517

Source: U.S. Bureau of Census, *7th, 8th, 9th, 10th, 11th, 12th, 13th, 14th Census of Population*, vol. 3, tab. 1b (Washington, DC, Government Printing Office, 1921), 85.

these immigrants and their children were forced to confront a delicate, controversial alchemy of race in Californian society, becoming themselves profoundly transformed when it came to thinking about their own identity and that of the many others with whom they came into contact. As will be seen, the strong concentration of Piedmont-born immigrants in the wine economy had much more to do with how notions of race were articulated in American politics and society than with the discursive images and ideas of continuity and cultural transplantation perpetuated by the Pavesian myth. The most convenient place from which to start rethinking the Piedmontese experience in California viticulture and winemaking, then, is the foundational tenet of that myth—the relationship between the immigrants and the land; between these Old World newcomers and both the imagined and the real geography of California.

CHAPTER TWO

Producing Winescapes
Immigrant Labor on California Land

The sense that individuals and groups have of a place, the meanings they attribute to what would otherwise be indeterminate space, are cultural formulations. Perception and human experience selectively define landscape and territory, which are in turn influenced by the ways specific places are represented—laid out in maps, described in novels and travel diaries, glorified by poets, reproduced in paintings, photographs, and films, or, as has occurred more recently, designated as historically relevant by state-run programs of heritage valorization and landscape preservation.[1] Indeed, the paradigmatic California-equals-Piedmont equation set out by Cesare Pavese and traditionally used to explain the success of Piedmontese winemakers in California, echoes a cultural formulation with its own precise history. Like any popular imagery, the Piedmontese version of the Californian myth was constructed by various texts over time, and as such may be historicized and deciphered.

The image of California as an American Mediterranean goes back to one of the state's founding fathers and the Republican Party's first candidate for president of the United States, John Charles Frémont. In 1845, Frémont crossed Mexican California, leading a line of men on horseback in which "four or five languages [could be] heard at once; . . . American, Spanish, and Indian dresses and equipment intermingled."[2] What began as an exploration of the springs of the Arkansas River turned into an occasion for inciting the patriotic feelings of the handful of Anglo Americans living in California at the time. These feelings would emerge violently the following year, in the Mexican–American War that led to the U.S. annexation of the entire Northern part of the land originally colonized by the Spaniards. The narrative that Frémont wrote about his experience, *Report of the Exploring Expedition to Oregon and North California* (1845), became an immediate best seller. In this book, as well as in his later *Geographical Memoir upon Upper California* (1848), Frémont extoled the climate, landscape, and natural products of the region by repeatedly comparing it to Italy, in turn transforming this resemblance into a metaphor for the possibility of developing a new and original regional culture. Frémont's analogy to the Mediterranean—a sun-drenched, healthy, and sensual South—swiftly embedded itself in the American imagination, thus stimulating the migration to California of thousands of middle-class Protestant Americans from the Midwest and the Northeast.[3]

While inhabitants of Piedmont's countryside, especially peasants, may have been ignorant of the identification between California and Italy being internalized by Americans at the turn of the twentieth century, they had various others means of geographic imagination at their disposal: letters and photographs mailed home by emigrants; descriptive tales from those who had returned; and a rich literature that was in the process of constructing an entire Italian fantasy about the American West, its people, and its nature. Emilio Salgari, the most important literary contributor to popular Italian exoticism, devoted a trilogy of novels to the American West: *Sulle frontiere del Far West* (On the Far West Frontier) (1908), *La scotennatrice* (The Female Scalp Hunter) (1909), and *Le selve ardenti* (The Burning Woods) (1910); as well as short stories like "Il re della prateria" (The King of the Prairie) (1896) and "Avventure fra i pellirosse" (Adventures Among the Redskins) (1900).[4] Such narratives translated places, landscapes, and exotic scenery into an intelligible geographic language for their wide intended audience. The sizeable consumption of adventure literature among the popular classes of Northern Italy at the time suggests that it significantly influenced the expectations of emigrants. Though seemingly centered on the struggles between Native Americans and pioneers, such literature projected compelling images of the American environment and the opportunities available to exploit it.

Asti, Sonoma County. Immigrants till the land before vines are transplanted, ca. 1890. The place where the Italian Swiss Colony was founded was originally covered with bush and used as sheep pasture. *Out West*, August 1902.

The idea of California as a sunny, rural Italy resting on the Pacific Ocean was certainly a constant in the many texts that sought to promote the immigration of Italian laborers to the state during the late nineteenth and early twentieth centuries. Especially after immigration legislation (the Chinese Exclusion Act of 1882) had drastically reduced the availability of Chinese labor, Californian farmers began looking at the growing influx of Italian peasants with great interest.[5] Winemakers like Andrea Sbarboro and Pietro Carlo Rossi of the Italian Swiss Colony played an especially prominent role in the campaign to support further immigration from the peninsula, and their efforts doubled once the opening of the Panama Canal (effectively completed in 1914) promised to lower the costs and times required to travel from Europe to California. Sbarboro, for his part, was stirred by more than just financial reasons, since he felt that his personal success story could inspire other immigrants and thus reinforce his role as a community leader. He also refused to hire Chinese and Japanese workers, whom he deemed inassimilable and prone to "orientalizing" California. According to Sbarboro, a mass migration of Italian peasants would therefore be the perfect antidote to the "yellow peril." The pragmatic Rossi, on the other hand, looked forward to expanding the company's reservoir of skilled, dependable, and inexpensive laborers (since most rural Italian immigrants would help limit the contractual power of the workforce and thus keep costs down), not to mention adding to the winery's consumer market. In 1903, Rossi participated in the International Congress of Agriculture held in Rome as both the president of the Italian Swiss Colony and an official California state delegate, in an effort to promote Italian immigration to California as soon as the Panama Canal opened. His arguments included the "model community" character of the Italian colony already in place, the richness of the natural resources, and, most of all, the extraordinary environmental affinity between the American state and Italy.[6]

The main Italian-language newspaper in San Francisco, *L'Italia*, edited by the nationalist Ettore Patrizi, similarly made frequent reference to the physical resemblance between California and the distant *patria* to stimulate the growing stream of Italian immigrants.[7]

The resemblance between the hills of the Sonoma and Napa Valleys and those of the Langhe or Chianti swiftly became an axiom adopted at face value by contemporary commentators. In *The Italian in America* (1905), Eliot Lord maintains that "perhaps more than any other state in the Union, California resembles Italy in climate and soil, and it is natural that the vineyard developments there should first have been pushed on a great scale by Italian labor."[8]

Some sixty years later, the paradigm would finally translate into the historiography of immigration to California, starting with Rolle's pioneering study, *The Immigrant Upraised*. Rolle opens the chapter titled "Italy in California: A Mediterranean America" by asserting that "all [the Italian immigrants] were invariably struck by the

The Russian River at Asti, 1900. *Out West*, August 1902.

similarities between California and ancient Tuscany or Campania. The terraced bluffs around Santa Barbara and headlands near Carmel reminded newcomers of the Riviera's Santa Margherita, San Remo, and Rapallo. Blue skies, olive trees, and craggy cliffs took immigrants back mentally to Posillipo. Even California's rainfall was much like Italy's—with the heaviest in the north. Scenery, and the mildness of the Golden State's seasons, proved a powerful attraction. In this 'Italy of America,' immigrants found that almost anything grown back home could be raised."[9]

Yet Rolle's geographical vignette does no justice to how profoundly Piedmontese immigrant winemakers actually transformed the land in California. The impact of immigrant work on the American earth

Asti, ca. 1900: immigrants prepare the land for vineyards. Viticulture at Asti was labor-intensive. *Out West*, August 1902.

and landscape is in fact a neglected dimension of the history of Italian migration to the United States.[10] Turn-of-the-twentieth-century Italian immigrants dug out train tracks, built roads, bridges, and dams, and excavated canals, sewage systems, and subway tunnels. Biella-born stonemasons in West Virginia and Vermont even hacked away at entire mountains.[11] Other immigrants leveled, tilled, and plowed vast tracts of land from coast to coast, intensely changing the physiognomy of rural America. In California, as Rolle himself suggests, not only did they introduce new grape varieties but also an amazing number of other crops—broccoli, artichokes, eggplants, and many other vegetables—thus profoundly changing the biological heritage of the region.

The early histories of Piedmontese wineries in California show just how much of an impact immigrant work had on the land. In 1899, Italian Agriculture Minister Guido Rossati completed a four-month trip across the United States to study the American wine industry. When he arrived at the Italian Swiss Colony's community of Asti, Rossati remarked on how much the land resembled the wine regions of Italy: "It is an undulating basin on the banks of the Russian River, protected from wind and bad weather by an elevated mountain range. Grapevines, olive trees, orange and other fruit trees thrive in its volcanic earth, just like in Italy's most favored regions, which it resembles in sweetness of climate and beauty of landscape."[12] Yet little was natural about the landscape that struck Rossati. For one thing, the grapevines, olive trees, and orange trees had been planted just a few years earlier. More important, as Sbarboro detailed in his autobiography, immigrants had worked long and hard to transform this area into a suitable site for grapevine cultivation. The site had actually been extensively researched and chosen more for its low cost than for the characteristics of the soil. In fact, in 1881 Sbarboro had acquired 1,500 acres of the Truitt Ranch for $25,000 (including $10,000 in cash) precisely because the area had been a bushy, barren piece of land used for sheep grazing. The ground from which his winery would rise had to be completely deforested. It was covered with so many dried trees and shrubs that Sbarboro even made a profit by charring them and selling them as charcoal.[13] The only acceptably fertile soil on the property was the relatively small part located right next to river. Sbarboro commanded that entire freight cars of manure to be brought in to Asti from San Francisco to fertilize the rest.[14]

The site in Sonoma where the Italian Swiss Colony first struggled and then thrived was an artificial landscape that did not naturally reflect the Italian landscape. The "model community" of Asti with its stretch of "characteristically Italian" tracts of land had been built on marginal earth that had been completely readapted by the work of immigrants. Even an advertising pamphlet published once the Italian Swiss Colony had become an established winery recalled that "That landscape of vines and villas, picturesque colonists' quarters, and rose covered wineries that has replaced the scrub oak of once uninviting foothills is, today, the great inspiration of the wine industry of California."[15]

During the company's early years, the immigrants' work entailed more than just making Asti's landscape "Italian." The winery was also confronted with a series of unexpected natural events. In the first year, the owners had some one hundred thousand seedlings planted only to see them destroyed by a flock of sheep. The following year saw locusts wreak havoc on the crop. By the time the first grape harvest came around, the vineyards produced pitifully few grapes. Later, the Russian River overflowed and caused even more serious damage. To top it all off, the looming threat of phylloxera, which struck nearby Napa Valley in those years, was a constant source of worry. Without the perpetual work to repair the land and the repeated loans by Italian American financiers in San Francisco, the Italian Swiss Colony would never have survived this initial phase. Contrary to what

Just planted vines of the Italian Vineyard Company in Guasti, early twentieth century. The effect of the relentless wind on the vines planted amid the "Cucamonga Desert" is noticeable. To protect the plants, laborers cut the prairie grass with a big steel scythe that worked a few inches under the ground, and let it dry between the vines. That, of course, was additional, exhausting work. Courtesy Cal Poly Pomona University Library Special Collections.

the Pavesian "Piedmont in America" myth leads us to believe, the history of the Italian Swiss Colony suggests there was no preestablished environmental condition to make the Piedmontese feel "at home" in California. Neither could the cultivation of grapevines be transplanted without cost. On the contrary, this involved high-intensity work to shape and alter the land.

The founding of the Italian Vineyard Company provides another example of how low-cost immigrant labor was the true value added that helped launch Piedmontese wineries in California by transforming marginal, inferior soil—not coincidentally ignored by farmers of other nationalities—into productive earth. In the summer of 1900, when Secondo Guasti, at the time the owner of a modest winery in Los Angeles, started assessing the area of Cucamonga for purchase so he could start cultivating grapevines, no potential financier would give him the time of day. A man who owned a few small vineyards in a neighboring area said to him, "Oh, pshaw! Give your money to charity if you're bound to get rid of it, and spend the time throwing horseshoes. Just one fine old sandstorm out yonder will bury your labors forever."[16] It really did require a stretch of the imagination to think such land could be used for a vineyard. The area known as the Cucamonga Desert was a vast, steppe-like rectangle beaten by the wind, completely uncultivated and uninhabited, located at the base of craggy hills with flowering orange groves stretching in every other direction around it. The layer of sand that covered its entire surface made it ill suited to the abundant irrigation needed in an area that received very little precipitation. In fact, there was so much sand that it completely covered the tracks of the nearby Southern Pacific Railroad when the wind lifted it up. To remedy the problem, the stretch of railway in this area was relaid by lifting the tracks onto a bed of stone.

Nevertheless, Guasti discovered that fertile soil lay not far beneath the sand, and he convinced himself that such dirt would not need to be irrigated. The grapevine roots could penetrate the soft sandy layer, which in turn could insulate the soil and keep it humid. Nevertheless, Guasti and the financial backers he finally found within the immigrant community took a considerable risk when they embarked on preparing this ground. Once again, the immigrant laborers charged with clearing the area faced the additional problem of having to transform inferior earth into something cultivable, in turn braving blinding sand storms and the attack of an army of rodents that had to be totally cordoned off from the vineyards.[17]

Also in this case, the story of California as an American Piedmont was so hegemonic that, despite all evidence and all the intense

Picking time in Guasti, ca. 1907. Looking north, in the background is Cucamonga Peak. The crates with grapes are going to be loaded onto the cars of the narrow-gauge train and shipped to the winery. Placing the rails was extremely hard work, requiring four men for each section of rails. Courtesy Cal Poly Pomona University Library Special Collections.

landscaping, it even penetrated the imagination of the protagonists themselves, and for decades to come. In 1977, David Correggia, who was born and raised in Guasti by immigrant parents from Asti in Italy, thought that his hometown "was named after Asti, Italy, because it reminded [immigrants] so much of their area. And I feel that this is probably why they came to this particular little community."[18]

The lack of any direct correlation between the natural configuration of California's land, the winemaking knowledge of Piedmontese immigrants, and the possibility of developing successful wineries is further suggested by the story of Giuseppe/Joe Gallo. Joe had been one of those Piedmontese immigrants who initially came to California as part of a second migration after staying elsewhere in the

United States, attracted more by the image of gold mines and the associated economy than some bucolic ideal.[19] It was only when the prospects of getting rich quick on the mining frontier proved to be an illusion and the idea of staying in California took definitive shape that young, unaccompanied male immigrants like him decided to embrace agriculture as a second choice.[20] For Joe, farming was actually a third choice: he had quit his work as a miner as soon as he could to become a saloon keeper. But when Prohibition took effect, his job in the saloon business vanished and he was forced to look for a new career with better prospects. Only at that point did he venture into viticulture. He thus set about cultivating and shipping grapes to urban markets full of consumers wanting to make wine at home.

In so doing, however, Joe encountered overwhelming difficulties. In their autobiography, his sons Ernest and Julio refer repeatedly to the poor quality of the land their father bought in his enterprise as a grape grower. Not only was his first piece in Antioch completely infiltrated by clay from the nearby river but, according to his sons, Joe chose the wrong kinds of grapes to cultivate. He preferred Zinfandel and Alicante Bouschet for their thick skins because this made them suitable for long-distance shipping, but they refused to grow in such barren land. Young Ernest and Julio were thus required to work long hours every day after school, on the orders of their authoritarian father, uselessly trying to obtain a crop from clearly infertile soil.

While Joe's next purchase in Escalon, in the Central Valley of California, was somewhat better, the land still required the zero-cost labor provided by his wife and sons for him to have any success with it. Further, grape-growing had now become little more than a side dish to Joe's new core business of producing illegal liquor. Yet this bootlegging venture would not last long either. Federal agents soon arrived at the scene of the crime, promptly taking a hatchet to the barrels, tanks, and tools for the distillation, and arresting Gallo the elder. Only later, after he began shipping the grapes themselves to Chicago, would Joe finally secure the capital he needed to buy better land on the edge of the city of Modesto.[21] On the downside, each new purchase once again required substantial, almost desperate, injections of work to turn a profit. As Ernest recalls:

> My father bought 160 acres across the street from what was now 70 acres on the Maze Road, from Ella Maze. And that 160 acres was bare, rough land. He paid $200 an acre for it. We wanted to plant it into a vineyard. So he rented a caterpillar tractor and a Le Tourneau scraper on a daily basis. The number of hours that a day consisted of was not specified in the agreement, so I took the equipment from eight at night and drove it until eight in the morning, and my brother would take it at eight in the morning and run it until eight at night. So we ran it around the clock, and did the land leveling in very short order and planted the grapes.[22]

An extreme culture of work thus became the trademark of the Gallos and especially the mystique that surrounded Ernest, who took a six-month leave of absence in 1936 due to exhaustion from overworking (a fate to which Julio would also succumb in 1941).[23] Such extraordinary effort glaringly contradicts the Pavesian image, according to which "you don't hoe in California. It's more like being a gardener."[24] Yet their struggles pale in comparison to the dramatic fate of their father, who killed his wife, Susie, in 1933 and then turned the revolver on himself, possibly driven by financial hardship. This shocking and violent end to Joe's story throws an entirely different light on the risk factors and the probability of failure tied to the winemaking business of so many Piedmontese immigrants in the United States during the late nineteenth and early twentieth centuries.

CHAPTER THREE

The Culture *and* Economy *of* Wine
in Italy *and* California

THE WINE CULTURE AND ECONOMY IN
NINETEENTH-CENTURY PIEDMONT

The tragic experience of Joe Gallo clearly challenges the notion that Piedmontese winemakers succeeded in California because of a wine culture they brought with them from the Old World. The idea of a painless transplantation of former knowledge and skills undervalues in fact the various ways Piedmont-born immigrants distinguished themselves in the world of California winemaking, a trade with origins dating back to the colonial Spanish period.

By the time the Piedmontese exodus to California began in the late nineteenth century, Piedmont vied with Tuscany for the title of most illustrious Italian wine region. These were the only two Italian regions with both significant portions of land devoted to the specialized, market-oriented cultivation of grapevines and a wine industry that could be considered modern. In the Piedmontese countryside, grape growing, winemaking, and wine drinking were also recognized as centuries-old traditional practices that were deeply rooted in the identity and culture of its people. But the development of the wine industry was recent, and rural winemaking traditions had little to do with disseminating updated enological knowledge and practices.[1]

Throughout Mediterranean Europe, grapes have been grown to make wine since time immemorial. There is even evidence that quality wines were produced in Piedmont as early as the late Renaissance period. Yet nothing that could be considered a large-scale winemaking industry existed anywhere, not even in France, before the eighteenth century. Until then, wine (to be distinguished from the more affordable beverage of pressed grapes and water consumed by most Southern European peasants) was a product enjoyed by very few people, except during rural cycle and religious festivals. Wine's economic value was thus very limited. Moreover, its high perishability made it difficult to sell beyond a local market, thereby further inhibiting any development of a wine industry. Even the concept of the vineyard was vague. Grapevines were cultivated alongside other crops, were generally allowed to grow to any height, and were supported by pergolas or trees.

When the grapes matured at the end of the summer, grape bunches would be harvested and brought to a cellar, where a group of men—never women—would stomp on them inside large vats. For white wine, the crushed grapes would be transferred immediately to a hand press to extract the juice, thus initiating the first phase of fermentation. To produce red wine, the skins and pulp were fermented together with the juice, thereby bestowing it with the color, tannins, and other chemicals required for its maturation. The resulting must would be separated from the residue and placed in barrels for further maturation and preservation. This last phase distinguishes traditional winemaking from its modern version since a number of variables, due to ignorance of chemical processes and lack of suitable equipment and space, put the fruits of the harvest most at risk. This was when dirty barrels or lack of filtering could cause the wine to take on the taste of the dead yeast from the sedimentation. The wine could also turn acidic, which is what would occur immediately upon contact with oxygen if the wine was not properly insulated. Summer heat was still another ruthless enemy. The commercial production of wine therefore remained a fragile, risky, and inevitably underdeveloped enterprise until well into the nineteenth century.[2]

The Piedmontese hills of Langhe and Monferrato were not extensively cultivated with vineyards until the 1860s, when grapevines began replacing the mixed crops typical of subsistence agriculture. In some areas, grapes even came to supplant all other crops, leading to the creation of a wine region. Various concomitant factors led to this transformation: the growth of an urban population thirsty for wine; the improvement of communication networks that permitted distribution over longer distances; the political unification of the Italian peninsula as an integrated market, where previously duties and tariffs imposed by single states had been in force; and, finally, the epidemic of phylloxera that struck French grapevines first. This last factor caused a spike in the price of grapes on the European market, thus driving Langhe and Monferrato farmers (along with those in Puglia, Sicily, and Tuscany) toward an economy based solely on grape growing.

Until then, grapes had just been a secondary crop grown primarily for personal use or a small local market. Now, suddenly, the rural economy depended on grapes' position in the market and the related fluctuations in their supply, demand, and price.[3] According to Francesco Meardi, who drafted the report on Piedmont for the Italian Parliament Commission on the current state of the Italian countryside and the living conditions of the peasant classes (better known as *Inchiesta Jacini*, 1878–1886), this overnight development concealed serious inefficiencies, even downright errors. Most Pied-montese landowners were habitually absent members of the nobility and the urban upper middle class who did little more than manage the transformation of their holdings distractedly and from a distance. The high profits being garnered by grapes encouraged farmers to buy every plot of land available, especially those belonging to ecclesiasti-cal bodies, which thus gave rise to heavy speculation and excessive fragmentation of funds.[4]

This early boom lasted only about two decades before the spread of phylloxera beyond the Alps, the resumption of French viticulture, and the tariff war between France and Italy brought it to an abrupt end in the late 1880s.[5] Nevertheless, at this time—also marked by the rapid growth of transatlantic emigration from the region—wine had already become a thriving sector of Piedmont's economy, a develop-ment sustained by long-lasting circumstances.

The first factor was the establishment of Piedmont's international prestige for its particular vineyard areas and its high-quality grapes. Nebbiolo, for example, was the main grape used to produce high-grade wines like Barolo and Barbaresco in the area of Alba. Parts of the Cuneo province and the areas around Alexandria and Casale Monferrato formed a wine district that came to be known interna-tionally for its production of distinctive wines like Barbera, Dolcetto, and Freisa. The area of Asti was also recognized for its nascent indus-try of spumante, a sweet sparkling white wine produced with grapes grown by the Moscato family.[6]

Further factors to support wine's emergence as a vital trade in Piedmont's local economy were the improvement of enological knowledge, the birth of the professional expert, and the creation of specialized institutes like the School of Viticulture and Enology in Alba (1881). Yet this advanced, professional knowledge was passed down only to a tight circle of educated and well-to-do individuals, associates, or representatives of the large wineries and the budding winemaking industry. Farmers, most of whom owned small plots of land that were inadequate for participating in market-oriented agriculture, continued to be excluded from this kind of formal information and therefore relied mostly on the traditional expertise handed down from their forefathers. The specialized literature of the new elite of formally trained enology experts never missed an occasion to emphasize the deficiencies and ignorance of that popular tradition. "Most peasants harvested too early; they crushed grapes with dirty feet in unclean vats; and they fermented their grapes too long, for their aim was to obtain alcohol and color in preference to savor and finesse," reported one trade magazine.[7] This orally transmitted and trial-and-error expertise was the same "winemaking tradition" that most Piedmontese immigrants brought with them to California. Joe Vercelli, a winemaker at the Italian Swiss Colony for nearly forty years, recalled that in the early twentieth century his mother had made wine in the basement of her house in San Francisco's North Beach with just the "equipment" of a bathtub, where Joe and his brother would press the grapes, a bag of whole cane sugar, and some recycled casks. That wine would eventually end up on the market in Little Italy.[8]

The third long-term consequence of the wine boom in 1870s and 1880s Piedmont, besides the mounting international prestige of Piedmontese wines and the improvement of local winemaking knowledge, was the emergence of a large-scale capitalist winemaking industry, complete with factories, machinery, and equipment for mass production, which absorbed the wine production of the countryside. The burgeoning industry also involved a new class of merchant intermediaries who acted as the true direct interlocutors of both the large wineries and the small independent wine producers.[9] These middlemen were the ones who bought most of the grapes and wine during the maturation phase from the original producers. With the advent of industrial winemaking, the production of anything more than a paltry amount of wine slipped from the hands of those living on the land to a small number of capitalists and merchants located in towns and cities. From a social point of view, this caused severe friction between rural producers and urban intermediaries. Small grape growers and wine producers paid a high price for their entrenched, reciprocal distrust and reluctance to cooperate, putting them at the mercy of cosmopolitan merchants who exploited their weak position on the market and imposed predatory conditions. During market depressions, such circumstances could become downright unsustainable.[10] It is therefore likely that rural Piedmontese immigrants would have arrived in California with a deep-rooted suspicion of intermediaries, along with their traditional respect for the social value of landowning and a work ethic based on postponing material gratification and limiting expenditures.

Interestingly, none of the key figures in the early development of the Italian Swiss Colony, the Italian Vineyard Company, or the Gallo Winery was directly involved in wine production before they left for California, either as growers or as vineyard owners. Seeing as technical winemaking knowledge did not spread sideways throughout the rural society of Piedmont, contrary to what impressionistic images have conveyed, these immigrants therefore had little to no specific skills in the field. What they did share—and what helped their future work in California—was their membership in merchant or professional middle classes located in small- or medium-sized urban centers within the Piedmont wine region. While their families had not yet produced wine, nor had they even been directly in the business of selling it, they had been close enough to have firsthand knowledge, albeit external, of the strategies, capacities, and risks involved in this kind of work.

Pietro Carlo Rossi, one of the leading authorities in the early California wine industry, had no winemaking experience before he emigrated. In 1875, at just twenty years of age, he graduated magna cum laude from the pharmacy department at the University of Turin, a future in pharmacy firmly on his horizon. Then, in 1881, squabbles with his family (one of the most affluent in the small town of Dogliani) spurred Pietro Carlo and his brother, Domenico, to leave their native country. Apparently, the young Rossis were on poor terms with the woman their father had married following the death of his first wife. The two brothers joined Alessandro Zabaldano, an uncle from their mother's side who had immigrated to San Francisco, and opened a pharmacy in the city. There was in fact little affection between Pietro Carlo and Domenico, and the two would go on to lead separate lives without ever doing business with each other. Pietro Carlo, for his part, gained an important entry into the mercantile world of the city with his marriage to Amélie Caire, the daughter of a French merchant (Justinian Claire) who had arrived in San Francisco through Cape Horn in 1850. But it was a fellow Piedmont native, Dr. Giuseppe Ollino of Rocca d'Arazzo in Asti, who would fatefully introduce Rossi to Italian Swiss Colony owner Andrea Sbarboro. By then, Sbarboro was convinced that making wine from the grapes he produced was the only way to save his shaky company, and he asked chemistry expert Rossi to oversee the new operations. Rossi took over in 1888 and from that point on, he almost never stopped studying and keeping himself abreast of the most recent developments in winemaking, both in California and abroad. He also made frequent trips to Italy, France, Spain, and Algeria to sharpen his enological skills, since initially these had been nothing more than those of a shrewd, self-taught man, albeit supported by pharmaceutical training.[11]

Secondo Guasti and Giuseppe Gallo came from similar social backgrounds. Guasti's father had been a well-to-do baker and merchant from Mombaruzzo d'Asti, a small but strategically located town on the main trade route between the Ligurian port of Genoa and Turin, the capital of Italy from 1861 to 1864. Only one biographical source, clearly inspired by Guasti himself, claims that his father had also been a winemaker.[12] Right after high school and the death of his mother, he was sent to work as an apprentice at the stores of relatives, first in Asti and then in Genoa. In 1881, Guasti set off for the United States from Genoa with a modest amount of money—fruits of the family business—but no professional experience or technical skills, save some limited training as a baker. He started working as a cook in a Los Angeles hotel owned by an Amillo, whose daughter he would later marry. Guasti's expectation upon leaving Italy had been to "make a fortune."[13]

Giuseppe/Joe Gallo's father, on the other hand, had traded horses and had owned a butcher's shop in Fossano, a large agrotown along the railroad between Turin and the sea. Young Giuseppe most likely had some notion of the technical aspects of selling wine since his family had also run a guesthouse with a restaurant attached. As mentioned earlier, however, the prospect that drove him across the entire American continent was the money he expected to make quickly in California's booming Gold Rush towns, not in the wine business. Giuseppe's complete ignorance of the theory and practice of winemaking is even one of the foundation myths of the E. & J. Gallo Winery. In their autobiography and several interviews, sons Ernest and Julio Gallo often claimed that they had learned everything they needed to know to start their business from a technical manual on winemaking borrowed from the public library in Modesto. "Had we taken a personal inventory at that time, our prospects would have looked very dismal," Ernest maintained. "Experience in producing commercial wine: none. Experience in marketing wine: none. Available cash: $900.23. Borrowed funds: $5,000. . . . *Confidence: Unbounded!*"[14] Their immigrant father had passed down scarce knowledge to them because he had possessed little of it himself:

My father had not been raised on a farm and had no aptitude for the work. He had to learn everything the hard way. He tried to plow in midsummer when the ground was dry and rock-hard instead of waiting for it to soften up after the rains. Since trucks were beginning to replace horses, he had gotten a good price on some giant dray horses. But the Clydesdales were too large and awkward for field work. Father succeeded only in repeatedly breaking the plow's moldboard. He soon traded the big horses for mules.[15]

Julio added other biting anecdotes about his father's farming skills:

Father decided the vines needed protection from the frost. I don't know where he got the idea, but he went to town and bought old car tires, which he brought back and directed Ernest and me to distribute throughout our vineyard. The next morning when the temperature dropped to near freezing, we were up at three A.M. setting the tires on fire. We raised the damnedest smoke, which at day-break covered the town of Escalon with dark black clouds smelling of burned rubber. When the smoke cleared away enough for us to return to the vineyard, we found the vines completely charred.[16]

Ellen Hawkes, the "unofficial" historian of the Gallo Winery, has noted how the Gallos may have used this negative legend as a rhetorical strategy to distance themselves from the enterprises of Gallo Sr., which were far more modest, not to mention compromising, as will be seen. After all, in California Giuseppe/Joe Gallo had trafficked in wine and cultivated grapes for nearly twenty years. According to Hawkes's reconstruction, he had even been preparing to open his own winery after the repeal of Prohibition.[17] Yet the inarguable fact remains that Giuseppe had brought no technical expertise in wine production from Italy.

The experience of the second- and third-generation children of these winemaking families would be quite different, destined as they were to be instructed in top American universities upon completion of their training at home. By 1909, twins Edmund and Robert Rossi had already graduated with degrees in viticulture and enology from the University of California. After graduating from the department of viticulture at UC Davis in in 1948, Edmund's son Edmund Jr. was offered the prestigious position of President of the American Society for Enology and Viticulture. The Gallos also sought to prepare their children to succeed them in running their winemaking empire by having them complete the proper academic training. Ernest's sons, David E. (1939–1997) and Joseph E. (1941–), both graduated with economics degrees from Stanford. Julio's son and successor as the head of production and quality, Robert J. (1934–), studied food science at Oregon State University, as did his sister, Susan (1936–).[18] Several of the founders' numerous grandchildren who work for the company today also completed university courses in enology.[19]

The amount of education required to successfully carry on the businesses of these Piedmontese winemaking families makes the accomplishments of their pioneering predecessors all the more remarkable. Indeed, the ability and willingness of these first-generation winemakers to co-opt resources and take risks, which they had inherited from the urban, merchant-class milieu—however provincial—back in Piedmont, turned out to be crucial for offsetting their scant or nonexistent previous winemaking knowledge. All things considered, the most important aspect of the "winemaking legacy" that Pietro Carlo Rossi, Secondo Guasti, and Giuseppe Gallo brought with them to the United States was the fact that they had all grown up during Piedmont's grape-growing boom and were therefore aware of wine's commercial potential. This is certainly the perspective from which they viewed the conditions of the local wine industry upon their arrival in California.

THE WORLD THEY FOUND: THE CALIFORNIA WINE INDUSTRY AND CULTURE IN THE NINETEENTH AND EARLY TWENTIETH CENTURIES

When the first Piedmontese immigrants to California entered the trade in the 1880s, winemaking was a potentially profitable but highly risky business. Though already mature, with several active medium- and large-sized wineries, the market was continuing to expand and was highly competitive; they would soon be significantly contributing to its expansion and participating in the competition as aggressive actors. Perhaps more than anything else about California's wine world, the new arrivals from Piedmont would surely have been struck by the predominance of European immigrants (notably German, French, and Scandinavian), many of them Catholic, working in the field. Coming from and serving wine-drinking ethnic communities, these immigrants played a vital role in the early development of the California wine industry. However, as this and chapter 10 will explore in more depth, the ethnic diversity of the winemaking world was both cause and consequence of the growing importance of the prohibitionist discourse in Californian and American public debate. Since the early nineteenth century, a widespread moralizing movement tried to introduce regulations to prohibit or limit the production and sale of alcohol, including wine. By the turn of the twentieth century, the temperance movement had singled out new European immigrant groups (especially Italians and other Catholics) as the main producers and consumers of wine and liquor, calling "demon rum" an "immigrant problem" and identifying the struggle against alcohol with the struggle against all anti-American elements in U.S. society. The chances, choices, and actions of Piedmontese immigrant winemakers had to be measured against the backdrop of such a specific economic, social, and cultural framework of California wine in which race, ethnicity, religion, and notions of foreignness and Americanness were very relevant factors.

Even the popular *vitis vinifera* grape, whose widespread presence on the West Coast was another crucial symbol in the California-as-American-Mediterranean myth, was itself an immigrant plant. The first homegrown California wine grape had instead been the Mission—a descendant of the first Spanish varieties grown by Jesuit missionaries in the vast area of the Spanish empire north of Mexico from the early seventeenth century on, and first cultivated in San Diego in 1769 by Franciscan friars from the local mission. The missionaries had needed wine to conduct mass in the indigenous communities they evangelized, and the native grape—the *vitis americana*—was unsuitable for winemaking. For nearly a century, this wine was produced solely for liturgical use and the private consumption of the missions. If nothing else, this pioneering stage of California winemaking established the warm, flat area around Los Angeles as the state's first wine region, specializing in strong sweet wines.[20]

While many pioneers of commercial winemaking in Southern California were Yankee settlers (sometimes of Irish descent) who came to California in the early nineteenth century and used wine to diversify the production of their farms, the scene was soon peopled with European immigrants like Bordeaux native Jean Louis Vignes, who started importing grape varietals from France via Boston and Cape Horn as early as the 1830s, and Rhenish Charles Kohler and John Frohling, whom history credits as the first California wine merchants on a national scale. In the north, where an enological development comparable to that of the area near Los Angeles would not happen until the 1850s, a similarly heterogeneous group of former fishermen and farmers from Maine and Illinois prevailed, along with winemakers who arrived "with their trade in tow" from Bourgogne, Alsace, and the Rhineland.

When the production of a marketable wine in California really began taking off in the mid to late nineteenth century, it straddled two distinct phases in the state's rural development. The first historical phase of California's market agriculture closely followed the Gold Rush of 1848–1849, stimulated by the need to feed the rapidly expanding population in the Northern Californian mining fields. Thanks to the great expanse of cultivable and grazeable land and the richness of the fertile virgin soil, the task was accomplished brilliantly. The old Mexican ranchos and even more so the new, American-owned capitalist and mechanized farms, began immediately to ship large quantities of meat, grains, fruits, and vegetables from the Central Valley across San Francisco and the Sacramento River to the boomtowns of the mining frontier. The state government also began promptly and intensely promoting agricultural work, for example founding the California State Agricultural Society in 1854.

The start of the second phase of rural development was marked by the completion of the transcontinental railroad (1869), which definitively transformed the market for California agriculture from a regional scale to a national reach. Grain was the first crop to enjoy such benefits, together with livestock raising (though competition with spacious Midwestern prairies would make both unsustainable by the late 1880s). When it became clear that the mining economy was lagging (around 1880), California agriculture began heading more steadily toward a range of typical crops, eventually specializing in select, extensively grown fruits and vegetables. This secured California a valued place on the international market, aided in no small part by its year-round temperate, stable climate and the great variety of its microclimates—as demonstrated by the different characteristics of the areas in which the three wineries discussed in this study were planted. An innovative legislation on water use introduced in 1887, which let farmers organize themselves into irrigation districts that sponsored the construction and management of canals, was crucial to Californian agriculture's shift toward horticulture and crop specialization within a wide-ranging national and international market. These districts were given the power to expropriate water-use rights from private companies and finance the canalization projects by issuing bonds. This legislation led California to become the number one state in the Union for both irrigated acreage—more than a million acres by 1890—and agricultural productivity. The first local crops to take advantage of this rapid agricultural growth were fruits, especially citrus, and vegetables—of which California remained one of the world's main producers for decades—with grapevines not far behind.[21]

As had recently occurred in Europe, the birth of a modern winemaking industry in California was stimulated by the existence of a sufficiently large market of wine drinkers and the ability to ship merchandise across long distances to reach those customers. While corn-based whiskey had long been successful, and statistics on imported wines and vermouth show that a U.S. wine market had already existed since before the Revolution, attempts to develop native wine production in the Eastern and Southern United States had failed rather miserably. In California, on the other hand, the grapevine found favorable conditions, just when the demand for wine started growing among various groups of consumers in the emerging urban–industrial society of the late nineteenth century. Members of the upper middle class were seeking to emulate the lifestyles of the European aristocracy, whose dinner tables often featured bottles of quality wine; young bohemians in New York and San Francisco were likewise contesting Victorian models of respectability with anticonformist styles of conspicuous consumption that included wine drinking; and for new immigrant workers from Catholic, Southern European countries, drinking wine was an integral part of everyday sociability. For decades to come, the real problem for California wine would be one of image, marketing, and price rather than the lack of a potentially large market. Even when the product's quality was excellent, California wine suffered from a lack of prestige compared to imported European wines, and it was bought by large merchants in the east mainly for distribution to the lower brackets of the market.

The arrival on the scene of the Hungarian immigrant Agoston Haraszthy (1812–1869) marked a turning point in the history of commercial wine production in California. Celebrated today as the founding father of California enology, Haraszthy is also responsible for mythically tying the immigration of European technicians, entrepreneurs, and laborers to the development of the state's wine industry. The liberal Hungarian nationalist had first arrived in the United States in 1840 as a political refugee. In 1849, following a brief, unsuccessful stay in chilly Wisconsin, Haraszthy reached San Francisco, where he found work at the state mint. His real interest and object of fascination, however, was the agricultural potential of the

The Board of Executives of the Italian Swiss Colony as they appeared in a promotional booklet, 1900. *Out West*, August 1902.

American continent. Contrary to his claims of having descended from counts, his family was not noble, though they had served in the imperial Hapsburg administration and owned land. They also had a long tradition in grape growing, which fueled the Hungarian immigrant's dream to reproduce the most prestigious European vintages on North American ground.

Haraszthy's entry into viticulture was marked by his forced retirement from the mint after being accused of having contributed to the disappearance of $130,000 in gold. Shortly thereafter, Haraszthy planted some four hundred acres of vineyards on his estate in Sonoma County, the Buena Vista Ranch. It was the first time the hills of Northern California were covered with grapevines as far as the eye could see, an unprecedented "European" landscape soon publicized as such by newspapers and the nation's first illustrated magazines. Haraszthy's winery was also known for the large scale of its production; its mass use of Chinese labor; its futuristic underground storage cisterns and redwood casks; and, last but not least, the unusually high quality of its table wines. Indeed, Haraszthy's wines would go on to win first prize at the annual fair of the California State Agricultural Society in 1858. It was at this time that the society asked Haraszthy to write what would become the first enological treatise published in California, *Report on Grapes and Wines in California* (1859). Finally, in 1861, the State Assembly would name him "Commissioner on the Improvement and Growth of the Grape-vine."

Strengthened by this mandate, Haraszthy traveled throughout Europe in 1861–1862, including stops in Turin and Asti, where he acquired Nebbiolo vines to bring back to the United States. By the end of his voyage, he had compiled several reports and shipped to California nearly 200,000 grapevine seedlings representing 1,400 varietals—a mass botanical migration with few precedents. The resulting handbook, *Grape Culture, Wines, and Wine-Making* (1862), would remain the classic introduction to California enology for years to come. Certain grape varietals imported by Haraszthy are still among the most important in California viticulture—Cabernet Sauvignon, Carignane, Pinot Noir, Sauvignon Blanc, Semillon, Riesling, Sylvaner, and Gewürztraminer. Curiously, this is not the case for the most common of all, Zinfandel, a black Hungarian grape that had already arrived on the Pacific Coast before Haraszthy.[22]

Stockholders of the Italian Vineyard Company, ca. 1910. In the background, the main winery; on the right, a partial view of the distilling plant. Courtesy Cal Poly Pomona University Library Special Collections.

Not everything came up roses for the ambitious Hungarian wine-maker who faced the same dilemmas that would later afflict other immigrant wine entrepreneurs, including those from Piedmont. As a recent immigrant, Haraszthy wisely sought to create important relationships in political and financial circles by using the strategy of marriage. Indeed, he encouraged two of his sons to marry the daughters of the landowner and leading political figure (not to mention fellow wine producer and Catholic) Mariano Guadalupe Vallejo. Yet despite all his skills in diplomacy, Haraszthy proved incapable of penetrating the subtle connections—characteristically American and Protestant—between moral values, racism, and political action. The politicians with whom he associated most closely were Democrats who supported California's entry into the American Union as a slave state; looked disdainfully on his use of Chinese labor; and harbored strong reservations about the morality of alcohol production. Haraszthy also made a ruinous assessment of how much financial support California politicians would be willing to grant the newborn wine industry. While such direct public support may have been possible in Europe, it was illusory to hope for in California. He never got back the $12,000 he advanced to cover the costs of his European journey and the plants he shipped across the ocean, thus contributing to his financial collapse. Like many immigrant entrepreneurs after him, Haraszthy tried to make up for the extra economic risks inherent in being foreign-born by trusting in the faith and solidarity of his family. He, his sons, and his widower father were the sole managers of the Buena Vista Ranch until financial hardships ultimately forced Haraszthy to sell the property to a corporation.

The Hungarian winemaker died shortly thereafter in a mysterious accident in Nicaragua. In the end, his greatest legacy was to spread the idea of California as an ideal environment for grape growing, promising success and ample profits. He also instilled winemakers with a positivist trust in science and technology as the means for producing high-quality wine on a mass scale. He thus conferred on California winemaking the dignity and faith required to compete with European wines—ever the undisputed standard of quality against which to be measured. On the other hand, his personal experience represented a warning on the additional hardships that awaited immigrant entrepreneurs wanting to try their hand at what remained for better or for worse a niche market. By the time of Haraszthy's death in 1869, U.S. public opinion was already starting to view alcohol consumption as the receptacle for the religious, social, and political tensions and anxieties that would eventually lead to national Prohibition.

Nevertheless, Haraszthy's vision was on the verge of being realized by the late 1860s with vineyards covering much of the hills of Sonoma County and Napa Valley. By the winter of 1867, more than four hundred thousand vines had been planted in Sonoma alone. This marked a turning point when the throne of California's most important wine region began shifting from Southern California to the area north of San Francisco. In fact, another of Haraszthy's lessons entailed the suitability of the humid hills of Sonoma and Napa for accommodating the European vines required to produce an acceptable table wine. The combination of semidesert heat and a specialization in the old Mission grape made the same task demanding for Los Angeles and Orange Counties. In fact, the "Anaheim disease" that struck the vineyards of this area in the early 1880s sealed its declining fate. The center of Southern California viticulture would then gradually move east toward the San Bernardino and San Gabriel Valleys, and in particular Cucamonga, thanks to Secondo Guasti's daring decision to plant vineyards in that area's sandy earth (which is precisely what saved them from the aforementioned disease). Guasti's "largest vineyards in the world" helped to turn a previously underpopulated and semidesert area into a wine district by the early years of the twentieth century.

By the early 1870s, the devastating spread of phylloxera in Europe signaled California's definitive takeoff in wine production by guaranteeing it a stable and dominant piece of the world market. The price and production of grapes and wine skyrocketed during the first half of the decade, thus creating the fortunes of a new generation of immigrants. Many of these names are still known to California wine lovers today: the German Jacob Gundlach in Sonoma; the Germans Charles Krug, Jacob and Frederick Beringer, and the Finnish Gustav Niebaum in Napa; the Frenchmen Charles Lefranc and Pierre Pellier in Santa Clara; and the Hannover native Carl Heinrich Wente in Livermore Valley. Most of these producers specialized in sparkling, sweet, and dry white wines, which were closer to their own experience and the taste of their markets. In fact, the production of a "perfect" California champagne was their personal Moby Dick.[23] In the great central grain-and-fruit valley down south, the combination of generous allotments from the U.S. government and the excessive financial power of the railroads over farming land had given rise to massive estates run via extensive capitalist agricultural systems employing armies of workers in a semi-slavish state. The ranches of French and German winemakers in Sonoma, Napa, and Santa Clara, on the other hand, were medium-sized properties with wineries run as part of a family economy. A variety of German, French, Portuguese, Mexican, and Chinese laborers looked after the vineyards under comparatively better conditions than what could be observed in the fields of the state's Central Valley.

By the mid-1870s, the pioneering age of California viticulture was therefore coming to a close. In 1876, a devastating crisis due to the uncontrolled overproduction that had marked the boom of five years earlier inaugurated a series of growth and depression cycles in price that would last into the 1890s. The immediate consequence was a drastic reduction in the number of wine producers via bankruptcies, mergers, and cartels. The wine industry was inclined to concentrate itself in a few dozen of the largest wineries. Moreover, the roles of grape growers, wine producers, and wine sellers, hitherto characterized by various shades of gray, became more differentiated and specialized.

A further element in the development of the California wine industry, as Piedmontese immigrants would encounter it at the time of their arrival, was its growing institutionalization. Associations of producers were established to support California winemaking through concerted price policies, coordinated promotion, and especially political lobbying aimed at attaining from the U.S. government protective customs tariffs on foreign wine imports. The California Wine-Growers' Association was formed as early as 1862, followed by the California Vine Growers' and Wine and Brandy Manufacturers' Association (later renamed the California State Vinicultural Association) in 1872. Locally based groups were also formed, such as the Grape-Growers' Association (1870), which assembled the winemakers of Napa, Sonoma, and Solano Counties. The state, for its part, promoted the creation of a special government agency for enological development in 1880—the Board of State Viticultural Commissioners (BSVC), whose first president was Arpad Haraszthy, son of Agoston. In addition to promoting the state's wine industry and devoting itself to fighting the threat of phylloxera, the board opened an experimental station in San Francisco that explored problems related to land selection and grape varietals, pruning, grafting, fermentation, and aging. The University of California's entry onto the field was fundamental when it came to advanced research. The same law that had created the BSVC established a department of viticulture in the College of Agriculture at Berkeley, which in turn proceeded with an extensive research project. Finally, the California Assembly passed the Pure Wine Law, which imposed serious quality controls on wine and established significant penalties for those guilty of adulterating it. A winemaking machinery industry also emerged at the same time, thus freeing producers from the need to import crushers, pressers, stemmers, elevators, pumps, and even barrels and vats from Europe.[24]

Most significantly for the upcoming experience of Piedmontese immigrant winemakers and for Italian immigrants in general, even during this time of intense development, and for decades to come, the sinister shadow of Prohibition would constantly hover over the fate of California's wine industry. Campaigns for temperance against the consumption of any inebriating beverages had originated in the Second Great Awakening of the early nineteenth century. This religious revivalist movement involved much of the Protestant population in New England and the Midwest, a large percentage of which were women. The supporters of this religious renaissance—largely a response to the social change brought on by industrialization and urbanization—believed in the active engagement of the faithful in Christian evangelization and the moral reform of society. Alcohol and the saloons in which it was copiously consumed became their main targets. Revivalists considered alcohol consumption to be a sin and the main drive behind the most despicable social ills: poverty, domestic violence, and family dissolution.

Societies and associations for temperance spread rapidly throughout the states of the Union. By the mid-1830s, there were some five thousand of them, comprising a million members. Unions like the American Society for the Promotion of Temperance (which organized converted ex-drinkers), the Cold Water Army (whose members were children), and Martha Washington Societies evolved quickly and successfully into political pressure groups that sought to persuade state, county, and city administrations to halt liquor consumption using legislation. Maine prohibited the production and sale of non-medicinal alcohol as early as 1851, followed shortly thereafter with similar laws by several other states in New England and the Midwest.

The campaigns for temperance were tinged with xenophobia and religious intolerance from early on. Many reformers considered alcohol an evil introduced to the United States by Catholic German and Irish immigrants. Some even believed that it represented the weapon with which the papists aimed to undermine the foundations of democratic American society. From the start, the struggle against alcohol blended with widespread anti-Catholic and racist sentiments.[25]

The temperance movement picked up momentum in the late nineteenth century and became the central theme of the national political agenda during the Progressive Era. The progressives were a composite coalition of politicians, philanthropists, social activists, scholars, and clergy with a significant female component. It was natural for them to identify the opposition to the free sale of alcohol as an instrument for their actions against the distortions of industrial capitalism. Many came from rigorously Protestant, middle-class backgrounds, and the ideal that united them most was a moderate social reform that would produce decent, concerned, and independent citizens. New, powerful associations like the Woman's Christian Temperance Union (WCTU), founded in 1873, and the Anti-Saloon League, formed in 1893, dedicated themselves to sensitizing the public not only to the individual, physical, and moral damages caused by alcohol but even more to social ills in terms of poverty, work accidents, and loss of productivity.

Of course, these arguments sounded nonsensical to most Italian immigrants, in particular the Piedmontese, whose often proclaimed work ethic happily coexisted with their general fondness for wine drinking. The twelve-hour days worked by the Gallo brothers in the family vineyards witness how ideologically distant the accusations of temperance activists may have resounded in the ears of Piedmontese Californians. Northern as well as Southern Italian laborers appreciated wine as a vital source of calories in their diet, effectively keeping their working bodies functioning, besides being a very relevant means of sociability, recreation, and, sometimes, intoxication. As will

Interior of the main winery of the Italian Vineyard Company in Guasti, ca. 1910. Workers are removing and cleaning the filters in the center. Courtesy Cal Poly Pomona University Library Special Collections.

be seen in more detail, in the first decade of the twentieth century Sbarboro campaigned and published vigorously against the misconceptions of the temperance movement by claiming that a moderate consumption of wine from a very early age was what kept Latin populations of Europe safe from the more widespread alcoholism that, he claimed, affected Nordics and Slavs.[26]

The war against saloons and alcohol production let loose by the Anti-Saloon League and the WCTU once again drove several communities to adopt or revive restrictive laws regarding the provision of liquor. By 1900, almost one-fourth of all Americans lived in a region where it was illegal to buy or sell alcohol, and by the start of World War I, influential people like Supreme Court Justice Louis D. Brandeis and former U.S. President William Howard Taft had become fervent supporters of Prohibition. In fact, the introduction of a national law prohibiting the production, marketing, transport, and sale of alcohol (though not its purchase, possession, or consumption, which were never subject to bans) became the objective of the progressive prohibitionists. They finally reached their goal in 1918 with the congressional approval of the Eighteenth Amendment, which was ratified by the required number of states in 1919 and effected in 1920 with the act named after Andrew Volstead, the Chairman of the House Judiciary Committee and the legislation's sponsor.

Prohibition got off to a reasonably successful start, especially in the areas of the country that had historically supported the reasons for temperance. In large Northern cities, on the other hand, the Volstead Act proved too dissonant and incompatible with modern, urban, cosmopolitan, and mass culture. Violations were so widespread that serious efforts to enforce it were rare, limited to the actions of a few motivated federal officers who were working with severely limited human and financial resources. In fact, the illegal trafficking of liquor yielded enormous sums for organized crime, whose ranks swelled with first- and second-generation Italian, Irish, Jewish, and Slavic immigrants. The thousands of Americans who took up the small-scale domestic production of whiskey, brandy, beer, and wine were also predominantly immigrants. By the end of the 1920s, Prohibition had lost much of its political support and moral credibility. Indeed, Franklin Delano Roosevelt's first important act as president was to initiate the procedures for its repeal in 1933.[27]

As discussed in chapter 10, from the late nineteenth century to the introduction of the Eighteenth Amendment and beyond, Prohibition caused a serious cultural war that split the United States in two. The temperance movement ultimately put Anglo-Saxon/Northern European/Protestant/rural America head-to-head with urban/multiethnic/Catholic/Jewish America. The working class, in which Southern and Eastern European immigrants were overrepresented by the turn of the twentieth century, spent most of their social and leisure time in saloons. According to prohibitionist reformers, saloons were centers of political and social corruption, where the powerful electoral machines of the party bosses arranged votes in exchange for favors and workers wasted too much of their meager wages, ruining their chances of social mobility and making themselves easy prey to radicalism and syndicalism.

By the late 1910s, a cohort of scientific racism popularizers had deftly spread the fear among white Protestant Americans that the Anglo-Saxon race would be made extinct through the invasion of Latin, Jewish, and Slavic hordes, which only perpetuated the wave of unconditional patriotism inspired by the U.S. intervention in World War I and the Red Scare that followed the Bolshevik Revolution in Russia. Added to this boiling cauldron, then, Prohibition inextricably overlapped with nativist, xenophobic, and racist motives. During the 1920s, both federal agents and members of the Ku Klux Klan roamed the American countryside, assaulting the houses and farms

Workers of the Italian Vineyard Company in front of the shop where barrels were made, ca. 1910. Courtesy Cal Poly Pomona University Library Special Collections.

of Southern and Eastern Europeans—including many Italians— and destroying the barns and sheds where they produced wine and liquor, usually illegally. More generally, the concurrent characterization of wine as a traditionally and culturally Catholic drink turned the new immigrants who consumed it into the ideological targets of a significant and influential part of American society.[28] The concentration of non-WASP immigrants in the production, marketing, and consumption of wine only served to reinforce the stigma of the alien that had already long accompanied the product of the grapevine, thus contributing to the plethora of regulations, limitations, and bans—first locally, then at the state level, then nationally—that already hindered the full development of the wine industry. Despite Agoston Haraszthy's efforts, wine would have to wait until the end of the twentieth century before consumers would start to think of and fully accept it as a legitimate American beverage.[29]

In essence, right on the eve of the Piedmontese immigrants' arrival on the scene, California winemaking had developed into a mature, complex, and highly risky system. Sbarboro and Rossi, Guasti not long after, and the Gallos a generation later would learn that while the California wine world offered them the chance to make their hopes and dreams of success come true, this would depend on their ability to mobilize the capital required for large-scale operations, considering the ruthless struggle to survive on the market that was already underway. Given their limited starting capital, they must have realized and accepted early on that their best chances lay in their ability to cooperate and synergize with other individuals and institutions.

The latter notion was not alien to them. In their small- and medium-sized home towns in Piedmont and Liguria, there had already existed an associationist tradition related to mutual-aid societies and cooperatives, themselves based on a foundation of solidarity and cooperation tied to the older trade guilds of the ancien régime. There was in fact a spirit of collaboration between the Piedmontese mercantile, professional, and landowner classes and the local public administrations—among the most advanced bureaucracies in the recently unified Kingdom of Italy. This was because local politicians generally owed their survival in Parliament to their abilities to protect the interests and values of the same exclusive citizen base that had elected them. The uninominal nature of the constituency, even if it bound the political struggle to the personalities of the candidates, served to guarantee that the opinions of the "productive classes" would be represented, while a public sphere formed of

THE OVERLAND LIMITED

Guasti, ca. 1910. The stockholders of the Italian Vineyard Company in front of the main dorm for single workers. At the time, many of the permanent workers of the company were single immigrant men from Piedmont. Courtesy Cal Poly Pomona University Library Special Collections.

associations, electoral committees, and newspapers served to mold them. The region of Piedmont therefore comprised a relatively broad civil society.[30]

While the bourgeois and religiously inspired socialist and utopian forms of organization that had shaped the first labor movements in Northern Europe had little influence in rural Southern Piedmont, despite the experiences of France next door, the world of California viticulture filled this gap with the various experimental communities that supported themselves with the products of their own wineries. In 1875, for example, the millenarian community of the Brotherhood of New Life, led by founder Thomas Lake Harris, traveled from its headquarters in upstate New York to Santa Rosa, in Sonoma County, where it acquired four hundred acres of land on which it began to grow grapevines. In 1888, the brotherhood reached a production of some two hundred thousand gallons of wine. Scandal forced the colony to close and Harris to return to his native England when his bizarre sexual notions came to light, including his profession of God's bisexuality and the existence of a "celestial spouse" that was to be sought in the body of whomever one supposed hosted it. Not far north, in Cloverdale, literally a few steps away from where Andrea Sbarboro was founding Asti at the same time, the Icarians, a group of French immigrants who professed a utopian communism inspired by what they considered the true Christianity, founded in their turn a winery called Icaria Speranza. After a promising start and a good ten-year run, the same rapid fluctuations of the grape market that initially plunged Sbarboro's Italian Swiss Colony into crisis would prove unsustainable and cause the experiment to fail.[31] Against the backdrop of the Icarian utopia's unfortunate end, it becomes even clearer how much Sbarboro and Rossi's enterprise depended on the circle of Piedmontese immigrant investors, the access to credit through personal connections with Italian American bankers, the ready availability of a vast immigrant workforce, and the presence of a sizeable ethnic market.

CHAPTER FOUR

One Nation

The Importance of Ethnic Cooperation

In addition to the Pavesian myth, which emphasizes the traditional winemaking skills of Piedmontese immigrants and California's optimal environmental conditions for their transplantation, another strong case has been made to explain why Piedmont-born winemakers were so successful on the Pacific Coast. The historian Sebastian Fichera, who chronicles San Francisco's Italian community, attributes this success to the winemakers' participation in an ethnic economy that integrated fellow Italian entrepreneurs, financiers, workers, middlemen, retailers, and consumers. According to Fichera, winemakers benefited in particular from privileged access to financing as members of an upstanding circle in which Italian banks granted plentiful credit to Italian wineries, whose Italian workers in turn deposited their savings into the same banks. He considers the case of the Italian Swiss Colony to be especially paradigmatic of how influential this cooperative spirit was in determining the economic and social success of the Italian immigrant community in San Francisco compared to its trouble-ridden sisters in New York and Chicago.

In his essay "Entrepreneurial Behavior in an Immigrant Colony: The Economic Experience of San Francisco's Italian Americans, 1850–1940," Fichera favors sociocultural factors to explain the success of the community as a whole by assigning full credit to the presence of a solid initial core of Northern Italian immigrants in San Francisco.[1] These trailblazing immigrants were already distinguished from their East Coast counterparts by arriving in California with some starting capital and some education. However, they brought something even more important with them to the United States from the rural towns of Piedmont, the countryside of Tuscany, and the seaside hills of Liguria: cultural capital, a predisposition for collaborating with and trusting one another. This cooperative ethos was henceforth strengthened via osmosis by the widespread associationist culture that Alexis de Tocqueville famously identified as a central feature of the "American spirit."[2] Moreover, unlike what occurred in the Little Italies of the large industrial cities of the East and the Midwest, this community did not dissipate when San Francisco became the destination of vast numbers of considerably less well-to-do Italian immigrants at the dawn of the twentieth century. On the contrary, not only did the original nucleus of "cooperative" entrepreneurs maintain its leadership, but it also imposed this ethos onto the rest of the community as an attribute to be emulated.

Fichera does considers Andrea Sbarboro and Pietro Carlo Rossi not only the most important pioneers of the Italian adventure in California winemaking, but also some of the best representatives of the group of middle-class merchants, bankers, and businessmen who spread crucial cooperative spirit among San Francisco's Italian American community. The Liguria-born Sbarboro was certainly very active in this regard. Having arrived in San Francisco in 1850 and inherited from his brother a drugstore in the heart of North Beach's Little Italy just as the neighborhood was taking shape, Sbarboro patiently built up his network of relationships with the most important members of the city's (Northern)

Italian community. In 1858, he helped organize the Italian Mutual Benefit Society, a thousand-member association that would form the foundation for an Italian hospital ten years later. Sbarboro also joined the local Masonic lodge and figured among the most convinced promoters of the initiative to establish Columbus Day as a national holiday.

After learning of the success of building and loan associations at a routine lunch one day at Campi's restaurant (a popular meeting place for San Francisco's middle-class Italian American merchants in the 1870s), Sbarboro decided he wanted a piece of the action. Such associations allowed small groups of partnered investors to buy monthly shares until reaching a sum that would in turn be loaned back to them as mortgages for building homes. Sbarboro earned an important reputation by acting as the secretary for some of these groups, especially when he fought against the fraudulent initiatives that threatened the industry's credibility, thus bringing the case to the attention of the State Assembly.[3] The operating model for these building and loan associations went on to serve as inspiration for Sbarboro's organization of the Italian Swiss Colony:

It was in 1881 that I became interested in the viticultural industry. A copy of one of the reports of the State Board of Viticulture came into my hands, and the outlook for the grape growing in California was pictured in such favorable light, that I began giving the subject considerable thought.... One paragraph stated that the average production of grapes in California was five tons per acre and that as grapes were selling in the market for $30 a ton, with the cost of production only $20 per acre, the profit per acre was $130. At that time, laborers frequently came to my office asking for employment. As they were *contadini* [peasants], who understood thoroughly the growing of grapes, I thought some of the money of one of my building and loan associations, which we had on hand and could not place advantageously, might be properly invested in buying a tract of land for the association with a view of putting these Italian vineyardists at work [*sic*].... [M]y attorney, Mr. David Friedenrich, who has been my faithful counselor for over thirty years,... stated that it could not be done, as the by-laws of the association stated that the money received by the members should be used only in procuring homes for members and their families. "But," he added, "you can organize an independent association and make your by-laws with the conditions of the new project." I immediately talked the matter over with a number of my friends and was encouraged to go ahead.[4]

The first "friend" to respond positively to Sbarboro's call was the Ligurian merchant Marco J. Fontana—shortly thereafter the founder of the vastly successful California Fruit Canners' Association—who underwrote a share purchase plan of $50 a month for five years. Sbarboro eventually managed to get various partners to underwrite a total of 2,250 shares for the company's capital. The first ten shareholders, including Sbarboro and Fontana, formed the company's board of directors, with Sbarboro taking on the role of secretary.

After completing his search for partners, Sbarboro decided to take things a step further by extending the company's risk and profit sharing to its future workers, who were to be employed on the basis of their ethnic affiliation. Not only did this hiring prerequisite reflect Sbarboro's nationalist idealism, but it also promised to increase the company's value in terms of fidelity, solidarity, and winemaking expertise (however limited). But the profit-sharing scheme did not work out as Sbarboro had hoped. After having bought land and prepared it for grapevine transplantation:

I summoned a number of laborers and explained the plan to them. Their wages, I told them, would be from thirty to forty dollars a month, with good food, wine at their meals, which was a necessity for them, and comfortable houses to sleep in. But in order to inspire an interest in the work and desiring that the Colony should be strictly co-operative, I explained that each laborer must subscribe at least to five shares of stock, to pay for which, five dollars a month would be deducted from his wages. In fact our by-laws provided expressly that all permanent laborers on the grounds must be members and the preference would be shown to Italian and Swiss laborers who were either American citizens or had declared the intentions to become such. Few of the thrifty immigrants, for whose benefit the Colony was formed, could speak English. I explained again and again to them our plan. They were ready to work for us, but they did not understand anything about co-operation and objected to becoming members. They thought cash for their work was better than any part in stock. I assured them that they could withdraw at any time they desired just the same as in the building and loan associations, and receive all they had paid in and such earnings as the directors might from time to time to declare. But it was no use, and we finally had to declare that section of our by-laws a dead letter and employ laborers without their being shareholders.[5]

Sbarboro's failed initiative shows the extent to which class determined the expectations, choices, and actions of both the laborers and the Piedmont-born businessmen who played leading roles in California winemaking. Far from forming a socially compact group, these immigrants interpreted and responded to their American experience according to needs, attitudes, and values that were rooted in their respective pasts and experiences in Italy. Class differences even conditioned their objectives for immigrating to the United States. Like Eel, the protagonist in Pavese's *The Moon and the Bonfires*, many proletarian

Piedmontese migrants looked at migration as temporary and came to California for the sole purpose of making money with which to return to their homeland. Sbarboro's stigmatization of workers who "did not understand anything about co-operation" reflects both the paternalism of ethnic entrepreneurs and how little the ethnic middle class knew about the variety of needs and motivations of other immigrants, not all of whom had come to California to pursue the American dream of individual success and Americanization.[6] In his positive view of the cooperative spirit among San Franciscan Italians, Fichera undervalues the degree to which class conditions weighed on the cost–benefit distribution of the various participants of the ethnic economy. This point will be explored further in the discussion of the wage situation of immigrant winemakers in chapter 7.

The importance Sbarboro placed on the constant weaving of social networks was proven again when disappointing crops and a fall in the market price of grapes in 1886–1887 brought the young Italian Swiss Colony to its knees. As Sbarboro commented significantly, "I saw ruin staring us in the face and I was indeed a very disappointed man, not so much on account of the money I had put in, although considerable, but because I had induced many of my friends to join my new venture."[7] This was precisely when Pietro Carlo Rossi, the most highly educated and socially privileged of Italian immigrant winemakers, came onto the scene. Like the Ligurian self-made man Sbarboro, Rossi was adept at maximizing relationships, forming associations, and seeking institutional support. After being called in to save the Colony after another market crash had driven shareholders to play their last desperate winemaking card, the Piedmontese pharmacist turned out to be even more skilled as an organizer and a diplomat than as a winemaker. Exasperated by the paltry sum offered by San Francisco merchants for his first harvests, Rossi led the Colony to its third transformation in just a few years—after having already gone from grape growing to winemaking—by organizing direct distribution through a network of independent agents in New York, Chicago, and New Orleans. He also expanded the Asti cellars and bought new ranches in Central and Southern California, all the while performing the delicate work of convincing the shareholders to continue placing their trust in him.[8] As a promotional booklet published by the Italian Swiss Colony in 1911 recounts, after Rossi took over the reins, "for sixteen consecutive years improvement and additions to the property continued, the shareholders never getting a cent in return. But the

Andrea Sbarboro (*center, with the hand in his coat*) with a group of visitors in front of Villa Pompeii, his neoclassical residence in Asti, ca. 1900. Courtesy Center for Migration Studies, Staten Island, New York.

co-operative spirit was by them carried through with both courage and intelligence."⁹

Rossi did much to prove his sagacity as an organizer and a negotiator when the Italian Swiss Colony became engaged in the so-called Wine War from 1894 to 1898. In 1894, seven of the most important wine merchants of San Francisco joined forces in an effort to control the market and regulate the frequent fluctuations, thus giving rise to the California Wine Association (CWA). Convinced that the CWA would use its firepower to create a substantial monopoly that would keep the winemakers at its mercy, Rossi immediately set about promoting an analogous association of producers—many of whom were Italian—that would eventually become the California Wine Makers' Corporation (CWMC). Rossi's plan was to absorb most of California's harvest through collective contracts with grape growers, to produce wine in wineries outside the CWA's circuit, and to store it until market conditions were more favorable. Asti's famous gigantic underground cistern, which Sbarboro later wisely used to promote the Colony's image, turned out to be perfect for storing the 1897 harvest until the market improved. The associated producers hoped this would allow them to contract with the merchants from a position of power rather than be forced to submit to conditions dictated by the latter.¹⁰

Interestingly, Rossi's behavior parallels the rural hostility and mistrust for intermediaries characteristic of the Piedmontese wine market back in Italy. Indeed, the view of merchants as parasites, rapaciously interposed between producers and consumers, permeated most of the subalpine agrarian world at the time. In any case, the vertical organization of all the winery's endeavors, from grape growing to barrel making to wine selling, which was key to the company's success and would inspire both Secondo Guasti and the Gallos, was all Rossi's work. Further, not only was he resolute in leading the CWMC and the Italian Swiss Colony through the Wine War, but he also played a vital role as mediator in the agreement that would finally bring it to an end. In 1898, the four major distributors of California wine—the California Wine Association, the Italian Swiss Colony, the Claus Schilling & Co., and the Gundbach-Bundschu & Co.—joined forces to become the Associated Wine Dealers, effectively sanctioning an end to the battles between CWA merchants and CWMC producers that had had such harmful effects on the industry. While the accord may have signaled the end of the Italian Swiss Colony's total independence in the distribution of its products, it nevertheless secured the winery's position as an industry leader for the decade to come.[11]

The following year, in 1899, Rossi became the protagonist of Sbarboro's new consociational financial enterprise, the Italian American Bank, established on the impulse of the same Italian American ethnic elite that had already supported the Italian Swiss Colony. The bank's foundation had both symbolic and material significance for San Franciscan Italians since it not only showed how much the community had grown numerically and economically (see table 2), but also represented the promise of further social progress in the future. On March 20 of that year, Sbarboro was nominated president of the bank, with his son Alfred as secretary and Pietro Carlo Rossi as one of its directors.[12] The financial institution was immediately put in the service of the Italian Swiss Colony, granting the winery such sizeable loans as to attract the attention of the supervisory state banking authority. In 1912, the State Superintendent of Banks advised the Italian American Bank to recover the winery's loan of over $400,000 as soon as possible since it was too high a risk. While the bank remained fundamentally sound, this incident clearly indicates the synergies that existed between credit systems and wineries within the Italian American business community of Northern California.[13]

Table 2

ITALIAN IMMIGRANTS IN SAN FRANCISCO COUNTY, 1852–1960

Year	Born in Italy	Total population
1852	141	36,154
1870	1,621	149,473
1890	5,212	298,997
1900	7,508	342,782
1910	16,918	416,912
1920	24,924	506,676
1930	27,311	634,394
1940	24,036	634,536
1950	20,051	775,357
1960	16,131	740,316

Source: Adapted from Hans Christian Palmer, "Italian Immigration and the Development of California Agriculture," PhD diss., University of California, Berkeley, 1965, 374–393.

Basing his thesis primarily on the biographies of Rossi and Sbarboro, Fichera theorized that the "associationist spirit" of an entrepreneurial elite of Northern Italian immigrants and its placement in service of the larger community was enough to explain the success of Piedmontese winemakers:

No group of immigrants benefited more from [Northern California's Italian American] ethnic economy than the Italian winemakers, who by 1910 were already well on their way to dominating their industry. In the Italian American Bank alone, some half-dozen wineries were borrowers, generally of sums over $10,000. . . . An analysis of industry personnel, moreover, makes it clear that intra-group workers had undeniable benefit to gain from such an expansion. . . . The much smaller number of Italians in [non-Italian]–owned firms . . . were largely confined to the unskilled jobs category. In the Italian wineries, all levels of the occupational structure, skilled, unskilled and managerial, were mostly filled from within the group. . . . Here then was an excellent example of an ethnic group economy at work: Italian-run banks would loan money to Italian-run wineries; such wineries would hire mostly Italian workers; who would in their turn place their savings in Italian-run banks. Such perhaps is the nature of the force that best explains the unexpected Italian strengths in so much of California's food production chain.[14]

The factors Fichera highlights are surely important. But they portray a situation that was equally advantageous for all the actors involved, with class playing a secondary role to ethnicity. Such a portrayal contradicts the reality, as will be discussed in the following chapters. Fichera's argument also does little to explain why Piedmont-born immigrants in particular achieved such significant results in the domain of wine. As mentioned previously, the market these immigrants encountered upon their arrival in the 1880s was already mature, crowded, and battle-worn. In such a context, entrepreneurs of other nationalities could also put synergetic strategies like those referred to by Fichera into action, and starting from a stronger position. In fact, the difference between the consortium skills of Italian winemakers and those of other ethnic communities was yet to be proven. In turn-of-the-twentieth-century California, a tendency toward ethnic economic association was certainly not the monopoly of Italian immigrants. The Japanese, for example, demonstrated an attitude that was at least equally remarkable in this sense.[15] Further, immigrants from Piedmont seemed to outstrip those from other Italian regions in this regard. Only the Mondavi family from the Marches, the Cella family from Emilia-Romagna, and the Petri family from Tuscany could be placed on a comparable plane with the Rossis, the Guastis, and above all the Gallos. More important, if the Italian wineries' key to success consisted purely of ethnic synergies, why could this model not be replicated in other food industries in which these immigrants had no lack of sufficient cultural background and technical know-how? Why did Secondo Guasti, for example, who

Ernest Gallo discusses
the quality of his wines.
Livingston, California,
1992. Courtesy Corbis.

had come from a family of bakers, not become a great bread industri-
alist in the United States? Why did the butcher's son Giuseppe Gallo
not apply himself to transforming the meat industry upon his arrival in
California?

Fichera is misguided when he implies that the common ethnic
affiliation of bankers and winemakers automatically supplied the latter with easy and favorable access to credit. The mechanism worked
when bankers and winemakers were essentially the same people, as
in the case of the Italian Swiss Colony, and it is also true that this was
extended to a number of other wineries. Yet such examples were not
the rule. When Ernest and Julio Gallo decided to open their winery in
1933, they turned to Amadeo Giannini's Bank of America (formerly the
Bank of Italy), assuming this credit body would be the most willing to
help them start their business. Italians had founded the bank, its directors included several Italians, and many Italian immigrants—including Ernest and Julio's parents—had long deposited their savings there.
Yet the bank's Modesto branch denied them the loan. A few months
later, empowered by the fact that they had already sold a batch of wine
on the Chicago market and just needed money to ship it, Ernest went
back to the bank and obtained the credit they required, though only
as a result of exhaustive negotiations that were unjustifiable for a loan

with practically no risk. Finally, in response to a third request the following year with an eye to acquiring vineyards, the Bank of America granted the Gallos only a small fraction of the funds they required. By this point, Ernest was convinced the bank bore a grudge against them and tried to find out why. Lo and behold, it turned out that Alfred Sbarboro—the son of the Italian Swiss Colony's founder, one of the bank's directors, and a member of the powerful mortgage committee—had defined the Gallo brothers as "newcomers who shouldn't be financed." In the end, the much more modest Capital National Bank, whose director George Zoller showed faith in the two young Italian Americans, would be the main bank to support the E. & J. Gallo Winery.[16]

While the Italian American credit sector's inclination to support Italian American businesses certainly played a role in the Piedmontese winemaking success in California, the Gallos' story shows there were also significant exceptions. Perhaps of greater note in Fichera's citation above, then, is the date of 1910, which he notes in passing as the year when the Italian leadership in California winemaking really took off—the same year the clouds of Prohibition began threatening their descent on the American wine industry. The fact that Italian Americans, and especially Piedmont natives, emerged collectively at the head of the wine trade just as it began to acquire a much more negative connotation is cause for serious reflection. In fact, in some cases, synergies between Italian banks and wineries forced the former to assume the supplementary risk of financing a dangerous and controversial niche economy, which is exactly what wine became in twentieth-century America. Even by 1953, decades after the repeal of Prohibition, when the Gallos considered buying the Italian Swiss Colony from the National Distillers, an official at their bank responded, "I'm not sure we want to lend on wine."[17] The picture of how Piedmontese winemakers emerged as leaders in the California wine industry would not be complete without a close look at why they were willing to take such risks.

CHAPTER FIVE

The Spirit *and* Social Ethics *of* Ethnic Entrepreneurship

While the widespread cooperative behavior in the Italian American business community and the privileged ethnicity-based access to credit, were not the sole reasons for the success of Piedmontese wine-makers in California, these entrepreneurs were heavily affected both by the mobilization of social networks inside and outside the Piedmontese community as well as by their status as immigrants. Were their financial endeavors facilitated or complicated by the ideals, attitudes, and values included under the umbrella of their "culture"? This chapter aims to unwrap a few analytical categories—ethnic entrepreneurship, ethnic economy, social capital, and cultural capital—which are relevant to address this question.

Immigrant entrepreneurship and ethnic economies have recently attracted much scholarly attention. Ethnic entrepreneurs are defined as business owners or managers whose membership in a group is tied to common origin or cultural heritage and is recognized as such by nonmembers of the group. Central to the concept are the intrinsic ties these entrepreneurs have to specific social structures that influence individual behaviors, interactions, and economic transactions under capitalism. Ethnic economy is a broader category that encompasses all the entrepreneurs, professionals, and workers of a particular immigrant or minority group. The notion essentially refers to two levels of functionality: the group's control of the labor market and the ethnic management's ability to employ members of that group; and the ethnic group's ability to direct its members into broad and important labor-market sectors of nonethnic enterprise, or even into the public sector.[1]

The concepts of ethnic entrepreneurship and ethnic economy both emerged out of evidence showing that the way ethnic and immigrant individuals and groups fight to gain limited resources "in the real world" does not correspond to that anticipated by the postulates of capitalism and classic economic theory. According to the latter, the behavior of economic actors in the market is and must be guided exclusively by a pure, rationalist cost–benefit calculation in the quest for economic profit, since any deviation from that ethos prevents the laws of supply and demand from functioning freely. Ethnic entrepreneurship and labor, conversely, are the most obvious examples of an economy that is socially oriented—that is, wholly or partly governed by moral and value considerations that influence personal objectives and the means to achieve them, in which the pursuit of material accumulation interacts with the search for approval, status, and power in relation to specific "others."[2]

Social capital—one's access to limited resources specifically in virtue of one's membership in certain networks of relations and loyalties based on occupational, family, cultural, or affective ties—therefore takes on particular relevance in ethnic entrepreneurship and economy. Borrowing money to start a business, a case repeatedly encountered in the story of the Italian Swiss Colony, represents the classic example of the difference between "pure," impersonal market transactions and those involving the social capital of the economic actors. Money can be borrowed either through a bank, which applies market interest rates; a long-term business associate, who may apply lower interest rates; a friend, who may not take any interest; or a close family member, who may not even expect the money back at all and consider it help for a loved one in need. Social capital resides in one's ability to obtain these graduated types of "gifts," which in turn depends entirely on one's social relationships with others rather than one's access to money (material capital) or education and skills (human capital).[3]

Another typical manifestation of social capital in the sphere of ethnic entrepreneurship is the ability of ethnic employers to obtain long work hours in difficult conditions at lower-than-market salaries, or even for free, from relatives or members of the same immigrant or minority group, as part of a common ideology based on blood ties and community. In the United States, many small ethnic businesses in retail food sales or service have historically survived competition against rivals with more capitalization precisely because of their conversion of personal feelings, solidarity, and loyalty—via low-cost and low-conflict labor—into an economic asset.[4]

The social capital of the ethnic entrepreneur and the ethnic business is therefore represented by their *embeddedness* within the social fabric in question, which in turn influences the form and results of the entrepreneurial endeavor. In terms of ethnicity, networks of social relations develop among individuals who interact with one another on the basis of familiarity derived from a reciprocal intelligibility of meanings, values, and norms. Social capital therefore presupposes the existence and exchange of intangible forms of knowledge that derive from a shared cultural background—cultural capital.[5] According to the definition of Alejandro Portes used here, cultural capital comprises the repertory of symbols that develop in social interaction and come to be used by individuals in ethnic or immigrant groups to interpret and give meaning to their own experience, including in the economic sphere.

Ethnic food and drink manufacturing, sales, and service provide clear examples of how cultural capital is crucial to ethnic entrepreneurship. In fact, cultural capital, in the form of specialized knowledge about "exotic" foods that are unavailable, unknown, or unappealing to an indistinct mass of consumers, has allowed ethnic entrepreneurs in niche markets to enjoy a marginal advantage over competitors with more financial capital but less of that particular, exclusive expertise. Food served by ethnic restaurants is a cultural commodity, as much a set of gastronomic, symbolic, and imaginary knowledge as a dish of nutritious substances. The economy of ethnic restaurants is so strongly influenced by the fact that what they sell is primarily a product of cultural identity that ethnic entrepreneurs can behave ways that may seem irrational from a conventional economic point of view—for example, by hiring or firing kitchen and wait staff because of who they are rather than what they can do. The weight of cultural capital is likewise evident in the case of Italian winemakers in California. Along with their wine, these ethnic businessmen offered fellow Italians throughout the United States the unspoken and intangible value of their ability to interpret the needs and tastes of their consumers, since their common diasporic affiliation implied an obvious cultural familiarity.

The centrality of social and cultural capital for ethnic entrepreneurship also incurs costs. The denser and more complex the networks of social relations, the more individual behavior (of both entrepreneur and worker) is subject to regulation in terms of observance of shared moral precepts and conformity to models of economic action accepted by the community. Cohesive groups prosper together, but they also fail together. On the one hand, internal solidarity supplies resources to individual entrepreneurship; on the other hand, it imposes clear-cut limits on personal initiative. As a result, the ethnic business community tends to occupy well-defined productive or commercial niches and to remain faithful to them even over several generations.[6]

Driven by the need to explain the relative economic successes of various minorities and the speeds at which different immigrant groups advance from a socioeconomic point of view, studies on ethnic entrepreneurship in the Unites States have led to the theorization of *modes of incorporation*—that is, the forms and processes with which immigrant groups of a certain nationality or race integrate into American society as workers, professionals, or entrepreneurs. The idea is that the overall performance of a specific group depends on both the conditions of *exit* (the reasons why the migrants left their country of origin; the legal or illegal conditions of their migration; and the economic and human capital they brought with them) and

Asti, Sonoma County, ca. 1890s. The labor of immigrants transformed the valley on the Russian River into a "winescape." *Out West*, August 1902.

those of *entry* (the state policies regulating immigration; citizenship and social policies; preexisting ethnic communities; and the society's attitude toward that particular group).[7]

When it comes to the conditions of entry, discrimination and racism have played a structural role in the formation of ethnic economic and occupational niches. Not only are immigrants prepared to perform tasks that those born in the United States or the members of other groups are no longer willing to perform, but they also fulfill the request for goods and services that the general economy is unprepared to or uninterested in fulfilling, eventually creating an informal economy (involving economic endeavors that are not illegitimate per se, but are effected outside the law). This is a central notion for this case study, particularly when it comes to how Piedmontese winemakers in California survived, and in some cases even prospered, during Prohibition.

Labor-market discrimination and intrinsic disadvantages like a limited grasp of English can actually act as incentives, rather than deterrents, for immigrants to concentrate themselves in independent businesses. This in turn encourages the formation of niche economies that are both new and unpredictable, since they cannot be related necessarily to the experiences, knowledge, and cultural materials brought by the immigrants from their countries of origin. For example, in the 1970s and 1980s, skilled, educated Korean immigrants in the United States found it impossible to find white-collar work commensurate with their training, mainly because of their lack of fluency in English. They were thus forced into opening small, family-run businesses, typically stores and supermarkets in neighborhoods of large urban areas populated by blacks and Latinos.[8]

The following chapters will address the specific modes of incorporation practiced by Piedmontese immigrants in California in order to explore how the socioeconomic conditions they encountered there—especially the controversial ideas about race and the stigma attached to the production and sale of alcohol—not only guided them toward the niche of winemaking but even favored their primacy in this industry. Rather than constituting a solid and enduring cultural heritage, the unique practices, ethics, and visions of the world transported by immigrants from Piedmont and recirculated in transnational social fields between Italy and California were gradually adapted and molded to a new social reality.

CHAPTER SIX

The Ethnic Edge

The Economy of Matrimonial Strategies
and Family Culture

This chapter and the following two examine how Piedmontese wine-makers Pietro Carlo Rossi, Secondo Guasti, and the Gallo brothers attempted to create and then dominate a mass wine market in the United States by investing in various family, community, and ethnic relational networks and by exercising sensibilities, expectations, and visions of the world that were rooted in their ethnic heritage. These immigrant winemakers had little choice but to accumulate such social and cultural capital, and use their imaginations to make the most of it, due to their late arrival on the California wine scene and their lack of significant startup capital or winemaking skills. Their behavior and mentality represented a unique combination of attitudes that had been shaped in the rural culture of Piedmont, on the one hand, and new, original responses to the socioeconomic conditions they encountered in California. The latter included an enthusiasm for the kind of Americanism that was defined by the individual pursuit of economic success, capitalism, the mass market, and a positivistic faith in technology and innovation. As with their "cooperative spirit," addressed in chapter 4, the concentrated investment in social and cultural capital of Piedmontese winemakers was only one of the reasons they stood out among other, equally motivated competitors, though it did characterize and propel their agency to a significant degree.

Marriage choices and strategies represented one of the most popular ways for Piedmont-born immigrants to build their social capital, as proven by their remarkably high rates of endogamy. The biographical entries included in Cleto Baroni's *Gente italiana in California* (Italian People in California) and the interviews collected in Maurizio Rosso's *Piemontesi nel Far West* (The Piedmontese in the Far West) both reveal that the vast majority of immigrants from this region who arrived in California in the late nineteenth and the early twentieth centuries chose spouses who were also born in Piedmont. Some of the male immigrants even returned to Italy for the sole purpose of marrying a woman from their hometown and bringing her back with them to California.

Endogamy among Piedmontese immigrants was partly the consequence of a deep-seated rural culture that disapproved of marriage to people from other towns or villages—worse yet from other Italian regions. Such unions were considered a dangerous personal hazard and a threat to the native community, which would be impoverished by the loss of someone eligible for continuing social reproduction. Not only did a number of nineteenth-century Piedmontese proverbs stigmatize marriage with "foreigners," but in some parts of the region, those who violated endogamy rules were subjected to an age-old ritual of public mockery and verbal abuse known throughout the subalpine area as the *ciabra* or the *scampanata*.[1] In California, however, such traditional attitudes were also attended by limited access to other brides or grooms due to differences in language, ethnicity, religion, class, and neighborhood.

In the specific case of those who entered the wine trade, the inclination toward endogamy coincided with matrimonial strategies meant to optimize available resources and join forces between families active in the same trade. The marriages of Pietro Carlo Rossi with Amélie Caire and Secondo Guasti with Louisa Amillo were crucial for the two men's careers: not only did their wives guarantee them new and important social connections, but they also turned out to be excellent business partners. Another relevant example is the case of Edoardo Seghesio, whom Pietro Carlo Rossi summoned to Asti, California, in 1886 (the two had grown up together in Dogliani, and Rossi's father's second wife was a Seghesio). In 1892, Edoardo was about to return to Dogliani to look for a wife when the daughter of Luigi Vasconi, the Italian Swiss Colony's head winemaker at the time, arrived in Asti, California, from her birthplace on Lake Maggiore. The two families arranged a wedding shortly thereafter. By 1902, Edoardo and Angela Seghesio had used their family resources to open a winery that is still running today, led by a third generation of Seghesios.[2] One of Edoardo and Angela's daughters also married Enrico Prati, the superintendent at Asti in the late 1910s who later (in 1923) bought the entire block of Italian Swiss Colony shares with brothers Edmund and Robert Rossi.[3]

Not long after Edoardo Seghesio and Angela Vasconi's wedding, Giuseppe/Joe and Michele/Mike Gallo, two modest, recently immigrated wine merchants, began diligently visiting the Hanford home of one of their suppliers, the Piedmont-born immigrant Battista Bianco, and courting his daughters, Susie (Assunta) and Celia (Celestina). Against the wishes of Battista and his wife, who boycotted both wedding ceremonies, Susie and Celia married Joe and Mike, respectively, in 1908 and 1909. For Joe, marriage was a boon. Not only was Susie a tireless partner who did most of the manual labor in the

Pietro Carlo Rossi and his wife, Amélie Caire, ca. 1890. Courtesy Center for Migration Studies, Staten Island, New York.

guesthouse–saloons and farms that he bought and sold up and down the Central Valley, despite his brutal mistreatment of her, but her family also taught him the rudiments of viticulture. (Ernest and Julio Gallo also had their first contact with vineyards in Hanford, having spent most of their childhood with their maternal grandparents because of Joe and Susie's stormy relationship.)[4]

Second-generation Gallos were similarly shrewd in their choices of brides. In 1931, Ernest married Amelia Franzia (1910–1993), the daughter of the Savona-born immigrant Giuseppe Franzia, a rich winemaker from Escalon who played a key role in helping the Gallos market grapes and later wine to the big East Coast cities.[5] In 1933, Julio married Aileen Lowe (1913–1999) in a union that would prove crucial for opening the doors of Modesto high society, which was known for its strict Protestant observance and its aversion to non-Anglo-Saxon immigrants.

Like other immigrant entrepreneurs in the United States—see the paradigmatic case of Agoston Haraszthy discussed in chapter 3—Piedmontese winemakers sought to put a family stamp on their companies and use the capital of solidarity and trust inherent in kinships to their full advantage. While this partly reflected a familist ethos imported from across the Atlantic, it served primarily as an antidote to the hostility they experienced as relative latecomers to an already well-established industry. In fact, as will be seen, family relationships functioned only occasionally as valuable business assets for Piedmontese winemakers, and family management often proved at odds with national, mass-market distribution. Further, none among Rossi, Guasti, and the Gallos had actually set up their migration projects in concert with their native families or invited any of their relatives to follow them to the United States. Nor did they establish any lasting transnational family relations between California and Piedmont or make any effort to circulate capital to or from Piedmont, unlike the majority of participants in other modern Italian diasporas.[6]

Pietro Carlo Rossi, for one, actually used migration to *sever* ties with his family of origin. While he had indeed migrated to San Francisco because his maternal uncle lived there, he swiftly branched out on his own, both personally and professionally. He even distanced himself from his brother Domenico, who had emigrated with him. His children, on the other hand, were a different story. Rossi started early preparing his twins, Edmund and Robert, to succeed him in running the Italian Swiss Colony, which they did after his premature death in 1911. Unfortunately, the Colony's roots as a cooperative financial venture among San Francisco's Italian elite left the company ill prepared for being strictly family run. As noted earlier, Rossi had already decided by 1901 that the Italian Swiss Colony needed to merge with the California Wine Association, paradoxically to preserve significant virtual autonomy (Rossi would remain in charge as president of the former and director of the latter). The Association went on to take control of all the shares from 1913 until 1923, by which time Prohibition had forced the company to stop pressing their Asti-grown grapes and the owners decided to liquidate. Only at this extremely critical point did Edmund and Robert Rossi come back into the game by purchasing the company in partnership with

Ernest Gallo (*right*) with his wife, Amelia Franzia, and Robert Mondavi. Livingston, California, 1992. Courtesy Corbis.

former employee Enrico Prati, going on to run it with admirable skill through the Prohibition years under the name Asti Grape Products. The Rossis and the Pratis ultimately sold the Italian Swiss Colony to National Distillers in 1942 for the impressive sum of $3,673,000. While Edmund and Robert remained in charge as president and vice president for the next five years, no one could still refer to the Italian Swiss Colony as a family business in any way, shape, or form.[7]

Secondo Guasti also appears to have migrated from Mombaruzzo to break away from his family of origin. In fact, rather than strengthening relationships with family back in Piedmont, Secondo and Louisa Guasti's trips to Italy in the 1920s were intended primarily for partaking in "high" Italian culture by visiting the great art cities; satisfying Louisa's Catholic devotion; and buying conspicuous consumer goods, including several works of art with which to furnish their luxurious villa in Cucamonga. Apparently, the only relatives in Italy that the Guastis visited faithfully were members of a wealthier Milanese branch of the family in the notary business.[8]

Nevertheless, Guasti sought to involve as many relatives as possible in the Italian Vineyard Company, even more than Rossi did. When sisters-in-law Rosa and Aurelia Amillo married Emilio Castellano (born in Casale Monferrato, Piedmont, in 1857) and Nicola Giulì (born in the province of Chieti, Abruzzi, in 1885), respectively, Guasti gave all four relatives jobs in the company. Giulì in particular would become the vice president of the Italian Vineyard Company from 1937 to 1939 and the president until 1945.[9] In an interesting parallel with Rossi, not only did Guasti also designate his (only) son, Secondo Jr., to succeed him, but once Prohibition was enacted he, too, understood that his company's survival would depend on powerful external alliances. Thus, in 1920, he pushed for a merger between the Italian Vineyard Company and Fruit Industries Ltd., a large cooperative of wine producers that controlled much of the country's sales of grape juice and concentrate, vinegar, and wine-based tonics. (Fruit Industries Ltd. and the Italian Swiss Colony would dominate the American wine market after Prohibition's repeal, representing the Gallo brothers' strongest competitors.)

Secondo Jr. found himself in a difficult situation when he became president of the Italian Vineyard Company upon his father's death in 1927. Not only were grape prices in free fall (due to the major agricultural crisis that preceded the Wall Street Crash and the onset of the Depression), but Prohibition was placing increasing strain on what had already been a volatile market. To make matters worse, the young Guasti had inherited neither his father's tenacious character nor his business sense. Indeed, he felt more in his element among Los Angeles high society than dealing with the less glamorous, everyday tasks involved in running a winery. By 1934, Secondo Sr.'s dreams of keeping the winery in Guasti hands were dashed when the long-sickly Secondo Jr. passed away, having survived his father by only six years. After his death, James Barlotti, the company's first secretary, took over the reins, followed by Secondo Jr.'s brother-in-law, Nicola Giulì. Louisa Guasti acted as vice president from 1933 until her death in 1937. By this time, the Italian Vineyard Company had already entered a phase of substantial decline that concluded with its sale to the New York–based Garrett & Company in early 1945, though it would return partially into Piedmontese hands when it was acquired by Philo Biane and Joe Aime's Brookside Winery in 1957.[10] Just like with the Italian Swiss Colony, family management proved as incompatible with the company's growth in a national market as did Prohibition.

The E. & J. Gallo Winery, on the other hand, would have a far different fate than either the Italian Swiss Colony or the Italian Vineyard

Women workers in Asti, ca. 1900. *Overland Monthly*, October 1909.

Company in terms of family involvement. In fact, few other large businesses today have more reason to boast of being a family-run company than this Modesto, California, winery. The founders' very business ideology was about keeping the company in family hands at all costs. Ernest and Julio's proverbial reluctance to speak to the media, along with the veil of secrecy that has surrounded the company's endeavors over the years, were just two repercussions of that attitude. In his autobiography, Ernest Gallo described their approach in quasi-spiritual terms:

Since we started our winery in the summer of 1933 . . . it has always been our philosophy to do whatever was to the long-range benefit of our company, regardless of its effect on current profits. Our attitude is considered fairly unusual in this age of often overpaid managers of public companies, whose primary interest is a favorable earnings comparison to the previous quarter or year in order to earn a current bonus, too often regardless of the long-range effect on the company. We have been able to maintain this philosophy because we have kept our business private, entirely in the family. We do not like to answer to anyone for our mistakes. (My advice to a group of young company presidents was this: "Keep your company private, and if it has already gone public, buy it back.")[11]

The Gallos were systematic in preparing their children and countless grandchildren far in advance to run the company and its various divisions. They also used the symbol of the clan to construct a family/business ideology that gave life and meaning to the company's family culture. Such symbolic creativity is epitomized by the Gallo Christmas ritual, observed each year, in which three generations gather to consume *bagna cauda*—a Piedmontese dip made with garlic, anchovies, and walnut or olive oil.[12] Yet there are also numerous, substantial cracks in the Gallo Winery's self-representation as a homestead in which blood ties find the perfect metaphor in bonds created by wine. Ellen Hawkes' 1993 anti-biography, *Blood and Wine*, brings these cracks mercilessly to light, revealing in her pertinacity how American middle-class culture maintained a morally prejudiced, and covertly nativist, attitude toward alcohol production until as late as the 1990s. The book is mainly an account of the judicial controversy that pitted Ernest and Julio against their younger brother, Joseph Jr. (1919–2007), in a precedent-setting case regarding the use of a personal name as a registered brand. The conflict began in April 1986 when Ernest and Julio denounced Joseph's illegitimate use of the Gallo name for his dairy business. As emerged during the trial, Joseph had always remained on the margins of the business (and profits) of the E. & J. Gallo Winery. He responded with a countercharge, hinged on his right to obtain a third of the company, considering that it represented an extension of the farm inherited from their parents, even if the original business had grown into the largest private winery in the world. But Ernest and Julio's defense team was successful in proving that the E. & J. Gallo Winery's foundation in 1933 had been entirely financed by the two older brothers and had nothing to do with the winery run by their parents, who had died tragically that same year. According to Hawkes, this is precisely why Ernest and Julio always insisted on their condition as self-taught and nearly propertyless when they had started their winery and never emphasized their origins in a winemaking family, unlike many of their competitors. Joseph's counterclaim was defeated in late 1988, and a few months later the court prohibited him from using the Gallo name on his cheeses any longer. Walking out of the courthouse, a disconsolate Joseph commented, "I have only got one name. I don't know how I'm supposed to look for another one."[13]

After opening her book with this devastating case for the company's family image, Hawkes goes on to detail a whole series of moral troubles masked by Ernest and Julio Gallo's apparent familism. As Hawkes reveals, Susie Bianco's life with her husband, Joe Gallo, was punctuated by domestic violence and abuse, driving her twice to seek divorce (only to withdraw her requests under Joe's pressure) before dying brutally at his hands in the apparent homicide–suicide on the Fresno farm. Uncle Mike's numerous arrests for bootlegging in the 1920s earned him a solid reputation as a gangster, and after

World War II his wealthy nephews left him living in a trailer park near Las Vegas as an embarrassing relic of a time with which they wished to sever all ties. When Ernest and Julio had needed loans to start their business ventures, their "family" had likewise closed the door in their faces. As Ernest explains in his autobiography, in 1933, both his aunt Celia and his father-in-law, Giuseppe Franzia, denied him the few thousand dollars he needed to buy the property for his first winery.[14]

While Ernest and Julio had long harbored plans of passing the company to their sons, when this finally happened, the transfer did not go smoothly. The most dramatic case was that of Julio's second son, Philip, who took his own life in 1958 after being tormented for years by the clan's lurking doubts about his sexuality. In the 1980s, business journalists would remark that Ernest's sons—mainly his first son, David, but also his second son, Joseph (the current copresident of the E. & J. Gallo Winery with Julio's son, Robert J. Gallo, and son-in-law, James Coleman)—were pale imitations of their father. One 1986 article in particular, in the authoritative *Fortune* magazine, went so far as to alleging that "David's behavior [is] occasionally bizarre. He habitually pokes his eyes and nose with paper clips."[15] The article angered Ernest tremendously and the E. & J. Gallo Winery immediately withdrew $650,000 in advertising from the magazines of *Fortune*'s publisher, Time Inc., and subsequently issued a press release upholding the important roles Ernest's sons played in the company and the unconditional trust placed in them.[16] Even in light of the fortunes reaped by the next generation of Gallos (a full sixteen of them are currently involved in the company), such tribulations create the overall impression that a familist ideology and a strategy of dynastic transfer of leadership were used only when they could effectively reinforce the strength of the management, especially that of patriarch Ernest Gallo.

Little in the way of a "Piedmontese family culture" can therefore be identified in the actions of Piedmontese winemakers in California. Far from being an inherited ethnic cultural trait, family ideology was more often bent toward a company's needs or determined by the context in which the ethnic entrepreneurs were embedded.

CHAPTER SEVEN

White Labor *and* Happy Families
Race, Social Capital, and Paternalism

The flexibility and pragmatism Piedmontese winemakers showed in adapting their family culture to economic circumstances similarly characterizes the way they used their ethnic origins to help them develop profitable social relationships. Indeed, it has already been noted that a common cultural identity activated crucial channels of solidarity between people from the same town or region: the Piedmont-born Giuseppe Ollino presented Pietro Carlo Rossi to Sbarboro; Secondo Guasti found partners among the tight-knit circle of Piedmont natives in Los Angeles to support his idea of transforming a desert wasteland into a vineyard; and the intractable Joe Gallo freed himself from manual labor by managing guesthouses whose main customers were immigrants from Piedmont, and generally moved within an immigrant milieu, before and after his pivotal encounter with his in-laws, the Biancos. In Escalon, for example, Joe's main contact was Dante Forresti, an Asti, Italy–born immigrant who had also managed a boardinghouse in San Francisco and had acquired a sizeable stretch of vineyards with his earnings. Despite their refusal to recognize any paternal inheritance, at the outset of their endeavors Ernest and Julio made broad use of the circle of contacts their father had built for himself among Northern Italian winemakers and sellers in Modesto and environs. Forresti in particular turned out to be vital for Ernest in obtaining a license to produce alcohol just weeks before the Eighteenth Amendment was officially repealed, thereby saving him precious time for the launch of his winery. Indeed, Forresti had trafficked in wine during Prohibition, knew the loopholes of alcohol legislation, and had influential connections in the city.[1]

While this "group mentality" was undoubtedly important, the area in which Piedmontese winemakers got the best return for their social capital was surely in the recruitment and control of their workforce—another point, along with associationist skills and access to credit, on which Sebastian Fichera insists. This ethnic asset is especially evident in the cases of the Italian Swiss Colony and the Italian Vineyard Company, both of which operated during a time when new Italian immigrants represented a potentially unlimited reservoir of labor, and before the racist Immigration Act of 1924 established national immigration quotas and blocked the flow of immigrants from Southern and Eastern Europe.

Both Pietro Carlo Rossi and Secondo Guasti initiated chain migrations by activating channels of personal contacts to attract rural Piedmontese workers to their California vineyards in San Francisco and Los Angeles, respectively. The large number of migrants who came to Asti in California from Rocca d'Arazzo (a village in the Italian province of Asti) can be explained by the presence of Giuseppe Ollino, the Italian Swiss Colony's vice president and a native of that town. The first arrivals were often followed by relatives and friends, thereby forming the "chain."[2] The 1920 U.S. Census reveals that while the town of Guasti's population included single male workers, it was mainly composed of a few relatively large Piedmontese families. In

Workers of the Italian Swiss Colony eat in barracks used as a canteen, ca. 1900. *Out West*, August 1902.

his research, the historian Maurizio Rosso identified one substantial village-based chain in particular that had arrived in Guasti from Bosconero, a small rural town in the province of Turin. In fact, the Italian Vineyard Company employed entire families from this one town.

The existence of and familiarity with such channels of recruitment was an obvious advantage for any peasants who wished to become migrants. As soon as they got off the boat in the United States, such workers already had a place to go and a job that awaited them. Their lack of English, which could otherwise have impeded many of their aspirations, posed few problems. For some, working for fellow townspeople was the pathway to relatively swift upward mobility, either as winery employees (Rossi and Guasti mostly tried to bring experienced winemakers from Piedmont who could take on semiskilled

Andrea Sbarboro (*center, under the sign*) with visitors to the Italian Swiss Colony at the Asti train stop, ca. 1895. Courtesy Alfreda Cullinan/San Francisco Museum and Historical Society.

and skilled jobs); or, later, through their own grape-growing and winemaking businesses.[4] But the ethnic economy based on grapes and wine did not benefit all the actors in the same way. Hiring Piedmontese workers was primarily an advantage for the ethnic entrepreneurs in terms of having access to a large pool of low-cost labor, an absence of unionization, and the ability to prevent conflicts through paternalism.

A useful source for understanding the wage situation encountered by Piedmontese immigrants is a report on the California wine industry drafted by the United States Immigration Commission (better known as the Dillingham Commission) in 1909. Aimed at gathering information to help Congress draft the first general immigration law in U.S. history (later formalized in the Immigration Act of 1924), the commission's work was inspired by an overall selection process to separate socially "valuable" races from "harmful" ones, which was itself culturally influenced by current studies in scientific racism and eugenics.[5] Significantly, the report divides California wine-industry workers into "whites" (Americans, Brits, Scots, the Irish, the French, Germans, and Scandinavians), representing 43 percent of all employees; Italians (40 percent); Mexicans (5 percent); the Chinese (4 percent); and the Japanese (3 percent).

According to the report, Italians were mostly employed by Italian-owned wineries and constituted the majority of their workforces. This ethnic concentration was reflected by the workers' engagement in every occupation, including semiskilled and skilled jobs, as Fichera has emphasized. But they were also clearly overrepresented in unskilled jobs: "Of the white employees a little more than one-half are 'general laborers' and 'cellarmen,' while more than two-thirds of the Italians are engaged in these two occupations. Of those engaged in more skilled and higher paid occupations the number of 'white' persons exceeds the number of Italians." The figures in the report reveal that 34 percent of Italian workers were paid $1.00–$1.25 a day; 37 percent were paid $1.25–$1.50 a day; and 9 percent were paid $1.50–$1.75 a day (all salaries included room and board). Moreover, a full 14 percent were paid less than a dollar a day, a salary bracket that included just one other race, the Japanese: "Of the men reporting earnings with board and lodging included, the Japanese and Italians show the lowest rate, there being 4 out of 11 Japanese reporting less than $1 per day with board, while 18 of the 127 Italians are in the same group. The Japanese and the Italians are the poorest paid races."[6] The median wage was thus little more, and in some cases less, than what Sbarboro claimed to have offered the Italian Swiss Colony's first workers nearly thirty years earlier: "Thirty to forty dollars a month, with good food, wine at their meals."[7]

Joe Aime, an Italian Vineyard Company employee who had immigrated to Guasti from Entraque, Piedmont, in 1913 at just eight years of age, recalled that in the early 1920s, the wage of the (Italian) men employed by the winery was $1.75 per eleven-hour workday. Aime also asserted that no labor unrest ever took place during his years in Guasti, let alone any strikes. The only dispute Aime could recall was one instigated by the boys his age who protested against being paid $0.75 a day for the same hours worked by the adults, and that this was settled with the provision of a small increase.[8] But even recollections of minor disputes and struggles are exceptional. Other oral histories of Italian winemakers insist on a total absence of work conflicts in both Asti and Guasti.

How was such an unnatural convergence of low salaries and low conflict possible? One explanation lies in how fully Rossi and Guasti adhered to American capitalism's overwhelmingly racist approach to labor management. Both the Italian Swiss Colony and the Italian Vineyard Company based their hiring, wage, and task-distribution policies on race, to the full benefit of the employers. As the Dillingham Commission report shows, in the early twentieth century each race was in competition with the others for access to the best jobs in the U.S. labor market. Each was considered more or less suitable for certain occupations and wages and had different prospects of social mobility. At the top of the pyramid drawn by Dillingham Commission inspectors were "whites," who proportionally occupied the highest-skilled jobs and enjoyed the best wages. Indeed, few white laborers remained in California winemaking by then, as a result of an inevitably upward social mobility of the racially privileged, which also propelled the entry of an increasing number of Italians into the winemaking labor market: "The numbers of ['miscellaneous white persons' and Italians] are now about equal, but formerly the proportion of Italians was smaller. Much of the work connected with wine making is disagreeable and many of the 'miscellaneous whites' have left this work to engage in more agreeable and better-paid occupations. Italians have become more numerous in the State and have engaged in this work in more numbers."[9]

As the Dillingham Commission survey reveals, Italians were poorly paid precisely because they mainly worked in Italian-owned wineries: "The difference in the earnings of Italians and those of the 'miscellaneous whites' is partly due to ... the fact that so many of the Italians work in wineries controlled by Italians, in the majority of which lower wages are paid than in other wineries."[10] Antonio Perelli-Minetti, a young but skilled winemaker brought over to Asti from Italy by Giuseppe Ollino, immediately experienced the impact of race on the rights and wage conditions of workers at the Italian Swiss Colony and within the California wine industry at large:

The crushing season started I think in August. During the grape season Asti employed a weighmaster, a name I can never forget, Shirley Black.... Mr. Rossi and Mr. Sbarboro were together.... I said to Mr. Rossi, "I have a man by the name of Shirley Black, but nobody has told me how much his wage is." So Mr. Rossi said to me, "$125 a month. You know, he is American, and if we don't pay them good wages, they criticize us." I said to myself, "I am in the wrong church. I am getting $75 a month because I am Italian and the other fellow is getting $125 a month because he is American." So Mr. Rossi must have seen the muscles in my face work. I didn't say anything.[11]

Why did Perelli-Minetti not say anything? To the full advantage of Rossi and Guasti, Italian vine workers had little hope of being paid any more in the non-Italian wineries precisely because they were Italian—that is, not only because they spoke little to no English or because they had recently arrived in the United States, but also for purely racial reasons. In fact, "in some wineries Italians are considered better as 'common laborers' and 'cellarmen' because they are satisfied with much of the work which is distasteful to natives and north Europeans.... On the other hand, other employers prefer the 'miscellaneous white' because they are considered the more temperate and also the more intelligent."[12] In other words, Italian grape growers and winemakers in California, like other Catholic and Jewish immigrants from Southern and Eastern Europe, took on what the labor historians James R. Barrett and David R. Roediger have defined as inbetween jobs. Such occupations were reserved for workers whose skin color was white—with all the positive legal and social implications this involved—yet not exactly "white" as defined by the complex and contingent social, cultural, judicial, and scientific criteria of early twentieth-century American racism.[13]

On the other hand, being racially "inbetween" may have provided Piedmontese immigrants in California with an important, supplementary motivational drive toward opening their own businesses. Indeed, the racialization of the labor market limited both their upward *and* their downward mobility. New European immigrants received a fundamental message with their inbetween jobs: that what was truly important in the United States was not being black or "yellow." Immigrants interiorized an awareness of the many advantages of a white identity via socialization in the workplace; sociability during leisure time; the prejudices and behavior of superiors; union policies and strategies; and the mass media. The dynamics of racial discrimination would have been obvious to late nineteenth-century Piedmont-born immigrants in California, as naive as they may have been about the meaning of the color divide when they first arrived in the United States. In 1882, Lorenzo Feraud recounted the experience of some Biella-born immigrant workers rubbing elbows with Chinese laborers in the repair of a sewer:

> Sometimes [the Piedmontese] felt dizzy, so they would lean against a wall dripping with a dark green liquid, wait for the faintness to pass, and then start working again. The Chinese remained quiet, their hair gathered in a braid around their head and hidden under a shabby cap, coming and going as if it were nothing.... Although our protagonists felt no particular sympathy for these people of the Celestial Empire, and like others hoped for their banishment, they were nevertheless forced to admire these fellow workers who adapted to everything and blindly obeyed every command, without complaint, working better and harder than the men of other races. They would leave around evening, washing and cleaning themselves as best they could, and would return to their rooms, tired and feverish but content. People avoided them in the street and many who passed them held their noses, whereas the Italians were treated with great respect, as though they were royalty. Such a comparison may sound exaggerated, but it is all true, and no one could ever say otherwise.[14]

Racial stigma made the Chinese, the Japanese, Filipinos, Mexicans, and African Americans *perpetually* destined for worse jobs, lower wages, and fewer civil and social rights than whites. Not only had racist legislation on immigration already excluded new arrivals from China in 1882, but by the end of the nineteenth century, both the Chinese and the Japanese (whose immigration was limited but not forbidden) formed a reserve supply of labor that was only to be used when there was a temporary lack of white labor, to be dismissed at the first opportunity.[15] "The general tendency has been to discriminate against Asiatics in winery work," asserted the Dillingham

Guasti, ca. 1910. Italian woman and girl in front of one of the houses the Italian Vineyard Company offered to workers with family. Before Prohibition, company housing was reserved to Italians. Japanese and Mexican temporary workers camped outside town, across the Southern Pacific Railroad. Courtesy Cal Poly Pomona University Library Special Collections.

Commission report.[16] Asian immigrants were effectively relegated to carrying out temporary migrant jobs like harvesting, for which they made up 92 percent of the workforce employed. Two-thirds of the grape gatherers were Japanese, a seventh were Chinese, and a fifteenth were Indian, the latter being "personally disliked because of their filthy habits, and [considered] the least intelligent among the races employed."[17]

The racialization of the Californian labor market allowed Rossi and Guasti to use their ethnicity (i.e., their Piedmontese origins) as a particularly potent weapon. On the one hand, the discrimination practiced by the "white" winemaking companies against Italian immigrant labor limited the alternatives available to the workers of the Italian Swiss Colony and the Italian Vineyard Company. On the other hand, the potential availability of a large, prejudicially underpaid workforce of Asians and Mexicans allowed the Piedmontese immigrant entrepreneurs to relativize the low wages paid to their Italian workers and, if need be, threaten to use it in retaliation against any demands for higher wages or better work conditions.

In Asti, as has been noted, Sbarboro insisted on inserting a ban against Asian workers in his company's statute, thereby making ethnic membership a prerequisite for employment. Over the years, the veto against Asian labor was blatantly upheld as proof of the Italian Swiss Colony's national communitarianism, which even bridged class differences. To further justify the company's racist hiring policy, Sbarboro

Italian workers in front of the main winery of the Italian Vineyard Company, early twentieth century. Courtesy Cal Poly Pomona University Library Special Collections.

described how an experiment to hire Japanese workers on a ranch in the southern part of the state had produced disastrous results:

> It is a well-known fact that the Japanese never keep their agreements unless they have to. Many farmers know this to their sorrow. Some years ago, the crop of the vineyard of the Italian Swiss Colony at Madera was so large that extra pickers had to be found. White people could not be had, so Mr. Rossi hired a company of Japanese to pick grapes at the high price of $1.50 a ton. They worked for a few days when they suddenly quit, without notice, and left for another place, where, we were informed afterwards, they obtained a little more. This naturally occasioned a large loss for the Colony, as we expected that the Japanese would finish the picking of the grapes and consequently had made no other provision for the work.[18]

The incident is revealing of the direct relationship between race and wages that existed at the Italian Swiss Colony and, in turn, of the delicate balance with which the Colony's management administered the economic and non-economic benefits that color and ethnicity carried. In this sense, it is telling that a wage issue was rationalized as a "betrayal of race" that strengthened the Italian Swiss Colony's resolve to pursue its ethnically based labor policy, leading it to promote several public initiatives in support of an immigration law that was both strongly anti-Oriental and generous toward Italian immigration. The winery's "Italianness" constituted a blood pact between the leadership and the workers. By signing it, however, the latter renounced any recourse to labor protest and struggle.

On the rare recorded occasions in which social peace was jeopardized at the Colony, employer repression ensued and restored order. In 1915, the local chapter of the Federazione Socialista Italiana (FSI), a radical Italian organization, invited the prominent labor organizer and editor Carlo Tresca from New York to do a propaganda tour in Northern California. On March 13, Tresca made an unannounced visit to Asti to try to talk to the winery workers—a bold move considering he knew that neither radicals nor union organizers had ever penetrated the Colony. After the guards had apparently driven Tresca out, many workers rose up, demanding the radical orator be allowed to speak. The FSI newspaper *Il Proletario* described Tresca's visit to the Italian Swiss Colony as "the most audacious undertaking possible in California," and called the unexpected reaction of the winery workers a major victory. "Never would I have thought," wrote the reporter, "that comrade Carlo Tresca's propaganda tour of California could have aroused so much enthusiasm even in localities where until today our propagandists have never visited."[19]

Vineyards of North Cucamonga (Guasti), ca. 1907. A Japanese woman picking grapes with her child. Courtesy Cal Poly Pomona University Library Special Collections.

The employer–worker relationship was similarly ethnicized in Guasti, though by different means. From the outset, the Italian Vineyard Company hired hundreds of non-Italian—and nonwhite—workers for the harvesting period. The Japanese made up this temporary migrant workforce until World War I, after which the workers were primarily Mexican. In the 1920s, when new immigration from Italy had reduced to a trickle, the Guasti company was forced to start recruiting several Mexicans on yearly contracts. But Secondo Guasti was careful to draw lines between Piedmontese workers, on the one hand, and Asian and Latino migrants when it came to distinctions in wages or benefits. When the journalist Lanier Bartlett visited Guasti in 1909, he described the composition and conditions of the company's workforce in predominantly racial terms:

> The permanent workers number 250, and most of them are direct from Italy, France, and Spain, where the best vineyard workers are to be found. The company provides them with model quarters—neat cottages for the married folk, and a club-house with two dormitories, showers and tub baths, and large social hall for the single men. A schoolhouse was built on the property by the company and presented to the county. During the crushing season, which lasts from late August until into November (the second crop on certain kinds of vines being very large), it is necessary to augment the regular workers with from two hundred and fifty to three hundred Japanese pickers. The owners of the vineyard are possessed of the usual dislike and distrust of Japanese, but it is next to impossible to get together enough white laborers who are willing to go out into the hot acres and stay on a job that is merely temporary.... The pickers are, therefore, furnished by Japanese contractors who establish camps in the vineyard, where are often to be found whole Japanese families, the women and children adding to the picturesque squalor of the bivouac.[20]

In the following years, Guasti's space came to be organized by race: "The village grew on both sides of the Southern Pacific Railroad. . . . On the other side of the tracks was a tent city where the Mexican people stayed and the Blacks and the Orientals were further down."[21] A differentiated distribution of rights and resources and a systematic, symbolic structuring of everyday life thus offered Italian workers the feeling of social superiority. Indeed, they were compensated for their modest salaries with an elaborate set of benefits based purely on their racial affiliation. This is an exemplary case of what the historian David Roediger has defined as the "wages of whiteness," which in turn harks back to the civil rights leader W. E. B. Du Bois's critique of all the European Americans who privileged white identity over class in the nineteenth and twentieth centuries.[22]

The case of the church of San Secondo d'Asti, built in 1924 on the wishes of Louisa Amillo Guasti, shows how the efforts to symbolically articulate the hierarchies of race in terms of space continued in Guasti until at least the death of Secondo Sr. Following a consecration ceremony in 1926 that ended with "an Italian dinner [that] was served to all those who had taken part in the dedicatory service and to the stockholders and their families,"[23] the church of San Secondo d'Asti was the focus of disagreements between the Guasti family and the parish priests who had been sent there by the local diocese. Four different priests would pass through its doors in the first year alone. According to Guasti's first preacher, Reverend Joseph Tonelli, the divergences were caused by the paradox of a church built for Italians who never attended—while the Mexicans came in droves. Further, the priest and the Guastis were at odds over how to spend the funds supplied by the latter. While the cleric wished to use them for religious purposes, the Guastis preferred that they be used to embellish the church according to their own tastes.

Picking grapes at the Italian Vineyard Company, ca. 1907. Pickers in Guasti were Japanese, Mexican, and sometimes African American seasonal migrant workers. They were hired in labor gangs and camped outside the village, by the vineyards. Courtesy Cal Poly Pomona University Library Special Collections.

The fourth priest, Joseph Cotta, abandoned his post after Louisa Guasti ordered him to remove all the ornaments he had used to decorate the church in honor of the sensibility of his most devoted parishioners, the Mexicans. In a testimony to the diocese, Cotta reported, "In the afternoon, the same Mrs. Guasti, Sr., came at 4 p.m., and I told her everything beginning with the words: 'You killed me and everything with my poor Mexicans... devotion, piety, fervor, faith, and everything.... 'Madam,' I said, 'ask any of these poor Mexican girls and boys... Ask the whole Mexican colony...' but she said, 'Oh, after all they are all our servants!'"[24]

The concomitance of low wages and low labor conflict in Piedmontese wineries must be considered in light of the intersection between labor issues and race. When Bartlett concluded his long article on Secondo Guasti, he emphasized this very centrality of race in labor management by asserting that Guasti "is an ardent worker for social uplift, a fact which is practically demonstrated by his treatment of white labor on the great property which he controls." Bartlett's words also reveal how relative and viscous the idea of race was in early twentieth-century California. While Piedmontese peasants were not really white in the eyes of Irish, German, or Scandinavian winemakers, nor in those of the Dillingham Commission reporters on immigration, they became inarguably white when surrounded by a mass of seasonal Japanese and Mexican migrant workers.[25]

The second reason the Piedmontese wineries enjoyed both access to low-cost labor and relative harmony between management and workers was the dedication and commitment with which both Rossi and Guasti created an elaborate system of benefits for the worker–citizens of their company towns. As a whole, the various kinds of nonmonetary compensation enjoyed by the employees of the Italian Swiss Colony and the Italian Vineyard Company provide an interesting example of ethnic-based benevolent capitalism. In Asti, "the settlement of laborers, with their happy families, containing over 50 bright and healthy children, all born there, and attending a neat school house of their own, forms in itself a most pleasing moral picture. It has a post office, telephone and telegraphic communication, charming private villas and costly, artistic gardens erected by the Colony's directors as summer resorts for their families. There is perhaps no happier community on the face of earth. No doctors, no druggists. None are hardly ever needed—thanks to God."[26]

The expensive new boardinghouse built for (and by) the winery's workers in 1911 was publicized in wine trade journals as a state-of-the-art building. Completed with the help of brick- and tile-making machines purposely brought in from Milan, its construction was an occasion to recall that "the colony has always been solicitous about the welfare of its employees, and this handsome new lodging house will contribute much to their comfortable life at Asti."[27]

As highlighted in Bartlett's eyewitness account, Guasti invested just as much as Rossi and Sbarboro in the benefits reserved for the Italian workers of the Italian Vineyard Company. New arrivals could count on not only a permanent job but also decent lodging, typically divided into single-family homes with little gardens for the families and a communal structure for the unmarried men. Some of the women in Guasti even volunteered to prepare meals for the workers without families. A large two-story building was built to house the administrative offices, to serve as a meeting place for the shareholders, and to host receptions. It was also the first place to accommodate Guasti's school, which began operating in 1904 and offered classes for children up to the fifth grade. Secondo Guasti later sold the school to the local educational district for a symbolic price, on the condition it be called the Piedmont School in honor of his birth region. A grocery store and a bakery also opened in 1913 to sell Italian food specialties, and a reading-room/library was established for the workers in 1920.[28]

The sense of ethnic community and identity provided by the two company towns of Asti and Guasti was also periodically promoted through recreational activities such as receptions, picnics, banquets, dances, and parties. Sbarboro, Rossi, and Guasti mainly used such events to impress important guests—especially company sharehold-ers, influential politicians of various factions, and key figures in other industries of Californian society—with the results achieved by their wineries. But they also made sure to involve the workers and their families, who belonged for all intents and purposes to the picture of happy integration and self-sufficiency that the owners used such occasions to promote both inside and outside the Italian Ameri-can community: "A harvest festival, the 'marenda' [Easter Monday in Piedmontese dialect] and the anniversary of the discovery of America were also celebrated in Guasti.... The women cooked traditional dishes, there was a great roast and, of course, there were as many grapes and as much wine as anyone could want. People sang and danced in a high-spirited atmosphere, one person played the harmonica, another brought the wine, another still brought the food."[29] At Christmas, Secondo Guasti would host a large party in his luxurious home and invite all the town's children.[30]

Even Sbarboro, Rossi, and Guasti's opulent villas were organic parts of their paternalist program. Sbarboro constructed his Asti villa by copying the plan of the House of the Vettii in Pompeii, which he had visited on one of his trips to Italy. Doric columns framed the entrance gate of "Villa Pompeii," which featured the word "SALVE" (hello) in mosaic and led to an inner courtyard containing statues and a marble basin.[31] Pietro Carlo Rossi built his residence, which he pretentiously called "Buen Ritiro" (Fine Retreat), on top of a small hill, thereby reinforcing his leadership role geographically. The construction of Secondo Guasti's dwelling, "a fabulous Italian Renaissance revival (or Mediterranean) style executive mansion" surrounded by meticulously manicured flower gardens, was completed in 1924.[32] The classic styles of both Sbarboro and Guasti's villas added elements of rural harmony to the company towns. Asti and Guasti were organized and represented as villages in which the home of the enlightened patriarch and the modest but dignified houses of the workers stood together as symbols of the shared accomplishments of both Italian work and high Italian culture.

Finally, what truly helped to reinforce ethnic communitarianism and identity was the establishment of the towns' respective churches. Our Lady of Mount Carmel was built in Asti in 1907 on a piece of land given to the archbishop of San Francisco by the Italian Swiss Colony. Not only did the company and its employees provide the

Asti, California, today. The new Our Lady of Mount Carmel Church, built in 1960, stands a few feet away from the site of the original church. The old church had been built in 1907, was also barrel shaped, and was made with actual wood from the barrels of the Italian Swiss Colony. Photo Simone Cinotto.

funds and materials for the church, but they also offered to build it for free, basing its design on the distinctive shape of a wine barrel. (In 1950, the church was demolished and reconstructed a few feet away using wood from unused barrels.)[33] The church of San Secondo d'Asti in Guasti was supposed to be as close a replica as possible of the original one in Asti, Piedmont, even if the capacities of the two structures would inevitably be quite different (three hundred in California and two thousand in Piedmont). Masons and carpenters were called in from Piedmont and Mexico for its construction, while blacksmiths in Guasti prepared the iron parts. The bells were cast in Italy and transported to California. As noted earlier, the problems surrounding San Secondo stemmed from the fact that, unlike the priests sent by the Los Angeles diocese, the first generation of Guastis did not think of it as a generic house of souls—be they Italian or Mexican. Rather, they regarded it as a family chapel in which to celebrate the success of Secondo's winery and the ethnic community he had built around it.[34]

In sum, Piedmontese winemakers articulated a narrative of ethnic identity that benefited from the specific racial and racist structure of California society on the one hand, and aimed at interclass national solidarity on the other. This attitude is epitomized by a two-page, Italian-language flyer, "Un appello alla popolazione italiana e svizzera degli Stati Uniti" (A Call to the Italian and Swiss People of the United States), which was printed by the Italian Swiss Colony and circulated to thousands of Italian Americans around 1910. To encourage consumption of the Colony's products among its ethnic audience, the flyer did more than just emphasize the quality of its wine, produced as it was by Italians familiar with Italian tastes. Replete with images from the Italian nationalist iconography of the time, the leaflet also stressed that the winery employed many fellow Italian Americans, that it created wealth for the Italian community in the United States, and that it upheld the "good name" of Italians in the United States in general. Each of these points would have resonated strongly with an ethnic group struggling to carve out its place in the racially structured hierarchy of American society.[35] Heavy doses of paternalism clearly ran throughout such efforts. Proletarian immigrants paid for the nonmonetary and immaterial benefits bestowed on them by ethnic winemaking entrepreneurs with modest wages and meager possibilities of reproach. Seen in this light, the description of Secondo Guasti by a sympathetic journalist like Bartlett has even greater impact: "[Guasti is] a beaming, humorous, jolly good fellow in the company of his intimates, and generous to a marked degree toward any worthy person who comes to him in distress; but short-spoken, incisive, and brusque when it concerns the days' work. Indeed, he is tremendously American in his adherence to the national motto: Business is business."[36]

CHAPTER 8

Italian Winemakers *and* *the* American System

THE IRRESISTIBLE APPEAL
OF MASS PRODUCTION

During the late nineteenth century and much of the twentieth, Piedmontese winemakers operated under unique conditions dictated by the U.S. wine market. Not only was the industrial production of alcoholic beverages shadowed by the moral and religious condemnation of American politics and society, but Italian winemakers also rarely hired non-Italian workers or sold their products to non-Italian customers. Yet despite all this, or perhaps precisely to counterbalance the fact that they traded in a product that was so disputably "American," Piedmontese winemakers earnestly embraced the dictates of U.S. capitalism and the mass market. They constantly innovated and mechanized their methods of production, preservation, and long-distance transportation. They also integrated their companies into the country's economic system by paying close attention to the dynamics of both the wine market and public regulation. Indeed, they often represented the avant-garde of American winemaking in fields like research, product development, marketing, and advertising.

In the historiography of California wine, the Italian Swiss Colony, and more specifically its first president, Pietro Carlo Rossi, is unanimously considered a leading figure in the modernization of the American wine industry. The giant size of its wine-storage tanks, for example, was widely publicized by industry journals as a clear indication of the Asti company's production power. By 1891, "the twins"—two large tanks as tall as two-story houses, with the capacity of twenty-five thousand gallons each—had already transformed the Asti site into one of the main attractions of Sonoma County.[1] A few years later, the company built a cistern that was promptly baptized the largest in the world. Made of Portland cement and located underground, the enormous tank could hold up to five hundred thousand gallons. Sbarboro had asked superintendent Luigi Vasconi to build it for him in a record forty-six days to store the exceptional harvest of 1897. Rossi had the walls covered in paraffin to maintain ideal conditions for the wine's insulation.[2]

The mechanized systems used in Asti were also decisively groundbreaking. The company was already using steam pumps by the turn of the century and introduced electricity to its grape-pressing process shortly thereafter. At a time when most other wineries were still lighting huge bonfires to ward off nighttime frost, the Asti company had already started using portable kerosene heaters.[3] The Italian Swiss Colony's new, futuristic premises, built in San Francisco in 1903 and housing high-capacity tanks, also made news. For one thing, the building was constructed using such advanced materials and criteria that it survived the devastating earthquake that destroyed two-thirds of the city three years after it was built. The survival of its structure and contents gave the winery a considerable advantage over competitors who had suffered serious damage from the quake.[4]

Visitors of Asti on the top of the "world's largest wine tank," built to store the 1897 harvest. In the background, the flag of the Kingdom of Italy waves. Ca. 1905. Collection of the author.

Rossi also applied the results of the most up-to-date chemistry research to the winemaking process. In particular, the Dogliani-born immigrant was one of the first to use sulfur dioxide to counter the effects of yeast on the grape must during fermentation and thus stabilize the wine. Thanks to him, the Italian Swiss Colony became a leader in the industrial use of refrigeration, which promotes the formation of tartrate crystals and better preserves wine. Rossi was in fact a tireless researcher who traveled throughout Europe to study the most advanced winemaking methods of the day. His interest in warm-climate wine production—stemming from the expansion of the Italian Swiss Colony's business to Madera and other vineyards in Southern California—led him as far afield as Algeria.[5]

Rossi's experience is an excellent example of how Piedmontese winemakers in California fervently sharpened their technical and merchandizing skills despite having inherited so little knowledge of wine from their early years in Piedmont. It also shows how, at the turn of the twentieth century, being a "foreigner" who spoke English as a second language gave immigrant winemakers a certain advantage when it came to identifying and importing technologies that were being developed outside the United States. During a trip to Europe in 1909, for example, Rossi secured the collaboration of Charles Jadeau, a winemaker from the Loire with extensive experience making Saumur Mousseaux wines, which are produced in a similar way to champagne. Rossi bought the proper equipment and convinced the Frenchman to follow him to California to head up a new line of sparkling wines. Jadeau, whose very presence in Asti notably enhanced the prestige of Rossi and Sbarboro's company, was the key figure behind one of the Italian Swiss Colony's most successful products: the Golden State Champagne.[6]

Secondo Guasti, the Italian Swiss Colony's declared admirer and imitator, was equally enthusiastic about using technological progress to streamline productivity. Guasti also experimented with unconventional techniques, like using narrow-gauge railroad tracks to transport grapes in gondola cars from the farthest vineyards of his vast holding to the crushing facility. He also consulted with enologists from the University of California regarding the best grapes for Cucamonga's hot, dry climate, and donated twenty acres of land to the university to establish a research center. Some of the varieties selected and developed by the scientists, including the Grignolino, became the cornerstones of grape cultivation in the area around Los Angeles.[7]

Technology, research, and development likewise formed the essence of the Gallo brothers' entrepreneurial credo. "A constant striving for perfection in every aspect of our business" is how Ernest put it, though this attitude developed primarily in the area of production, which was overseen by Julio.[8] As discussed below, the E. & J.

Gallo Winery's first major successes came from wine-based aperitifs and sparkling drinks that horrified many purists. Yet Ernest's main goal was to establish the Gallo brand on the national and international market as a guarantee of uniform quality. Julio thus made serious efforts to use the most advanced growing methods, winemaking equipment, and techniques to produce a decent, homogenous table wine at an unbeatable price. In fact, the Gallo Winery was one of the first producers to store its wine in tanks made of stainless steel—rather than redwood or cement—to inhibit bacterial growth as much as possible. Seen from above, their immense Modesto facility looked more like a futuristic refinery than a winery. Inside the facility, research on various aspects of the winemaking process proceeded at a frenetic pace. In 1942, the Gallos hired the chemical researcher Charles Crawford to work as an enologist. Supplying him with a research laboratory and a cellar, they called on him to develop "the best wine that could be made and [sold] at a reasonable price."[9] Charles and Julio's laboratory soon established a reputation for the extraordinary commitment required of its employees and the messianic devotion expected by its leadership, but also for being a veritable melting pot of the U.S. winemaking elite.

By the late 1970s, many independent winery owners and some of the most well-known winemakers in California had spent a good part of their career at the E. & J. Gallo Winery. "[That's where] I learned how to approach a problem and solve it by the application of scientific principles," recalled one.[10] In fact, the Gallos stood out among wine producers for their extensive funding of important research programs, especially those conducted in the viticulture and enology departments of Fresno State University and the University of California, Davis. As a result, these became two of the most prestigious programs in the world in their field and gave the Gallo Winery ready access to their best graduates in return.[11]

The Gallos also took a rational, scientific approach to select-
ing grapes and land, which they bought up gradually in and around
Modesto and in the most famous California wine regions of Sonoma
and Napa. Some of their projects were so ambitious as to verge on
megalomania. In 1986, on land they had just bought in the Dry Creek
Valley, Julio had two entire hills moved to give their vineyards perfect
exposure. The hills were literally razed to the ground and transported
several hundred feet away by giant bulldozers to create the new Gallo
of Sonoma Winery, which today produces the company's most prestigious wines.[12] Such a hyper-technical approach explains why Julio
Gallo would remark, after visiting some of the best wineries of France
and Italy in 1959, that "[Europe] was still stuck in the past, with old-
fashioned equipment and methods."[13]

Likewise typical of the enthusiasm of Piedmontese winemakers
for the dictates of American capitalism was the will to create a mass
wine market in the United States. Such a market was obviously the
exact opposite of the niche in which they were forced to operate both
when they first arrived and again during Prohibition, which nullified the results they had achieved thus far. Until the 1940s, the most
important markets for Piedmontese winemakers remained the immigrant enclaves of the large industrial cities of the United States. Their
companies thus specialized in products that satisfied the requests of
their urbanized customers: moderately priced bulk red wine made
with a mix of different grapes and suitable for being shipped in large
quantities over long distances. Italian winemakers enjoyed a near
monopoly in this niche, simply by virtue of knowing the tastes and
needs of their fellow immigrants. Yet they remained stubborn in their
attempts to expand the American wine market to mass dimensions
and reach the "average" American consumer. While the Italian Swiss
Colony, the principal and most advanced of the Italian winemaking
pioneers, would lead such attempts before and immediately after

Prohibition, the Gallo brothers would take them to an entirely new level after World War II.

MASS MARKETING AND ADVERTISING

To reach this goal, Piedmontese winemakers applied mass-marketing strategies to their industry, which they adopted from producers of nonperishable consumer goods and other mainstream sectors of the American food industry. Ernest Gallo would famously pronounce that he wanted to do for wine what Procter & Gamble had done for personal hygiene products or what Campbell's had done for canned soup. There were several areas in which the Italian Swiss Colony was the undeniable precursor to the Gallo Winery's winning model: vast national distribution to reach as many consumers as possible; the development of standardized product lines that were homogenous and easy to replicate; the cultivation of a particular image among an undifferentiated public to emphasize the value of the brand; and the intensive, creative use of advertising.

The determination to vertically integrate all operations of their business—from grape growing, winemaking, and bottle manufacturing to advertising, distribution, and sales—is in fact a distinguishing characteristic of all Piedmontese American winemakers. This strategic attitude likely stemmed from the late nineteenth-century confluence of a mind-set that was deeply rooted in rural Piedmontese culture (suspicion and hostility toward middlemen, brokers, and merchants); the example of the trusts in important U.S. food-industry sectors like meatpacking, which the pioneers embraced with a neophyte's enthusiasm; and the risky nature of a U.S. wine market that was riddled with regulations and prohibitions and burdened by a religious and social condemnation redolent of nativism, which thus made the utmost government control of every economic factor in the business especially necessary.

By the early 1890s, the Italian Swiss Colony had established a distribution network that stretched as far as China and Tahiti. Thousands of gallons of the company's table and dessert wines traveled each year by train from San Francisco to Chicago and New Orleans, and a small fleet of steamships brought wine to New York via the Isthmus of Panama. In June 1894, the ship *Alameda* carried 12,500 gallons in a single load. In fact, during that time, almost every ship leaving San Francisco with a load of wine was carrying products from the Asti-based company. One 1892 shipment to London contained

Wine of the Italian Swiss Colony arrives in New York, ca. 1905. Most of the wine of the Colony was shipped from San Francisco to many destinations in the United States and abroad. Collection of the author.

The head office of the Italian Swiss Colony in San Francisco, 1903. Courtesy Center for Migration Studies, Staten Island, New York.

5,000 gallons of wine, and even Central and South American routes were becoming increasingly important.[14] Nevertheless, the American market remained the most important one by far for the Asti winery, which even had its own network of Italian American wholesalers to market its wine in the big cities. This arrangement had clearly been orchestrated by Pietro Carlo Rossi, who by then was renowned for having defeated the "wine trust" (the group of major wine traders united under the California Wine Association) and winning the Wine War. He was also an implacable adversary to any San Francisco wine merchants who tried imposing their own prices on the winemakers' products.[15]

The Italian Swiss Colony had to strengthen its brand in the minds of consumers in order to integrate and control every link of its distribution chain. While the overwhelming majority of producers sold their wine wholesale, delegating the task of guaranteeing product quality to retailers, the Asti winery arranged to have its wholesalers bottle and label the wine before sending it to retailers. In 1911, Rossi even decided to build a large, modern bottling factory in downtown San Francisco so that he could directly distribute bottled wine up and down the West Coast.[16] Each bottle, which contained either red table wine or champagne, had a green, white, and red label featuring the coat of arms of the royal Italian Savoy family (a white cross against a red background) and the words "Italian Swiss Colony" in elegant script. This strategy had the profound effect of replacing the relationship of trust that had existed between consumer and retailer with that between consumer and producer, mediated by the brand. Moreover, it held particular weight at a time of increasing public concern over the authenticity of food-industry products, fueled by Upton Sinclair's muckraking exposé on the deplorable hygienic conditions of Chicago's meatpacking factories in *The Jungle*, published in 1906. That same year, in response to this and other similarly damning journalistic reports about the quality of the food and beverages ending up on American tables, the Pure Food and Drug Act was passed to forbid the adulteration of food and drink products.[17]

The Italian Swiss Colony enhanced its brand by launching well-defined, easily identifiable products. The aforementioned Golden State Champagne developed at Asti by Charles Jadeau was a considerable commercial and marketing success—the first branded champagne to appeal to a mass public.[18] But it was Tipo Chianti—a red table wine made of various Italian grapes and launched at the World's Columbian Exposition in Chicago in 1893—that matched the Asti winery's image more than any other product. The unprecedented popularity of Tipo Chianti among the American public went a long way in establishing the Italian Swiss Colony's reputation as the best producer of authentic California wine.

Products of the Italian Swiss Colony, ca. 1910. The company pioneered in national and international wine marketing. Collection of the author.

There was a certain degree of paradox in all this, since Rossi had chosen the name Tipo Chianti to evoke the popular Tuscan wine, adding the "Tipo" prefix to vaguely distinguish it from the original (*tipo* meaning "type" or "-like" in Italian). The wine was bottled in traditional wicker-covered flasks (imported from Italy) and affixed with the label featuring the Savoy coat of arms. Adding paradox to paradox, the word Tipo gained such notoriety that the Italian Vineyard Company and other California wineries started producing their own Tipo wines. After suing the Italian Vineyard Company in 1903 and winning the case in 1908, Rossi swiftly registered the precious Tipo name as a trademark.[19]

The Italian Swiss Colony also proved especially creative in the promotion of its products—an approach that was decidedly avant-garde

The most popular of the Italian Swiss Colony's products, Tipo Chianti featured a characteristic straw flask, ca. 1910. Collection of the author.

for the wine world of the day, both at home and abroad. Rossi's international prestige and multilingualism were crucial for bringing his company's wines to the attention of juries at important world fairs, thus helping them garner assorted awards and recognitions throughout the United States and Europe. In 1896, Rossi sent a collection of his wines to be analyzed and evaluated by the School of Viticulture and Enology in Alba, Piedmont. The favorable findings inspired Prince Louis of Savoy to visit Asti in 1901, followed by Prince Ferdinand in 1905. Italian Swiss Colony wines received an honorable mention and a silver medal at the Bordeaux Exposition in 1895, another silver medal at the Paris Exposition of 1900, gold medals at the expositions of Buffalo (1901), St. Louis (1903), Portland (1904), and Seattle (1909), and finally the Grand Prize at the Turin Exposition of 1911, awarded to the Golden State Champagne. The winery took great pains to publicize such recognitions, and thus authenticate the value of its table wines, among the larger public, which was still anchored for the most part to the notion that European wines and palates were superior to American ones.[20] The organizational, diplomatic, and rhetorical skills of Andrea Sbarboro contributed decisively to making the Italian Swiss Colony "the most well known national trade brand marketed by any element of the California wine industry."[21] The Ligurian entrepreneur developed a truly modern strategy for creating a corporate image. On his impulse, the Italian Swiss Colony produced and distributed a series of promotional pamphlets that not only highlighted the quality of its wines, but also described the difficulties the "colony" had overcome, the successes it had achieved, and the impressive guests it had received. One of them even went so far as to paint Asti as a "paradise of workers."[22]

This last point is particularly interesting, since it shows how cultural difference was already being commodified and marketed several decades before the "marketing of ethnicity" exploded in the multicultural America of the 1970s and 1980s.[23] Sbarboro's corporate propaganda exaggerated the philanthropic motivations and utopian ethnic character behind the company's endeavors over its more purely capitalist nature, transforming the wholly Italian identity of his workforce into a marketing tool. According to a 1911 promotional pamphlet, "The laborers at Asti are picturesque. They have handsome, happy, dark-eyed children and beautiful wives."[24]

Sbarboro was also brilliant in attracting local and national media attention. Indeed, his portrayal of the community in Asti as a "joyous and folkloric cooperative" appeared regularly in illustrated magazines devoted to tourism, travel, and nature.[25] But the Ligurian immigrant's masterwork was surely the official inauguration of the enormous underground cement tank built in 1897. On May 14, 1898, Sbarboro invited a few hundred of the most high-profile figures in

San Francisco and California to a gala ball held inside the tank itself, which had been emptied of wine just for the party. A special train was organized to transport guests from Sausalito to Asti, across San Francisco Bay. Inside the cistern, "Supreme Court judges elbowed San Francisco supervisors and foreign consuls reversed their steps to avoid collisions with millionaires," all to the sound of an orchestra and amid the camera-bulb flashes of photojournalists.[26] Not surprisingly, several local, national, and even international newspapers dedicated a good deal of space to the unique event.

Both the vertical organization of the Italian Swiss Colony and the ambitious marketing methods developed by Rossi and Sbarboro certainly served as benchmarks for Secondo Guasti's Italian Vineyard Company. By the 1910s, Guasti's winery was considered one of the most important in California, boasting as it did five thousand acres of vineyards, twenty thousand tons of grapes harvested each year, and the capacity to store two million gallons of wine. The company's sales office in Los Angeles marketed its wine to retailers, hotels, and restaurants throughout the United States and Europe, and its branches in Chicago, New York, and London guaranteed direct coverage of the most important markets. Guasti also came up with original marketing methods like offering sizeable discounts to customers who returned casks, vats, or corks bearing the brand "IVC." Such promotional practices, along with the quality of its wines, did much to spread the Italian Vineyard Company's reputation throughout the U.S. market.

Further proof of Secondo Guasti's inventiveness came once Prohibition was in force and he had a factory built to dehydrate grape syrup, with which to produce "wine bricks." Once dissolved in warm water and with the addition of yeast, these blocks of grape concentrate could produce about a gallon of wine. Sold as Vine-Glo, the product effectively skirted the ban on wine selling thanks to a derogation that permitted domestic winemaking for personal use. But its considerable success would last only one year, after which time the Justice Department expressly prohibited its manufacture.[27]

Despite the pioneering efforts of the Italian Swiss Colony, the dream of first-generation Piedmontese winemakers to make American wine a product of mass consumption would not be fully realized until Ernest and Julio Gallo came onto the scene. In fact, their winery's keystone was the unprecedented control it exercised over an exclusive network of wholesalers and representatives unlike anything the wine industry had seen before. The management was explicitly direct and oligarchic. "Most wineries in those days had an independent broker who handled their sales," explained Ernest. "We never used a broker."[28]

In the early 1940s, when the E. & J. Gallo Winery was still up-and-coming, its competitors were giants like the Italian Swiss Colony and Fruit Industries Ltd. (the mega-cooperative of wineries that had bought the Italian Vineyard Company), which together were responsible for more than half the country's total wine sales. Later formidable adversaries included Louis Petri's United Vintners and even Coca-Cola, which attempted a foray into the wine market during the mid-1970s under the brand Wine Spectrum. Ernest's strategy consisted in targeting one local market at a time, state by state, methodically unhinging the consolidated positions of rivals by offering wholesalers a "complete package"—an entire line of products, special offers, the assistance of a devoted sales team, and substantial advertising—until they dominated the entire national market. He called his strategy "total merchandizing," and its objective emerged during a meeting with area sales managers: "One time [Ernest] asked thirty of us to define what we thought total merchandizing was, and we all did it differently. Finally, there was one man from Ventura, California—his name was Conners—and he got up and said, 'Ernest, I think what you mean is' (and this was supposed to be sarcastic) 'if you have a great big supermarket, you open the door of that supermarket and you don't see any produce, you don't see any canned goods, you don't see any meat; all you see is Gallo wine.' Ernest says, 'That's total merchandizing!'"[29]

In 1972, the Federal Trade Commission fined the Gallos for violating antitrust laws with their "exclusive marketing policies"—that is, unfair competition based on them obligating their wholesalers to sell only Gallo products.[30] Their visionary strategy required partners who were exceptionally motivated or "hungry," as Ernest put it: "I felt that we would not be able to build our own brand unless a salesman went into a store selling only one product: our wine. This would require the creation of a sales force that would sell only Gallo. In this way, a salesman would not be inclined to accept no for an answer. If he didn't make a sale, he didn't eat."[31] Accordingly, Ernest chose wholesalers among small bottlers who were unhappy with the excessive power of the large wineries and recruited salesmen among young traveling agents who were already familiar with retail sales in products like detergents, drinks, and cigarettes. The latter were trained to look after both the wholesaler and the dealer with maniacal attention. In this they were encouraged by the example of Ernest himself, who, rather than analyzing graphs from the comfort of his office, spent much of his time on the road, visiting small stores in remote towns across the country in order to keep his finger on the market's pulse. As soon as salespeople were hired, they were given a manual with basic rules to abide by:

- Talk to retailers about the advantages of carrying our product
- Obtain the most visible position at eye level for Gallo wines
- Trim shelves with colorful point-of-sale materials
- Use bottle collars to attract consumer attention
- Rotate stock to ensure quality, and keep the Gallo shelves stocked

- Dust our bottles to keep them bright and clean
- Place counter displays in key traffic locations.[32]

The "no brokers" rule that distinguished the Gallos' entrepreneurial practice played out in their direct acquisition of various businesses related to wine sales and production. During the Great Depression, the two brothers began taking over the factories of local bottlers or wholesalers who had incurred debts with the winery that they could no longer pay off. Once these companies were on the verge of bankruptcy, the Gallos would offer to commute their debts by becoming controlling partners, thus transforming the failing businesses into their own establishments.[33]

In 1957, the Gallo Winery spent $4 million to build a glass factory from scratch that could produce some two million bottles a day. The company also bought three cargo ships, docked at the port in San Pedro, to transport wine to the East Coast. Shortly thereafter the winery further enlarged its property with the purchase of the largest road transportation company in California, Fairbanks Trucking Co., and the Midcal Aluminum Co. factory, which produced the foil coverings for the necks of the bottles produced by the glass factory.[34]

The fortunes of the Modesto winery stemmed primarily from its adoption of two U.S. marketing cornerstones from the 1950s, the zenith phase of Fordist mass marketing. Indeed, giving people what they wanted and bombarding them with direct advertising on a national scale became the foundations of the Gallo business credo, and, in turn, Ernest and Julio's role in the creation of a national wine market of unprecedented proportions. In an effort to satisfy the presumed tastes of the masses—that is, consumers formerly reluctant to drink wine—the Gallos developed product lines designed to reach as many retailers as possible. Their intuition about what those tastes were and how they would evolve took care of the rest.

To please palates accustomed to sweet and sparkling drinks—as the statistics of carbonated beverage consumption suggested—the Gallos produced wines like Paisano, a heavily sweetened red table wine; Pink Chablis, a sweet, fizzy table rosé invented for women and publicized as a "classy wine"; and Ripple, a fruit-flavored sparkling wine that came in small, single-dose bottles and was named after the whirl of foam that formed when it was poured.[35] When consumers became more aware of "serious" wines and began seeking products more on par with prestigious European brands in the 1980s, Ernest and Julio were quick to launch a new line of higher quality wine produced exclusively in the vineyards of Northern California. They called it Carlo Rossi Red Mountain after their former associate Charles Rossi, who had become famous after being chosen to appear in a television advertising campaign because he looked like an "authentic winemaker" and had changed his name to Carlo because it "sounded more Italian."[36]

The Gallos' first major success on a national scale, however, was Thunderbird, a lemon-flavored fortified white port, whose story once again reveals some interesting connections between the social and moral status of wine production and consumption, the ethnicity of the producers, and the dynamics of race in the United States during the twentieth century. The idea for Thunderbird came from sales director Al Fenderson, who remarked to Ernest how the residents of some black ghettoes in the big cities drank large quantities of white port with lemon juice added. Ernest decided at once that a wine replicating this preparation could attract "a broad spectrum of consumers—including the retired and elderly on fixed incomes," and he put his laboratory enologists to work to produce some samples.[37] Thunderbird was initially launched in select urban enclaves populated by African Americans. The promotional tactics used by the company were revolutionary in their way, such as discarding empty bottles on sidewalks so the brand would imprint itself on the imagination of ghetto residents. Thunderbird was an immediate and runaway success and opened the door to one of the Gallos' most important wine markets for several years: the "ethnic market," according to Ernest's definition; or the "misery market," according to his critics. Indeed, the Gallos' fortunes were long tied to cheap, fortified "hooch" or "street wine," theirs being the preferred brand of paper-bag-clutching alcoholics who wandered the most wretched streets of urban America. Poor people of color were for the Gallo Winery what Italian immigrants had been for the Italian Swiss Colony and the Italian Vineyard Company: an inevitable target market; faithful and important, but difficult to break away from so as to expand toward other, wealthier consumers. In the end, Ernest and Julio had to fight hard to refresh the negative image that had developed out of this early success.[38]

But the Thunderbird matter is also symptomatic of the Gallos' impassioned approach to advertising. In the years immediately following Prohibition, when 80 percent of American wine was still sold in bulk, Ernest had already begun paying close attention to label graphics and bottle shapes and colors.[39] After World War II, when available advertising space began growing exponentially in a variety of mass media, Ernest indulged his instincts for effective promotional slogans and a simple yet potent company message. He was inarguably the single most important pioneer in television wine advertising and launched several memorable campaigns. In addition to his aggressive tactics for marketing and developing the value of the brand was his widespread use of various means of publicity—everything from strategically placed billboards on California highways to cardboard displays and other promotional materials positioned with painstaking care in retail outlets.

No advertising campaign had more success, however, than the catchy tune played on the radio to accompany the launch of

Thunderbird. Its cadence purposely mimicked the current, popular slang spoken in the black neighborhoods of the U.S. metropolises: "What's the word? / Thunderbird / How's it sold? / Good and cold / What's the jive? / Bird's alive / What's the price? / Thirty twice." Ernest loved telling the story about a trip he took to Atlanta in 1957, the year Thunderbird was launched. He was driving through one of the city's more dangerous downtown neighborhoods when he spotted a black passerby crossing the street. He lowered his window and asked the man point-blank, "What's the word?" "Thunderbird!" the man replied without missing a beat. "Then," concluded Ernest, "I knew we had made it."[40]

SEEKING POLITICAL SUPPORT

Piedmontese winemakers also demonstrated the degree to which they had assimilated the dynamics of U.S. capitalism in the care they took to cultivate relations with influential political figures. Such backing was doubly important considering the controversial nature of the American wine industry, and extended far beyond the circle of their ethnic community. In fact, having allies inside the chambers of power—where decisions were made about not only the future of liquor production and sales but also ethnic issues like immigration policy—significantly counterbalanced the stigma wine carried as a foreign, un-American product for most of the nineteenth and twentieth centuries.

In this sense, too, Rossi's Italian Swiss Colony represented a model that Guasti's Italian Vineyard Company would soon emulate and that the Gallo Winery would significantly expand on and refine. The Asti-based winery used the inauguration of its giant tank in 1897 as an occasion to promote itself and establish lucrative contacts with the

Prince Louis of Savoy visits Asti in 1903. Pietro Carlo Rossi is third from left in the upper row. Collection of the author.

most well-known politicians of the day, and it continued to host similar public-relations opportunities for some time. Among its visitors in 1903 alone were a delegation of the American Bankers Association, Italian Ambassador to Washington Edmondo Mayor des Planches, a mission of the German government that included the ambassador in the United States, and a group of agronomic experts. Theodore Roosevelt was served Tipo Chianti during his visit to San Francisco in 1906, and President William Howard Taft tried the Golden State Extra Dry Champagne in 1911. Finally, on August 11, 1914, San Francisco Mayor James Rolfe made the official send-off speech from the dock when the SS *Nebraskan* set sail carrying the Italian Swiss Colony's first shipment to cross the Panama Canal.[41]

Dignitaries' visits to Asti always carried explicit political implications, as demonstrated in this account of the California governor's visit in 1910:

> When Governor J. N. Gillett alighted at the station at Asti at noon Friday, he was given an enthusiastic reception by the school children and residents of the district. An elaborate luncheon was served at the Colony House of the Italian Swiss Colony, where the Governor had an opportunity to taste some of the choicest wines of the State. In the afternoon, he was driven over the 2,500-acre vineyard of the colony and then inspected every department of the immense winery and storage vaults. The Governor was especially

The winery and distilling plant of the Italian Swiss Colony at Kingsburg, Fresno County, ca. 1905. Under the management of Pietro Carlo Rossi, the company expanded its operations in different areas of California. Collection of the author.

interested in the new two-story reinforced concrete building, 100 by 100 feet, which is nearing completion and is intended for the manufacture of California champagne.[42]

At this point, company president Pietro Carlo Rossi began to speak:

> Governor, you are in many ways responsible for the erection of this building, for if we had not been encouraged by the favorable new tariff of Congress on wines, we never would have dreamed of putting more of our time, energy, and capital into the development of this costly champagne enterprise. . . . Undoubtedly, one of these days we will have the satisfaction of having you as one of our representatives in the Senate of Washington, D.C., and very probably further discussions will arise on the benefits of a protective tariff. We hope you will remember the day you visited Asti and saw the inception of our production of champagne.[43]

Sbarboro, for his part, worked tirelessly to find and cultivate political support for the two issues closest to his heart: a pro-Italian/anti-Asian immigration policy and pro-alcohol/anti-Prohibition legislation. He contacted every politician he could regarding the first, including War Minister William Howard Taft as he passed through San Francisco on his way to the Philippine insurrection in 1905.[44] But Sbarboro was even more determined in his actions against the ordinance that, if approved, threatened to destroy the business to which he had devoted an important part of his life. He totally absorbed himself in a sweeping campaign to sway public opinion against the proposed prohibitionist laws and in 1908 published two pamphlets: *The Fight for True Temperance: Practical Thoughts from a Practical Man* and *Temperance vs. Prohibition.* In his writing and public actions, Sbarboro stressed Prohibition's lack of effectiveness in fighting alcoholism in the states and counties where it had already been adopted at the turn of the century. He also promoted, with obvious self-interest, moderate wine consumption as the ideal antidote to alcohol abuse, armed with a statistical survey on the matter in Europe.

On a trip to Europe in 1908–1909, Sbarboro contacted as many American consulates as possible, obtaining formal declarations of support from many of them for his appeals to the U.S. Congress.[45] He valiantly pleaded his case, championing wine as a remedy for alcoholism with the legislators and committees working to introduce restrictive rules on alcohol consumption all across the country. Sbarboro's biggest success came in 1908, when he traveled to Washington to speak at the Littlefield hearings regarding a bill being proposed to outlaw the shipment of wine and liquor from a non-prohibitionist state to a prohibitionist one. Sbarboro's impassioned deposition held some weight in the law's defeat, even if he is most remembered for the shocked reaction he provoked among the Women's Christian Temperance Union delegation when he claimed that dispensing a bit of wine at lunch to preschool children would make them immune to alcoholism for the rest of their lives, thus liberating the United States from a serious burden. He was nevertheless conscious that his victory on the Littlefield bill would be a minuscule obstacle to Prohibition's mounting tide. In his autobiography, he recalls with some regret how his awareness of the forthcoming amendment's inevitability was precisely what drove him in 1911 to give up any active role in the Italian Swiss Colony.[46]

Secondo Guasti's influential position in the Los Angeles business community also held weight with local politicians. Indeed, the Mombaruzzo-born immigrant was known for his familiarity with "heads of state, business leaders, financiers, bishops, and A. P.

Italian Vineyard Company, Guasti, ca. 1910. The narrow-gauge train used to transport grapes from the vineyards to the winery. The movable railroad was necessary because of the extension of the vineyards and the sandy soil, which made the use of draught animals difficult. Courtesy Cal Poly Pomona University Library Special Collections.

Giannini (founder of the Bank of Italy, later the Bank of America)," not to mention other famous people like Benito Mussolini's son, Vittorio, who visited the Cucamonga winery on more than one occasion.[47] However, neither of these trailblazing immigrant winemakers could come close to understanding the value of political connections in building a wine empire and struggling daily with local, state, and national legislators over alcohol production, sales, and consumption, to the degree that Ernest and Julio Gallo did. Throughout their long rise to the top of the American wine market, the two brothers were often at the center of legislative battles over the enactment of laws to which they would be the greatest beneficiaries, in turn revealing their knack at identifying and supporting key politicians for the approval of such actions.

In 1954, on the eve of their launch of Thunderbird and the rest of their line of sweet, flavored, fortified wines, the Gallos joined those supporting the Wine Institute (the industry's main association of producers, founded in 1934) in its pressure on the federal government to review the law on "special natural wines" (i.e., wines with added flavoring). Before then, the only wine in this category to enjoy ordinary regulation was vermouth, which had originated in Italy but

Italian Vineyard Company, Guasti, ca. 1910. After the picking, workers load grapes on the cars that will carry them to the winery. Courtesy Cal Poly Pomona University Library Special Collections.

Interior of the barrel-making plant at the Italian Vineyard Company in Guasti, ca. 1906. Courtesy Cal Poly Pomona University Library Special Collections.

had been produced for decades, in imitation form, in California. Every other wine that was "rectified," as the law defined it, had to pay a "rectification" tax, since it was no longer a raw product and could be produced only in specific "rectification establishments," not in common wineries. The new law nullified these taxes and limitations, paving the way for the Gallos to conquer this important new piece of the market.[48]

History repeated itself just before the launch of Ripple in 1959, when the Gallos convinced the government to change the law again, this time eliminating the heavy tax applied to champagnes for wine with a carbonation of less than 14 psi (pounds per square inch, the unit of measurement for air pressure in liquids). Once again, the law was adapted to the marketing needs of the Gallos.[49] In 1975, at the end of an exceptionally long and bitter union battle with the organized Chicano laborers of the United Farm Workers of America (the size-able Hispanic agricultural labor union led by Cesar Chavez), the Gallos also got the state of California to introduce the Agricultural Labor Relations Act, a measure to regulate union relations in agriculture written in terms they preferred.[50]

The Gallos were to play leading roles in yet another case of political pressure in 1990. This time, the two brothers sought to have the Bureau of Alcohol, Tobacco, and Firearms change the legal regulation regarding champagne labels. According to the law in force, any sparkling wine to be sold as "champagne" in the United States had to be produced according to the traditional *méthode champenoise*—that is, fermented in the bottle rather than in steel vats. If a wine was produced in the latter way, its label had to carry the designation "bulk process." According to the Gallos, who were trying to change their image as producers of low-cost wine, such a designation would lower the prestige of their brand. They therefore requested the wording be changed to the "Charmat method." Taking its name from its French inventor, Eugene Charmat, this method still involved bulk production in large steel tanks, but according to the Gallos, the French-sounding name made it sound like a "high-class" product.

Even though producers and consumers of champagne made in the champenoise method accused the Gallos of trying to defraud the public, the law was nevertheless modified in their favor, largely thanks to the support of two senators: Kansas Republican Bob Dole and California Republican John Seymour. According to Ellen Hawkes's anti-biography *Blood and Wine*, which meticulously describes this and other related lobbying efforts on the part of the Gallo family, the brothers had contributed a total of $112,000 to both men's senatorial campaigns over the three preceding years.[51] But Hawkes is even more lavish with details regarding the political matter for which Ernest and Julio received the most mass media attention: the so-called Gallo Amendment, which also featured Dole among the protagonists. In 1978, as they watched the number of their descendants grow along with their financial fortunes, Ernest and Julio began to worry about the tax laws that would affect the inheritance of their estate. At the time, family-owned companies with fewer than fifteen heirs benefited from favorable tax conditions, and because of their large number of grandchildren, the Gallos would be denied access to such a benefit. According to Hawkes's account, this was when California Democratic Senator Alan Cranston, a politician for whom Ernest Gallo had made election contributions since 1968, stepped in. First, a

Ernest Gallo (*right*) with other wine tycoons: Robert Mondavi (*left*) and the film director (and winery owner) Francis Ford Coppola (*center*). Courtesy Associated Press.

Washington law firm prepared a bill whereby families with more than fifteen heirs could pay their estate taxes in installments over ten years. Then Cranston carefully chose how and when to present the bill to the Senate. The final vote took place during an impromptu weekend session when few senators were present, thus ushering in the law that would prove so beneficial to the Gallos.[52]

In 1986, however, Congress decided to revise the tax regulation so that each generation of heirs would have to pay estate taxes on property, thus preventing a single taxation from being applied to the transfer of property from grandparent to grandchild, also known as the "generation-skipping transfer." According to a reconstruction in the *Wall Street Journal*, the Gallos called in favors from certain politicians to have an amendment passed that would benefit their position in relation to the planned revision. Newspapers would rebaptize

A large plant for wine storage and fermentation of the E. & J. Gallo Winery at Livingston, California, ca. 1972. Courtesy Corbis.

it the "Gallo amendment" in honor of its most famous beneficiaries, even if its main sponsor, Georgia Democrat Edgar Jenkins, claimed to support it because of personal conviction rather than as a favor to anyone else. In the late 1990s, journalists investigating the private financing Bob Dole received throughout his career considered the future presidential candidate to be the key player in the Senate's approval of the amendment. Indeed, the *Los Angeles Times* reported that between 1986 and 1996 the Gallos had contributed $274,000 to Dole and another $705,000 to foundations connected to him.[53]

While the exclusive (ethnic) social and cultural capital of Piedmontese entrepreneurs were decisive in the development of their businesses in many respects—most importantly their access to low-cost labor—in other ways they were no different from any other successful American capitalists. Italian winemakers were just as enthusiastic and inclined as were their counterparts in other economic sectors when it came to technological innovation, mass production, and the marketing and advertising of brands and products on a national and international scale. They also worked zealously to secure vital support among national politicians—going well beyond their circle of fellow Italian Americans. To fully explain the success of Piedmontese winemakers in California, therefore, it is necessary to look beyond cultural capital and the logic and dynamics of the ethnic economy, and explore once again how the dynamics of race influenced the "modes of incorporation" of these immigrants in the largest state on the West Coast.

CHAPTER 9

Wine *and the* Alchemy
of Race I
The Social and Cultural Economy
of Italian Regionalism

Notions and practices of race played a decisive role in helping Piedmontese immigrants achieve more success in the economic niche of California winemaking than anyone else—fellow immigrants and U.S. natives alike. In fact, race was a major factor in both "modes of incorporation" that substantially explain their emergence as leaders in the trade: their self-segregation from other Italian immigrants and their flexibility in adapting to the segregation imposed on them by the stigma and risks of wine production itself, which caused competitors of other nationalities to flee the industry.

Piedmont natives developed such responses and practices out of the specific ways they approached migration in the late nineteenth and early twentieth centuries, the meanings they attributed to that experience, and the new identities they forged in the process. The starting point for examining this distinct mode of migration has to be statistics: some two million people left Piedmont during Italy's "great migration" of 1876–1925, thus marking the region as one strongly inclined toward human mobility. However, breaking these results down into different periods and comparing them to the data on Italian emigration as a whole can help us draw more-nuanced conclusions. With 709,076 departures between 1876 and 1900, Piedmont's migrants made up 13.5 percent of the total number who left the Kingdom of Italy in the same period, second only to those of the Veneto (17.9 percent) and a good deal more than those of Southern regions like Campania (9.9 percent), Sicily (4.3 percent), and Calabria (5.2 percent). In 1901–1915, on the other hand, though the number of departures from the subalpine region was higher (831,088), they made up only 9.5 percent of the national total, as opposed to 10.9 percent from Campania and 12.8 percent from Sicily. While Piedmont stands out for the precocity of its sizeable migration flows, its predominance in this regard decreased after the turn of the century. Other factors that distinguish nineteenth- and twentieth-century Piedmontese migration include a prevalence of European destinations over transatlantic ones (59 percent of migrants from 1901 to 1913 left for other countries on the Continent); a high percentage of returning migrants (125,307 of the 807,276 who left between 1905 and 1925); a preference for Argentina among extra-European destinations (23.29 percent of the total immigration from 1876 to 1900, compared to 2.65 percent of that to the United States); and a progressive, gradual drop in the number of rural migrants after 1900. Such data mark migration to California as rather eccentric with respect to the general picture.[1]

As for the causes and composition of the migration flows, earlier studies have linked Piedmont's involvement in Italy's great migration to the late nineteenth-century agrarian crisis and its consequences. "Push" factors included the distorted relationship between industrialization, urbanization, and the countryside; plunging agricultural prices; tariff wars with France; the phylloxera epidemic; and silkworm diseases. Hardest hit by the crisis were areas considered to be the weakest links in the region's economy, like the Southern province of Cuneo (where Langhe lies) and the alpine valleys around Turin, whose exhausted rural populations were forced to leave their homes to seek a better life elsewhere.[2] However, more recent studies have begun to paint a more variegated and complex picture of the situation.[3] For one thing, it seems the reality of the alpine world and transborder migration was quite different from that suggested by Fernand Braudel's famous 1960s definition of the mountains as a *fabrique d'hommes*, an eternal reservoir of labor for the more fertile plains and more developed cities.[4] In addition to identifying established routes of temporary and seasonal migration with origins in the ancien régime, local studies on Piedmontese alpine societies have revealed comparatively high levels of literacy among the population and, in particular, expertise in specialized trades that could be applied elsewhere to supplement the limited resources provided by the land. In fact, newer research has essentially proven that "rather than 'fleeing' a poor, hostile environment, mountain dwellers cast themselves toward economic resources spread out over a wide geographical horizon."[5] As active subjects who could identify and seize opportunities within a fluctuating international labor market, these migrants gave rise to a widespread and long-lasting culture of mobility.

In-depth studies on areas with a marked early disposition for manufacturing, like the subalpine province of Biella, have been similarly revealing in their revisions of classical perspectives on Italian migration.[6] Such research has revealed mass emigration to coexist with an extremely advanced industrial economy; labor, union, and political unrest; a notable degree of immigration; and a substantial presence of entrepreneurs and specialized workers among those emigrating. For most migrants from these more developed and developing areas, mobility represented an attempt to resist proletarianization, in terms of both disciplination and devaluation of their preindustrial/ protoindustrial working skills (a particularly significant challenge for the gendered social status of men). Local historians have identified well-established chain migrations related to skilled occupations and professions practiced abroad (especially in the construction industry) that were continually enlarged by new arrivals from the same native towns. As a result, Piedmontese migration historians have also revealed the roles immigrant entrepreneurs played in activating "relational chains as part of establishing a business and recruiting a workforce," and contributing "to the economy of the arrival sites and the realities of departure."[7] Immigrant wine entrepreneurs in California deployed the same sort of social capital and acted within the same regional–diasporic framework. It would therefore be reductive and misguided to interpret the subjectivity and agency of Pietro Carlo Rossi or Secondo Guasti through the lens of the mass rural exodus caused by Italy's agrarian crisis.

Newer studies on Italian migration have also exposed a dimension that is of particular interest to the present analysis—that is, how Piedmontese immigrants represented themselves. Biella-born bricklayers who had photos taken of themselves holding their work tools in front of a house under construction in France or a newly erected bridge in West Virginia, for example, were clearly expressing pride in their professional skills and resourcefulness, not self-pity. Even migrant workers with arguably miserable jobs had a largely positive image of themselves based on their sense of superiority over fellow workers from other Italian regions. Seasonal coal men from the Piedmont areas of Val Chisone and Val di Susa working in Provence, for example, considered themselves better skilled, more experienced in the tools of the trade, and more productive than Lombard workers from Bergamo, thus superimposing a narrative of ethnic difference over an economic rivalry.[8]

While historians are still in the process of completing a detailed picture of the contexts and consequences of migration in all Italian regions, scholars focusing on the Piedmontese situation have already concluded by reinforcing a notion espoused by many contemporary observers of the great migration—that there were actually two Italian migrations, "an early exodus, typical of the Northern regions, and a later, less-skilled one from the South."[9] These researchers have used oral history and other qualitative sources to reveal that, when compared to migrants from other regions, especially from the South, the Piedmontese thought of themselves as characteristically gifted with initiative, autonomous, and possessed of a strong work ethic and a decisive drive toward accumulation and sacrifice. Such racial characterization of a difference between Northern and Southern Italians was part of the transnational ideology that was constructed alongside the spread of the Italian diaspora throughout the world at the crossroads of scientific postulates, ideals of nationhood, and dynamics of capitalism and imperialism.

This narrative of racial identity first emerged even before the great migration that carried millions of Italians away from the recently defined borders of the nation-state, right after Italy's unification under the Kingdom of Sardinia in 1861. Already in the years immediately following the Risorgimento, Northern travelers, Piedmontese public officials, and army volunteers returning from the Garibaldian campaign were describing the inhabitants of Sicily and other Southern regions as "wild," "barbaric," "Bedouin," and "African."[10] The bloody war that ensued between the Italian army and the brigands only magnified and spread the prejudice Northerners and Southerners already felt toward each other. By the end of the century, despite a widespread nationalistic and popular literature that emphasized the common national affiliation of Italians beyond their regional origins,[11] the Southern masses continued to have a poor reputation

among many Northerners, most of whom were rural or urban workers themselves.

Southerners, for their part, typically viewed Northerners as the
last in a long line of autocratic despots who deserved the same dif-
fidence, hostility, and deception reserved for their predecessors.
While Northern workers compensated their Southern counterparts
for their economic backwardness and political inferiority with some
degree of solidarity, they also considered them intrinsically dishon-
est, careless, and dirty—essentially an embarrassing burden that
other Italians were forced to put up with as citizens of a recently unified country. As late as 1926, Antonio Gramsci would argue, in his
unfinished essay "Some Aspects of the Southern Question," that the
Italian proletariat's prerequisite for forming a counter-hegemony lay
in the ability of "the masses of the North" to eliminate the:

> ideology [that] has been disseminated in myriad ways among
> [them] by the propagandists of the bourgeoisie: the South is the
> ball and chain which prevents the social development of Italy from
> progressing more rapidly; the Southerners are biologically inferior
> beings, semi-barbarians or total barbarians, by natural destiny; if
> the South is backward, the fault does not lie with the capitalist
> system or with any other historical cause, but with Nature, which
> has made the Southerners lazy, incapable, criminal and barbaric—
> only tempering this harsh fate with the purely individual explosion
> of a few great geniuses, like isolated palm-trees in an arid and
> barren desert.[12]

The public discovery of those who were radically other led Italians, who had hitherto felt at most a vague sense of regional affiliation—as Piedmontese, Lombard, Calabrian, or Sicilian—to add to
their identity the binary opposition of North versus South.

Such opposition was scientifically authenticated at the turn of the century when influential anthropologists like Giuseppe Sergi (1856–1929) and Alfredo Niceforo (1876–1960) carried on the criminological studies and phenotypic analyses initiated by Cesare Lombroso (1835–1909) by endeavoring to explain the origins of the cultural and socioeconomic differences between Italians in racial terms. While Sergi and Niceforo offered diverging historical interpretations of the "degeneration" of Italy's Mezzogiorno, they both theorized the existence of two distinct Italian races: the Alpine–Celtic and the Mediterranean.[13] Thanks in part to the considerable prestige Lombroso had enjoyed in the United States, the work of the younger Italian anthropologists met with similar success there. Important American scientists and politicians immediately adopted their work as supplementary material for their complicated mapping of European races, which was at the heart of a mounting political debate over the burdens being imposed on American society by the new immigration. From 1899 onward, the documents of the U.S. Commissioner–General of Immigration incorporated the scientific distinction between Northern and Southern Italian races proposed by the Lombrosian anthropological school. As a result, when Piedmont natives reached the immigrant screening station at Ellis Island, they were registered as Italians in the "Nationality" box and as Northern Italians in the "Race" box. When political conflicts over proposals to restrict immigration reached a fever pitch during and immediately after World War I, the most popular promoters of racist scientific thought, Edward A. Ross and Grant Madison, drew much from the works of Lombroso, Sergi, and Niceforo, especially their emphasis on the social dangers of Southerners. The Immigration Commission established by the U.S. Congress (1907–1910) inserted lengthy extracts from the Italian anthropologists' work on racial metaphysics in the voluminous proceedings it published in 1911. The immigration quota laws of 1921 and

1924, which would take the drastic measure of forbidding any new sizeable Italian immigration to the United States by indelibly marking Italians as racially undesirable, were a direct consequence of those debates and inquiries.[14]

In essence, Italian immigrants had internalized complex racist narratives even before stepping onto American soil, split as they were into groups whose borders were defined not only by local origins and dialects but also by racial principles. Being registered by the first public officials they encountered—that is, by the powerful U.S. government—as belonging to the Northern Italian race surely resonated with new arrivals from Piedmont as an authoritative confirmation of a notion that was already familiar to them. When these immigrants then proceeded to turn-of-the-twentieth-century California, they encountered a state where racist terminology and ideology held far greater weight, and the ethnic composition of the population was far more differentiated, than in states like New York or Illinois. While significant numbers of African Americans would not migrate from the American South to the major cities of the Northeast until the interwar years, the Golden State had already been hosting a large "nonwhite"—that is, Asian and Mexican—population since the late nineteenth century. And while the racial position and even the whiteness of Italians in California was subject to debate—as shown by the 1909 Dillingham Commission report on winemaking—the abundant presence of Asian immigrants, who were subject to far greater prejudice, meant Italians were never the "last on earth."

While Piedmont natives would come to redefine their identity in various ways in California, they initially continued to identify themselves by their *local* origin and identity, as they had done in Italy. One of the immigrants interviewed by Nuto Revelli in his ponderous oral history collection *Il mondo dei vinti* (The World of the Vanquished) describes his experience as a new arrival in search of work in the vineyards of Central California: "In Gilroy, near San Jose in California, I meet this cowboy in a Tuscan tavern who says to me: 'You look Piedmontese.' And I say: 'No, I'm not Piedmontese, I'm from Saluzzo [a town in Piedmont].'"[15] Various circumstances would lead Piedmontese immigrants to begin identifying themselves as such, including daily life and interactions; the search for solidarity and support, especially in the winemaking trade; and the desire to distinguish themselves from other immigrant groups who were also redefining their local identities in the regional sense. As will be discussed in greater detail below, this diaspora regionalism played a central role in solidifying a Piedmontese identity around the practice of winemaking, vineyard work, and winery jobs. And the concentration of Piedmont-born immigrants in the world of winemaking in turn

Italian Swiss Colony's Golden State Extra Dry Champagne, winner of many international awards, ca. 1910. Collection of the author.

reinforced their own image as Piedmontese rather than as natives of Asti, Dogliani, Bosconero, and so on.

The desire of Piedmontese immigrants in California to distinguish themselves from Southern Italian immigrants played a vital role in the formation of their identity, and their efforts to do so were aided greatly by their numerical prevalence in the state, since Northern Italian immigrants far outnumbered those from the South for quite some time. The applications for naturalization presented by Italians in San Francisco between 1903 and 1916 show that 80 percent of them had left for the United States from the Northern ports of Genoa and La Havre, while only 20 percent had embarked from Naples, the Mez-zogiorno's typical center of emigration.[16] According to the most reliable statistics available on Italian immigration to California—those

Children of Asti, ca. 1905. The picturesque image of the Italian Swiss Colony as an accomplished ethnic utopia was integral part of the masterful promotional work of Pietro Carlo Rossi and Andrea Sbarboro. *Overland Monthly*, October 1909.

compiled by Hans Christian Palmer in 1965—85 percent came from Northern Italy in 1904. It was not until later in the twentieth century that the numbers began to weigh more in favor of Southern Italian immigrants. The percentage of immigrants who came from Northern Italy to California fell progressively from 69 percent of all immigrants from Italy in 1910, to being on par with the percentage coming from Southern regions in 1918, to the historical lows of 45 percent in 1920, 38 percent in 1921, and 42 percent in 1922.[17]

Many Piedmontese immigrants in turn-of-the-twentieth-century California had internalized both anti-Asian and anti–Southern Italian sentiments as part of a general familiarity with the motives behind American racism and the acceptance of the principle that the "world is organized by race." As noted in chapter 7, new European immigrants in the United States swiftly learned the importance of distinguishing and distancing themselves from "nonwhites" in the workplace. The vigorously anti-Asian propaganda of Italian Swiss Colony's owner Andrea Sbarboro epitomizes the actively involved, almost militant racism practiced by Italian American entrepreneurs and merchants, partly in an effort to pander to the U.S. middle and political classes. On February 22, 1880, the *San Francisco Chronicle* reported that "a 'Swiss Italian Anti-Chinese Company of Dragoons' has been formed, numbering forty members.... A resolution to notify the city authorities that the company is prepared to render them any assistance in removing the Chinese was adopted."[18] Although they expressed their enthusiasm less publicly, leading figures in San Francisco's Italian American community also adopted anti–Southern Italian attitudes. The analogous objective was to show "Americans" the desirable racial characteristics they possessed in comparison to others represented as different and inferior. When the U.S. media began spreading racial prejudice against Southern Italians in the wake of troubling crime news that erupted shortly after the turn of the century, many members of the Italian American middle class, and the newspapers that served them, took great pains to differentiate the image of the "model communities" they led from that of the new arrivals, thus helping to form the public opinion that there were in fact two distinct Italian immigrations to California.

The idea of racially differentiating between Northern and Southern Italian immigrants, to the detriment of the latter, resonated with various strata of Californian society at the time. At the 1902 assembly of the country's largest union, American Federation of Labor Secretary Samuel Gompers emphatically supported the introduction of a literacy test to admit new immigrants to the United States, on the basis that "this regulation will exclude hardly any of the natives of Great Britain, Ireland, Germany, or Scandinavia. It will exclude only a small proportion of our immigrants from North Italy. It will shut out a considerable number of South Italians and Slavs and others equally or more undesirable or injurious."[19] Commenting on the murder of the police officer Joe Petrosino in Palermo, the March 16, 1909, issue of the *San Francisco Chronicle* likewise called for regulations to prevent a "horde of assassins" from reaching California via the soon-to-be-opened Panama Canal:

> Bloodthirstiness of this kind is not an attribute of the manly northern races, and while we receive murderous immigrants from all countries, the majority, and the worst, are unquestionably from Southern Italy, and especially Sicily. . . . The inhabitants of Southern Italy and Sicily are the descendants of more kinds of ancestors than those of almost any other district of the world, and the admixture of African and Asiatic blood, modified however, much by intermarriage with Europeans, has produced a race whose lower orders are about the worst in the world among races which are counted as civilized. These people bear no resemblance to

the inhabitants of Central and Northern Italy, from whom we get some of the best types of American citizenship.[20]

It is thus not surprising that the journalist James Bartlett annotated his opinion of Secondo Guasti's "Piedmontese nature" in entirely racial, almost Lombrosian terms in order to please the subject of his article: "From a rear or side view, this Italian is rather more Teuton than Latin in appearance—a big, short necked, round-headed, broad-shouldered, bluff-mannered man of middle age."[21]

In the Italian press, the concern that Southern immigrants would stain the image of the model community painstakingly built by the Ligurian, Piedmontese, and Tuscan colonial middle class was articulated through reproof not only of criminal behavior but also of what was considered eccentric with respect to the sobriety of Northern Italians. Many ethnic entrepreneurs, especially those in the agricultural sector like Rossi and Sbarboro, promoted new immigration from Italy as an inexpensive and manageable source of labor, provided it comprised individuals who were "strong, honest, and willing to work."[22] In 1911, the newspaper *L'Italia*, which was closely linked to the positions and interests of Italian American entrepreneurs in California, expressed its emphatic aversion to the procession of the statue of St. Anthony being planned by the Sicilian immigrants of San Francisco and the exhibition of "primitivism, superstition, and ignorance" this would involve:

> The appearance of a phenomenon new to our colony, as this projected procession of Saint Anthony . . . would cast a disagreeable light on our colony and threaten to transform it into a resemblance of the sister colonies of the East. . . . We do not want public processions; we do not want effigies of the saints carried through the streets: we want to preserve for our colony all its beauty and

enviable fame for seriousness, civilization, freedom from elements which represent the crassest ignorance and the most shameful superstition; who have no sense of dignity... and do not hesitate to make public show of that ignorance and superstition.[23]

By then, the prejudice of Northern Italians cut across all social classes and had been internalized well beyond the point of just worrying about what "Americans" thought. One of the second-generation Piedmontese immigrants interviewed by Maurizio Rosso recalled, for example, that "at the time, [having holes for earrings] was the mark of the southern immigrant, it was like bearing the stigmata. The Piedmontese felt superior to other Italians. My parents would refer to someone by saying 'what can you do, he's Sicilian.' They didn't want me hanging out with Sicilians any more than they wanted me hanging out with Mexicans."[24] All indications suggest that by the turn of the twentieth century, Italian immigrants in California had developed a racial identity that was based as much on being white as on being from a certain region, and especially whether that region was in the north or the south of Italy, a distinction that only grew in relevance as economic competition increased and pit one regional group against another.

Dino Cinel has placed special emphasis on this aspect of the Italian experience in California by devoting entire sections to it in his history of Italian immigration to San Francisco. Cinel uses the categories of civic pride and regionalism to describe how ethnic businesses endeavored to monopolize subsectors (niches) of California's economy, and he believes that regionalism was actually a new and fundamental form of social capital on which these immigrants based their daily interactions and economic survival, rather than an obsolete cultural burden. Not only did this represent a movement beyond village loyalties (civic pride), but it was also a model for an active adaptation to the needs and conditions of migration.

The predominance of Liguria natives in small-scale agriculture is a particularly telling example. Indeed, some 150 Ligurian immigrants were already running horticulture businesses on small plots of land around San Francisco by the 1870s. Some of the ways they managed to build their near monopoly in this industry included exclusively hiring fellow Ligurians, whom they recruited through chain migrations; taking full control of local distribution and sales; and imposing a fixed, regulated price policy. In 1874, for example, a group of farmers from the capital Ligurian city of Genoa founded the San Francisco and San Mateo Ranchers' Association, which was charged with the task of "coordinating" production and distribution in the local market.[25]

Interestingly, the multiregional Northern Italian ethnic elite who sought to lead the Italian enclave of San Francisco viewed the virtual monopoly of a particular market by a single regional group of immigrants as a stabilizing factor rather than something that would disrupt the construction of a national community. In 1869, the newspaper *La Voce del Popolo* even published a warning that legitimized Ligurians' exclusive right to practice horticulture: "New immigrants are arriving in the city almost every month. We advise these new arrivals not to look for work in horticulture; that industry is already saturated." Some thirty years later, the Italian American press would make similar references. In 1903, for example, *L'Italia* reported that "the practice of starting a business in competition with one that is doing well or the determination of a regional group to enter a line of work already controlled by another group is likely to ruin both groups and both activities, and to create unnecessary confusion."[26] For the various Italian regional groups in California, choosing to follow a distinct, antagonistic path from which to run one's business was considered the normal, natural way of doing things. Conflict could be avoided only by maintaining these separate paths. Natives of the

Tuscan town of Lucca—the second-largest regional group of Italian immigrants in late nineteenth-century San Francisco after the Ligurian Genoese—had originally tried to enter the horticultural trade in competition with the Ligurians but were effectively excluded by the latter. Then, from the late 1870s to the early 1880s, the situation changed. San Francisco's population grew; the range of agricultural products increased, resulting in greater turnover; and a large new fruit and vegetable market opened (the Columbus Market). In response, the Genoese allowed the Lucchesi to take on the subordinate but strategic position of selling their produce, first as street vendors and later as market-stall managers. The Lucca natives in turn came to monopolize this position and protect it fiercely from other competitors. Over the medium to long term, the compromise benefited both groups. The Genoese established a dominant position in the production and industrial transformation of fruits and vegetables in the California market, and the Lucchesi carts and stalls eventually became grocery stores, national and international distribution companies, and restaurants.

It is important to note that when an industry's market expanded from the local to the state or national level, the mass production required made discriminatory segmentation of the workforce and exclusive business dealings based on regional background impracticable. Mark J. Fontana's hugely successful California Fruit Canners' Association—which was founded in 1899 and merged with the California Packing Corporation, better known as Del Monte, in 1916—hired immigrants from various Italian regions and even borrowed from non–Italian American banks (another glaring exception to Fichera's ethnic-based financial cooperation theory). It was therefore the *initial* advantage that regional groups gained from having controlled exclusive niches that would prove so critical in the long run. Indeed, Fontana, an Italian Swiss Colony shareholder and native of the Genoese town of Cerisola, had opened his original business in the 1870s when the Genoese dominated San Francisco's fruit and vegetable industry. The only reason why he could even create the fruit-canning empire he eventually did was thanks to where he got his start: a fertile milieu of fellow ethnic entrepreneurs who had used tooth and nail to conquer and defend their limited niche market.[27]

The development of San Francisco's fish industry is another story. By the time Italian immigrants began arriving in San Francisco in large numbers, this market had already been monopolized by the Chinese since the days of the Gold Rush. Only in the 1880s did Ligurian immigrants manage to break that monopoly by virtue of their number, their trade skills, and, last but not least, their use of violence and intimidation toward their competitors. The general discrimination of San Francisco's white society toward the Chinese only made it easier for Ligurian fishermen to push Asian Americans out of the fish industry and take it over for themselves.

Once again the Lucchesi tried unsuccessfully to enter a trade dominated by Ligurians. This time, however, a large group of Sicilian fishermen succeeded where they had failed, albeit at considerable cost. In 1906, a Genoese fisherman would ascribe the resistance of these rivals, who risked their lives to protect their boats from vandalism, to their innate physical traits: "At night, when [the Sicilians] are not fishing, they curl up in front of their boats. They have a skin like a green turtle and never take cold."[28] Yet the Ligurian fishermen refused to compromise with their Sicilian rivals, unlike how they had eventually done with their fellow Northern Italians, the Lucchesi, in the horticultural industry. Instead, the clash between these two groups over control of the fish market turned into the bloodiest conflict in the history of the Italian presence in San Francisco. In 1907, the *San Francisco Chronicle* would report on its severity: "Boats were sunk, nets have been cut, and sometimes owners too have been cut. Launches have gone to sea and neither launches nor owners have been seen again."[29] The vanquished were forced to change occupation or move their fish business elsewhere. Many present-day fishing communities along the coast of Oregon and Southern California were actually founded by Sicilians expelled from San Francisco after the bloodiest phase of the "fish war" against the Ligurians. As usual, ethnicity was used to support the winning group's cause rather than to help mediate conflicts between fellow Italians. As *La Voce del Popolo* warned in 1898, "Newly arrived fishermen must obey the regulations of the Mutual Aid Society or go fish somewhere else."[30] The battle for control of San Francisco's fish market was never entirely settled. Ligurians continued to dominate it—especially the more profitable parts that required greater capital investment, like tuna and outboard fishing—and the Sicilians were confined to the remaining, more marginal businesses that dealt in shallow fishing and cheaper fish. Yet the latter's foothold in San Francisco's fish and seafood market had widened nonetheless due to their violent ways of operating, which soon attracted the attention of the authorities and the condemnation of local newspapers.

Therefore, the fish industry was distinguished from that of horticulture by the total lack of cooperation between the conflicting regional groups, especially the Ligurians' utter refusal to bargain with the Sicilians as they had done with the Tuscan Lucchesi. But this was not necessarily detrimental to—or lacking in mutual advantages for—all the actors involved in the intra-national economic war. On the eve of World War II, Italians controlled 80 percent of the fish industry in California overall—everything from fishing, to sales, to canning—despite their ongoing internecine battles.[31] In other words, the predominance of certain regional groups of Italian immigrants, be they entrepreneurs or workers, in certain niche sectors of the California economy came about regardless of whether they had either made the strategic choice to cooperate with one another or waged citywide battles against groups from other regions. Regionalism, quite simply, was an effective form of social capital with which to develop a business. The issue of race, especially when articulated as part of the North–South antinomy, steered interethnic economic relationships on a collaborative rather than a conflicting course. From this point of view, the dynamics of the battles to control the produce and fish markets of San Francisco can shed new light on how the Piedmontese won and used their predominant position in the California wine market.

The Italian Swiss Colony developed a model of collective economic interaction that was a lot closer to what happened in horticulture between the Genoese and the Lucchesi than what happened in fishing between the Ligurians and the Sicilians. Sbarboro and his fellow Ligurians, who made up the majority of the Italian American business community in San Francisco from the mid-nineteenth century onward, were the first Italians to take over the winemaking industry in Sonoma County. However, falling grape prices and crop volatility forced them to seek help from Piedmontese technicians like Dr. Giuseppe Ollino, who brought in new grape species from Piedmont; pharmacist Pietro Carlo Rossi, introduced to them by Ollino; and Novara-born Luigi Vasconi, who would become the Italian Swiss Colony's first head winemaker. As discussed in chapter 7, Ollino and Rossi both swiftly prompted important professional chain migrations from their native towns in Piedmont to Asti in California. The Ligurian investors maintained financial control of the company but gradually stepped aside to let the Piedmontese take over winemaking, marketing, and management, thus also sharing the wide margins of financial risk inherent in such an enterprise. Structured this way, the Ligurian–Piedmontese partnership worked quite well. A 1906 book about the most important Italians in the United States noted as such, placing typical emphasis on the racial characteristics of the protagonists Sbarboro and Rossi: "The first fully embodied the irrepressible restraint and acuity of a Ligurian; the second all the calculating, irresistible audacity of a Piedmontese who lets no obstacle stand in his way."[32]

Based on the statistics that exist on emigration from Northern and Southern Italy to San Francisco in the 1870s and 1880s, it can be reasonably surmised that the unemployed peasants with experience in winemaking who bombarded Sbarboro with requests for work (and thus sparked his idea to start the Italian Swiss Colony) were largely, if not exclusively, Northerners, and more specifically Piedmontese, Ligurians, and Tuscans. The names "Italian Swiss Colony" and "Asti" would certainly have held some philological and symbolic weight for them, especially considering how much race affected the reciprocal perception of Italian emigrants from various regions in the San Francisco of 1881, not to mention its repercussions in the context of the interethnic economic competition just delineated. The Swiss Italian Anti-Chinese Company of Dragoons, which in those same years got ready to attack San Francisco's Chinatown, marked with the choice of its name the Northern Italian identity of its members. Indeed, one of the immigrants interviewed by the anthropologist Micaela di Leonardo recalled that her family members regarded and narrated their identity as "Italian Swiss" to distinguish themselves from Southern Italian immigrants and their negative image.[33]

In the construction of their ethnic utopia in Asti, Sbarboro and Rossi doubtlessly took advantage of both the inclusive, cooperative behavior of Italian immigrants and their *exclusive* attitudes toward other regional groups. As in the case with the Genoese and the Lucchesi, who monopolized fruit and vegetable sales in San Francisco by joining forces and strenuously defending their turf from other potential pretenders, this racialized strategy helped mutually strengthen the dominant economic positions of the groups involved. For the Piedmontese of the Italian Swiss Colony, this meant securing the influential position of running one of the largest wineries in the United States for two generations. Considering the central role, symbolic and otherwise, that the Asti company would play in the overall adventure of Italian winemaking in California, this was significant indeed. When the Italian Swiss Colony took off at the state and national levels, Piedmontese entrepreneurs and workers assumed preeminent positions in the newly established winemaking niche. In the kaleidoscope of the economic specializations of each Italian regional immigrant group in California, winemaking was associated with the Piedmontese from the start.

As the Italian Swiss Colony grew and endeavored to establish a nationwide market based on the transcontinental presence of Italian American immigrants from every region, its characterization as a Piedmontese company began to play more of a strategic role, even as an effective marketing tool. As noted above, discriminatory hiring and business practices may turn out to be incompatible with mass-market production. Yet the importance of such practices in providing a crucial starting advantage cannot be overstated. Not only had they contributed significantly to the establishment, definition, and reinforcement of an ethnic economy with a distinct identity of its own, but they had also helped in forming a network of relationships, sources of capital, and ideas that led to a Piedmontese monopoly of the California wine trade. According to Hans Christian Palmer, the leading historian of the Italian contribution to California agriculture, such an identity was built according to an ethos that he defines as "clannishness,"[34] a textual and practical sense of affiliation that sedimented into discourse. Indeed, the high rate of marriage among Piedmont natives in general and those employed in winemaking in particular not only reflects the will of a slender ethnic minority to use every means possible to optimize its economic resources—as Palmer suggests—but also signals the importance given to race in its more primordial acceptance of a community of blood ties. Both economic *and* racial factors were involved in persuading Piedmontese wine-makers in California to associate among themselves (to the exclusion of others) with an enthusiasm that would have been unlikely in their native towns. In fact, the Piedmontese immigrants who entered the winemaking industry preferred doing business with other Piedmont natives despite the fact that they constituted a numerical minority, since the ultimate goal of such unprecedented regionalism was to reinforce and defend the ethnic niche market of wine.

After founding his vineyards and winery in Cucamonga, Secondo Guasti emerged as the leader of a group of Piedmontese entrepreneurs and investors who worked tirelessly to promote the arrival of new workers from Asti and other towns in Piedmont. Truth be told, Guasti also included men from Southern regions among his closest associates, like Basilicata-born James Barlotti and Abruzzo-born Nick Giulì (who was also a relative), probably due to the smaller size of LA's Italian community. On the other hand, the Piedmontese identity of his Italian Vineyard Company, and especially the company town of Guasti, was maintained and emphasized even more carefully than it was up north in Asti.

Ernest and Julio Gallo's father, Joe, similarly built much of his uneven and ultimately tragic career in winemaking within the confines of the Piedmontese immigrant milieu in California. Joe's encounter with his future father-in-law, Battista Bianco, with whom he regularly chatted in Piedmontese dialect outside the older man's house about grape prices and wine quality, was perhaps the most important turning point of his life. In fact, no matter where Joe moved throughout the San Joaquin Valley, he always found a way to connect with fellow Piedmontese immigrants within the microsphere of grape farming. Later, his eldest sons would likewise rely on this tight-knit network of relationships to help them launch what would become a hugely successful business. Despite being a generation removed from the immigration experience, Ernest and Julio would still list a strong work ethic, tenacity, restraint, austerity, frugality, virile corporate ruthlessness, and even a certain pessimistic worldview as their guiding values. Few Piedmontese immigrants would fail to recognize these very characteristics as their own, and as those belonging to the Piedmontese identity in general.

CHAPTER 10

Wine and the Alchemy of Race II
Prohibition

As a moment of profound caesura in the history of California wine-making, Prohibition also had distinct racial implications, pitting as it did a largely nativist, Protestant, and rural America against an ethnic, urban, and Catholic one. In fact, the Eighteenth Amendment would establish the image of winemaking as one in which Italian immigrants indulged in particular, adding to it the stigma of illegality. At the same time, it would also provide these recent arrivals with new and unexpected opportunities, which came as a result of their near monopoly of an industry that had taken on a semi-criminal status.

The origins of such circumstances can be traced back to the state of the political debate on the present and future of the American nation at the turn of the twentieth century. Ironically, with their anti-Asian racism, Italian Americans in California had helped forces that were essentially their own enemies. In fact, California itself was a hotbed for nativism and anti-immigration legislation. The state was the setting for the passage of the Chinese Exclusion Act in 1882— the first important triumph for the nationwide movement to restrict immigration. After intermediate victories, such as the Immigration Act of 1917 (also known as the Asiatic Barred Zone Act), this movement would achieve its main objective in 1924 with the introduction of the law that regulated immigration to the United States on the basis of national quotas—and strongly penalized Italians. In addition to upholding the ban against the Chinese and allowing only "free white persons" to naturalize, the Immigration Act of 1924 reduced legal entries of European natives from countries of more recent immigration, like Italy, to a pitiful number.

Scholars of scientific racism and many Americans alike viewed Italians—especially those from the South—as less than commendable for immigration by virtue of being Catholic; rural; poor; overly prolific; mostly illiterate; ill accustomed to liberal democracy and its institutions; and well represented among criminals, socialists, and anarchists. This last aspect was particularly relevant during World War I amid rampant doubts over immigrant loyalty to the national war effort. Such tensions only grew after Russia's 1917 October Revolution unleashed a violent, antiradical hysteria throughout the United States that came to be known as the Red Scare. The most famous emblems and victims of this repressive climate were two Italians—Puglia native Nicola Sacco and Piedmont native Bartolomeo Vanzetti—who were executed following a controversial murder trial. The event marked a turning point and caused the big American capitalists—formerly the most influential supporters of an open policy toward immigration—to join forces with the historical opponents of open immigration, the Protestant middle class and the big unions. The coalescence of this new social bloc in turn paved the way for the restrictive legislation of the Immigration Act, which included both Northern and Southern Italians among the races considered undesirable.

The ensuing prohibitionist movement thus became inextricably intertwined with these debates, drives, and fears: "Like the Red

Scare, Prohibition employed coercive means, the force of law, to impose cultural unity on an increasingly heterogeneous and complex society."[1] While the temperance movement had already been nurturing nativist sentiments from the early nineteenth century on, these began taking on distinctly racist implications in the climate of mounting aversion toward immigrants at the dawn of the twentieth century. The arrival in the United States of "foreign hordes" of mostly Catholic Irish, German, Polish, and Italian drinkers greatly concerned the predominantly Anglo-Saxon Protestant prohibitionist reformers, who wished to uphold ideals of sobriety, respectability, and productivity. For the latter, the saloon's rapid expansion as a meeting place for new immigrant workers represented an alarming attack on the democratic virtues of the American nation. In the prohibitionist imagination, the saloon became the principal breeding ground for the growth of Roman Catholicism, anti-American foreign radicalism, and the corrupt power of immigrant party bosses, as noted in the resolution of the General Baptist Convention of California in 1894: "That, as members of the denomination which was first to uphold the liberty of consciences and separation of church and state, we put ourselves on record as utterly opposed to any attempt to secularize the public schools, and to control our government in the interest of a foreign hierarchy, we believe in upholding American schools, American ideas, and American labor, and opposing the un-American saloon and the liquor traffic, and also the power of a foreign pontiff and a wily Jesuitism by our prayers, our efforts, and our voices."[2]

California occupied a unique place on the national scene due to the multifarious racial, cultural, and religious composition of its immigration. Around the turn of the twentieth century, the state was the destination of two different mass migrations: one made up of new, mostly non-Protestant, European immigrants; and the other composed of Protestant Americans from the East and Midwest in search of a healthier climate—both literally and metaphorically—in which to recreate rural communities of independent producers according to specific ideals of social organization being threatened by the vices of industrialization and urbanization. Thus there existed at least two different white Californias in terms of ethnicity, religion, and attitudes toward alcohol. In 1910, a good 60 percent of San Francisco residents had been born abroad and the Protestant population was a measly 15 percent. The city by the bay was in fact a veritable bastion for some of Prohibition's most resolute opponents. In Los Angeles, on the other hand, the situation was reversed. First- and second-generation immigrants represented a mere 35 percent of all residents, and 56 percent of the population was Protestant (a fact that becomes even more meaningful when one considers that most Catholics in Southern California were Hispanic and thus lacked significant political or social power due to racism). Indeed, Los Angeles and its suburbs constituted the action base for prohibitionist reformers. The rural areas of the state were equally differentiated. With the ethnic and religious balance of a local population determining the restriction policies of a county or a town, one that adopted embargo measures on the production, trafficking, and sale of alcohol could easily be found next to one that did not, thus producing a sort of leopard-spotted reality throughout the state.

Some municipalities totally prohibited saloons within their borders, while others drastically reduced the number of licenses granted.[3] Nevertheless, from the late nineteenth century on, it was clear everywhere that the fight for Prohibition was a fight against everything that could be identified as "foreign" in American society. Newspapers like the *California Voice* urged their readers to mobilize against "every sot who beats his wife, every ignorant beer-swilling Mexican, Italian, Polack, and other savage." According to the paper, the only possible cure for the degeneration of the "ignorant horde that Europe [sent] over to rule America" was the introduction of a prohibitionist legislation in the hopes that "if the brains of said rabble could be kept clear of stupefying beer and fiery whisky they would be better men, make better society, and not so many votes would go to the ballot box via the rum hole."[4]

The growing stigma of anti-Americanism affecting those who produced and sold beer, wine, and liquor prompted an exceptional proportion of Catholic immigrants from Central–Southern Europe to work in these trades. In 1870s San Francisco—already considered a modern Gomorrah by temperance activists—around 32 percent of those working in the liquor trade were German, 26 percent were Irish, and 5 percent were English. Only 19 percent had been born in the United States. However, fifty years of punitive legislation and the work of powerful pressure groups like the Anti-Saloon League and the Woman's Christian Temperance Union significantly accelerated the ethnicization of the alcohol industry. By 1916, half the wine and liquor merchants of San Francisco had a German name and 70 percent of the city's saloon owners were German or Irish. In the meantime, the industry had witnessed a constant, distinct retreat on the part of those born in the United States.[5]

The same thing had been occurring in wine production throughout California. In the last decades of the nineteenth century, Italians had joined German, French, and Scandinavian winemakers as late arrivals, taking the places in vineyards and wineries being abandoned by those, usually second-generation Irish or British originally from the East Coast, born in the United States. Wine entrepreneurs and workers alike were afraid of and demoralized by the censure their trade aroused in influential sectors of Californian society and politics. As the 1909 Dillingham Commission report on California winemaking revealed, the number of non-Italian European immigrants in the world of wine work was in rapid decline. Indeed, many Irish,

German, and Scandinavian immigrants had already made the move by then to easier, more profitable occupations with better prospects for the future, and the rest followed suit shortly thereafter.

The production of wine began to stand out from that of other alcoholic beverages like beer and whiskey—which continued to be dominated by Germans and the Irish—both for its increasing monopolization by latecomer Italians and its relationship to the prohibitionist debate in California. In fact, wine had a special importance for the state's economy, occupying as it did a symbolic position in the image of California as a sunny land dappled by orange groves, olive orchards, and vineyards. This status would become a crucial weapon for Prohibition opponents like Democratic Party representatives, whose consensus came primarily from the urban, Catholic immigrant population. As early as 1855, during a California Assembly debate over the proposed popular referendum to introduce Prohibition to the state, the "wets" managed to pass an amendment whereby "the provisions of this act shall not be made to apply to wine manufactured from grapes grown within the limits of this state."[6] The amendment crowded out and weakened the prohibitionist front, contributing in some measure to the referendum's defeat with 55 percent of the voters opposed. In fact, alcoholic beverage producers, and the wets in general, would continue to use the contra-indications of banning wine to help stall legislation for several years. While this made it easier for anti-prohibitionists to claim such an inclusion would be bad for California's economy, however, prohibitionists would continue to argue that any exception would throw the entire legal and ideological structure of their reform proposal into crisis.

As the 1910s approached and the introduction of prohibitionist measures at the state and even the national level began to seem inevitable, thus also signaling the fate of the saloons, California winemakers made the strategic move of distancing themselves as much

Mug shot of Michele/Mike Gallo, brother of Giuseppe/Joe Gallo and uncle of Ernest and Julio, 1913. He was arrested on the accusation of being the leader of a ring cheating money out of other Italian immigrants. Courtesy Butler Library, University of California, Berkeley.

as possible from manufacturers of beer, whiskey, and other liquors. Unlike beer, wine hardly depended on the saloons, where little of it was served. Moreover, not only did it contain less alcohol than whiskeys or brandies, but in many European food traditions it was also considered more of a complement to a meal than a means with which to become intoxicated. The latter formed the main argument with which Andrea Sbarboro made himself known as one of the staunchest advocates for the wets, investing all his political contacts and diplomatic skills into making table wine immune to nationwide Prohibitionist measures. By the mid-1910s, however, even Sbarboro was forced to acknowledge that this strategy was undermining the general front of alcohol producers among many smaller, weaker pressure groups, to the full advantage of the more radical prohibitionists. In 1917, winemakers supported a legal compromise (the Rominger Bill) that would abolish saloons and prohibit liquor sales in California, but would allow the sale of wine and beer with an alcohol content of less than 14 percent in restaurants, hotels, and clubs, and domestic consumption of fortified wines with an alcohol content of up to 21 percent. While the California Senate passed the law by a hair's breadth, it was defeated outright later that year in the State Assembly through the intervention of the most intransigent sectors of the prohibitionist associations and the Protestant churches, who by then were determined to fight until they reached the widest target possible.

During the campaign to support the Rominger Bill, it became clear that most immigrant and Catholic electorates in California would willingly abandon saloons in exchange for saving wine. The continued intransigence of prohibitionists in the face of any such compromise therefore smacked of outright sectarianism. On the other hand, this was hardly surprising considering the fact that dry exponents bitterly opposed even an obvious anti-prohibitionist argument like wine's liturgical function. In fact, already in the 1870s certain Californian Methodist theologians, who were also radical exponents of temperance, had begun to claim that wine's use in the Eucharist was the result of an erroneous translation of the Bible. According to their reinterpretation, Christ offered unfermented grape juice to his disciples at the Last Supper. The debate itself, which led to the use of nonalcoholic grape juice instead of wine in Evangelical churches, was one more sign of wine's controversial status in California at the turn of the twentieth century.[7]

At any rate, the Rominger Bill was rejected on the eve of the U.S. entry into the Great War, an event that would turn out to be decisive for the development of the Noble Experiment, as President Hoover later called Prohibition. In fact, through its food-conservation programs, the war provided the perfect occasion for the introduction of a "wartime Prohibition," which in turn proved the ideal legislative gateway for passing the Eighteenth Amendment. California, which despite everything was still one of the most anti-Prohibitionist states in the country, was the twenty-fourth state to ratify the amendment. On January 16, 1919, Nebraska senators provided the decisive vote to reach the two-thirds majority required. On October 28, the Volstead Act was passed, against the veto of President Woodrow Wilson, and the U.S. Congress finally turned Prohibition into federal law. As determined by one of the clauses, the amendment went into effect at midnight on January 16, 1920.

The war years would also prove quite significant for the formation of a distinctive ethnic niche within the wine industry. While German Californians had previously represented Italians' main competition in wine production and especially sales, they would suffer a severe blow by the violently patriotic ideological climate of the war period. After the declaration of war against Germany, anything German automatically became an enemy in the United States. The production and sale of alcohol by German immigrants came to be colored by tones of betrayal and sabotage in the minds of the larger public. As victims of extreme suspicion, Germans reacted by eliminating businesses that could identify them as anything less than model American citizens, and sometimes even this was not enough. Not only did the Anheuser-Busch brewery see its sales plummet, but the U.S. Treasury Department even went so far as to seize the estate of cofounder Adolphus Busch. Such repression, especially the self-inflicted kind, had therefore considerably reduced the historically important German presence in California wine production and sales even before the Eighteenth Amendment was introduced.[8]

Many Italian Americans considered the enactment well-nigh incomprehensible precisely because it extended to wine, a drink so profoundly connected to their history, culture, and religion. There was simply no substitute for wine in the food habits, conviviality, and social life of Italian workers. As a result, no other ethnic American group came to be more identified with the illegal production and sale of wine during Prohibition than Italians, especially the Piedmontese. Nor was any other group as persistent in making wine at home. In fact, the exception made by the Volstead Act for domestic wine production, apparently introduced to protect the production of all-American cider—a traditional drink in certain rural and Protestant American communities—only served to stimulate the enormous expansion of "production for personal use," which was flagrantly used for illegal trafficking. By the 1920s, one could easily recognize the Italian neighborhoods of the big American cities by the number of grape crates that were unloaded in front of houses and swiftly brought down to basements. Everyone knew that Italian restaurants served homemade, under-the-table wine, camouflaged in coffee cups or soft-drink bottles. The hand-processed bulk wine sold to the many Americans who continued to drink liquor as much as or more than before Prohibition, was even given its own name, Dago Red, in reference to the common ethnic slur for an Italian immigrant in the United States. In San Francisco, "a walk through the Italian quarter reveals wine presses drying in the sun in front of many homes. The air is heavy with the pungent odor of fermenting vats in garages and basements." According to the New York Times, practically every house in this most populated Little Italy of California had been transformed into a small winery.[9] Another contemporary observer reported that in Northern California, "Every [Italian] family sells wine and every cabin has its vat. The result is that an American laborer is always without money, and the Italian is always increasing his savings account."[10]

The near monopoly Italians acquired in the illegal trafficking of alcohol, including wine, depended in good part on organized crime, which had been established in the bosom of the Italian community and controlled alcohol sales using corruption and violence. While Italian Americans were already used to being depicted by the media as habitual criminals, the adjective "Italian" now appeared next to the names of criminals in the newspapers with unprecedented frequency. An analogous ethnic monopoly also developed in the legal (or semi-legal) world of wine production, in which several companies were duly registered and overseen by the authorities as producers of grapes, grape juice, grape concentrate, sacramental wine, and wine-based vinegar, tonics, and digestifs. Many non-Italian competitors had disappeared from this shady, semi-legal market, dissuaded by the severe legal limitations that would be imposed on their businesses; skeptical that the law would be repealed any time soon; or intimidated by the connection most people made between alcohol production and anti-Americanism, not to mention the blatantly nativist acts of persecution to which this could lead. The only reason Edmund and Robert Rossi (in partnership with former employee Enrico Prati) managed to reacquire all the shares of the Italian Swiss Colony from its main shareholder—the California Wine Association—at the favorable price they did in 1923 was precisely because the seller wished to divest itself of any participation in the wine industry as quickly as possible.[11]

Italians, especially those from Piedmont, were also the most willing to shoulder the risks and difficulties involved in conducting a wine business during Prohibition. In reality, nearly all the profits they would derive from selling wine would be thanks to its very illegality. Making it unlawful to traffic in wine caused prices to rise, thus sustaining the market for grapes and the imaginative wine substitutes that were sold within the narrow spaces permitted by the law. Far from halting wine consumption in the United States, Prohibition actually caused it to increase over the period of 1920–1933, from a maximum of 0.7 gallons per capita in 1911 to an annual average of 0.8 gallons. Nevertheless, wine remained closely associated with crime for fourteen long years. The only way for Italian winemakers to survive and prosper during that time was to "get their hands dirty" and assume all the risks of an informal business, doing their best to transform their reputation as the main transgressors of the Prohibition law into a marketing strength.

In addition to their lack of practicable alternatives and their status as relative latecomers compared to the Germans, French, and Scandinavians, the structural nature of the wine market itself prompted Piedmontese winemakers to take on such risks, and achieve such considerable success. Indeed, the market for shipping winemaking grapes to the large urban centers of the United States saw explosive growth after the enactment of the Volstead Act. Twenty-six thousand railway cars of the first vintage alone (that of 1920) were shipped from California to the rest of the country. Contrary to the catastrophic predictions of wet politicians, the price of the Californian grape shot up during the early years of Prohibition, with an average growth of 200 percent between 1920 and 1926 (after which it slowed considerably). The values of vineyards rose at an even more dizzying pace. Those selling for $100 before Prohibition were worth $500 by 1921 and were changing hands for $1,000 an acre by 1923.[12] For companies like Edmund and Robert Rossi's Italian Swiss Colony and Guasti's Italian Vineyard Company, shipping wine over long distances to the large immigrant markets in the East had already been a central practice of their business for a many years. With the advent of Prohibition, the only thing such companies had to do was replace their wine with grapes for domestic winemaking to ensure several more years of prosperity. Even Joe Gallo managed to achieve the first big success of his American career through the much more modest activity of farming grapes destined for the markets of Chicago and New York, with the help of his sons Ernest and Julio.

Italian and Piedmontese winemakers also remained almost entirely alone in the manufacturing of those grape products that managed to pass through the legislative mesh of Prohibition. With the proper license, wineries could produce grape juice, syrup, gelatin, and concentrate, all of which could be transformed into ersatz wine by adding sugar and alcohol. As mentioned in chapter 8, Guasti's Italian Vineyard Company specialized in producing "wine bricks" made of dried, compressed must, which produced something very close to wine once dissolved in water and with the addition of yeast. The California Padre Wine Elixir, produced by two of the Italian Vineyard Company's first shareholders, the Vai brothers, met with a success that could hardly be justified by the product's sole use as an iron-based tonic, for which it was marketed and advertised.[13] Even real wine, properly speaking, could be produced licitly, with a license, for use in Catholic Mass, for medicinal purposes, to make vinegar, and as a natural aroma to flavor food products, tobacco, and soft drinks. Italian American wineries adapted to these new product lines with great flexibility, a trait that was especially impressive considering the fickleness of the legislations (wine bricks were soon outlawed, for example), the precariousness of market forecasting, and the ephemeral nature of the line between lawful and unlawful.

The best examples in this sense were once again the Italian Swiss Colony and the Italian Vineyard Company. Edmund Rossi described the way his company had functioned during Prohibition in a 1971 interview with the oral historian Ruth Teiser, of which it is worth citing a lengthy extract:

TEISER: And you were shipping fresh grapes?
ROSSI: And making grape juices and grape concentrates.
T.: How did you learn to make concentrate?
R.: Oh, well, with a vacuum pan.

T.: It was not anything that you had done before though?

R.: No.

T.: Before Prohibition who were the customers for your bulk wines?

R.: Oh, everybody. Wholesalers in every town. . . . [We would sell wine in] barrels. Fifty gallon barrels. Eventually in tank cars. . . . We used to ship by water in 50 gallon barrels to New York through the Panama Canal.

T.: Did a large percentage of your wine go east?

R.: Yes.

T.: Then during Prohibition who were the customers for the grape juices and concentrates?

R.: That, see, I had to develop. That was work. That you had to ferret out, and induce people to get into it. We sold grapes more easily.

T.: And those were just the grapes from the acreage at Asti?

R.: No, we bought grapes too, neighbors' grapes. It was a risky business, oh yes.

T.: You must have felt all along that Prohibition wasn't going to last?

R.: Well, we were gambling on that. It was a gamble all right. Because it took capital all the time, putting hands in your pocket.

T.: You must have felt very loyal to the business to work that hard and put in that much faith and time and effort.

R.: Yes. Well, that's all we knew.

T.: Did you ship many grapes to San Francisco?

R.: Yes.

T.: Someone told me about the big wineries in apartment house basements here. Did you know about those?

R.: Yes, people used to . . . We used to have a plant at Broadway and Davis, where we'd crush the grapes that they'd buy and

then they'd deliver them home in kegs and ferment them.
We did the crushing for them.

T.: These went to the individual homes?

R.: Yes, family. We had French, German, Italians. I used to call on them at home.

T.: Did you help them bottle their wines . . . ?

R.: Yes. Well, we had two or three men that did that on their own.

T.: That really was a hard way to market wine, wasn't it?

R.: It was.[14]

Risk, danger, hard work: these were the daily components of doing business in the unique economic niche to which a racist ghettoization had relegated Piedmontese winemakers. They were also the costs to be paid for dominating the marginal, segregated, and informal market of wine during Prohibition. Now, in addition to the skills they had already developed in the decades before 1920, they also had to learn how to deal with the repression of an increasingly corrupt law enforcement system and how to cope with the consequences of violating the law.

In 1922, the Italian Swiss Colony—by then called the Asti Winery Company, but still the largest winery in Northern California—made the news in a case that illustrates the complications encountered by Piedmontese winemakers as they tried to profit from their leading position in this new, booming illegal market. That September, the federal agents George H. Crawford, Henry W. Meyer, and Waldo E. Curtis of the Prohibition Unit of the Twenty-First District Head-quarters in San Francisco, which was responsible for enforcing the Volstead Act in Napa and Sonoma, investigated the operations of the winery in Asti. Agent Crawford later reported:

Some time ago I received information that quantities of wine were being transported nightly from the vicinity of Santa Rosa,

Healdsburg, and Geyserville, and especially the Asti wine company. We agents figured that if we could devise some ways and means whereby we could get a truckload of wine coming directly from the Asti Winery Company we could pull over one of the largest transactions since Prohibition went into effect. [Asti is] the biggest wine concern there is, practically, in the United States. That is my understanding. It is a bunch of people that is worth several millions of dollars. It is composed of the richest Italians in the State. We thought that was the only way they could be caught. . . . If they were caught, it would be the biggest catch that ever has been known. That is what I understood.[15]

Crawford and the other "dry" officers thus stationed overnights just above Geyserville, on the north–south road traversing Sonoma, until they intercepted a truck fully loaded with wine. The driver refused to answer any questions, so the agents drove him back to the last house he had stopped at by following the truck's distinctive tire tracks. The driver claimed he had been there for a social visit, not to pick up wine. The agents proceeded to break into the house. As Crawford reported,

We found two men on the premises, awake, a light in the house, they were sitting eating some bread—I think it was bread and wine, but I don't know for sure . . . Immediately upon entering, this young fellow (from the wine truck) said something to those two men in Italian which I didn't understand. They pretended they did not talk much English, and denied they had ever seen him before, and said that they had not sold him any wine.[16]

The house turned out to be part of the Seghesio Winery and the two men talking to the truck driver in Italian (most likely in Piedmontese dialect) were Edoardo Seghesio and his son Arthur.

Edoardo had been a winemaker for the Italian Swiss Colony in the early years of the century before having established his own winery. From 1920 to 1921 he had also been a shareholding partner in the Asti winery along with the two Rossi brothers and his son-in-law Enrico Prati. The young driver stood handcuffed in the back of the room as the agents demanded menacingly to see reports from the Seghesio Winery. When Angela Seghesio came in crying and yelling, "What is the trouble, what is the trouble?" Edoardo hastily assured the agents he would have Prati bring his winery's reports from Asti.

At this point, the accounts of these events—as later assessed during a corruption trial waged against Crawford by a federal jury—diverge. Crawford claimed that Prati tried to bribe him with $10,000 when he got to the Seghesio Winery the next morning in return for guaranteeing safe passage for future wine shipments from Asti to San Francisco. Crawford went on to allege that he talked Agents Meyer and Curtis into pretending to accept the money so they could seize Prati's next convoy and thus incriminate the Asti winery, which was a much bigger prize than that of the Seghesios. When the San Francisco Prohibition Unit, which had been already monitoring him, questioned Crawford about failing to report the money, he claimed it was because the investigation of Asti was still under way. In the meantime, Meyer and Curtis had been alerted of impending trouble and had fled to Mexico. In court, Prati and the Seghesios charged that the federal agents had extorted the money from them, forcing them to sign for a $10,000 loan at a banker's home in the middle of the night in exchange for not arresting them on the spot and pressing charges.

While the federal judge found Crawford guilty of having accepted the bribe and sentenced him to eighteen months in jail, he also decided that Prati and the Seghesios had offered the money to the agents freely and refused to return it to them. More than two years passed before the winemakers were acquitted and the $10,000 was returned to Prati, in December 1924.[17] Whatever the "truth" may be, the Crawford–Seghesio case suggests that (Piedmontese) Italians in Northern California were widely recognized and singled out as the leading wine traffickers and therefore had to deal with the repressive and often corrupt hand of the state government—yet another form of social capital they had to accumulate. Indeed, once the Volstead Act had come into effect in 1920, these immigrant winemakers had felt that no other viable career options were open to them (a sentiment echoed in Edmund Rossi's aforementioned remark that winemaking "was all we know about"). However, they also recognized that Prohibition's unique socioeconomic context of illegality could provide them with unprecedented, if risky, opportunities for upward mobility.

Guasti today, 2010. The site is close to Los Angeles–Ontario International Airport, which claims most of the area where vineyards were. Photo Simone Cinotto.

Leading wine historian Thomas Pinney's account of California winemaking during Prohibition emphasizes how Italians exercised an unspoken hegemony over the state's devastated wine industry, something no one would have thought possible, at least to that extent, before the advent of the Volstead Act. Pinney focuses primarily on the position of the Italian Vineyard Company:

> Secondo Guasti's large enterprise at Cucamonga maintained itself mostly by shipments of grapes to the homemaking market from its huge vineyards (the "largest of the world," the company boasted), but kept the winery going too: it made concentrates, and when all other outlets were closed, it made wine. An inspection in 1925 reported that the entire plant was in full operation, and by 1930 the inventory at Cucamonga showed more than 2.5 million gallons of wine on hand. Perhaps this was the largest operation in all of California. It included wines under the whole gamut of borrowed names that characterized provincial California: claret, burgundy, riesling, sauterne, marsala, tokay, malaga, sherry.[18]

Prohibition drastically reduced the number of legally recognized wineries in California from 694 in 1922 to 177 in 1933, a situation that turned out to be relatively advantageous for Italian, and especially Piedmontese, winemakers.[19] If their position in the industry had already been significant at the turn of the century, it was downright preponderant now. By the time the Gallos entered the arena to relaunch and modernize the industry immediately after the repeal of the Eighteenth Amendment, their strongest competitors were either consummate companies that had successfully completed the fourteen-year journey through the desert of semi-illegality—like the Rossi brothers' Italian Swiss Colony, Guasti's Italian Vineyard Company (now controlled by Fruit Industries Ltd.), and the Roma Wine

Company of brothers Giovanni Battista and Lorenzo Cella—or beginners who, like the Gallos, were confidently entering the world of wine production after having taken advantage of the circumstances of Prohibition to sell large quantities of grapes in urban immigrant markets (such as Louis Martini, Giuseppe Franzia, and Antonio Perelli-Minetti).[20]

It is ironic but revealing that entrepreneurs like Rossi, Guasti, and the Gallos could pursue their universalist dream of creating a mass wine market in the United States thanks in large part to their very marginalization, their racial characterization, and a Puritan reformist condemnation of their trade that reflected widespread nativist sentiments. Prohibition's application to wine, a process with roots and extensions that stretch well beyond the period of 1920 to 1933, allowed the members of an inbetween race to create a relatively protected manufacturing niche, a semiformal ethnic economy that would allow them and subsequent generations of entrepreneurs to make substantial profits. It is also interesting to note how the pendulum of historical narrative, represented by two generations of historians of Italian immigration to California and of American wine, has swung more in the direction of admiring characters like Pietro Carlo Rossi, Secondo Guasti, or Ernest Gallo for their acumen as American businessmen, rather than focusing on the mistrust they engendered and the attempts made to segregate them from a national economy. The difficult, controversial, and painful ways these entrepreneurs managed to transform disadvantage into its opposite make for a unique and interesting story.

Conclusion

Work, Social Capital, and Race in the Experience
of Italian Winemakers in California

The story of Italian winemakers in California presents an interesting case for historians of ethnic entrepreneurship and immigrant work in the United States. The "Pavesian paradigm"—the discursive notion according to which Piedmontese immigrants came to the United States already possessing a wine culture that could then blossom in ideal environmental conditions under a placid Californian sun—is a convenient but misleading shortcut to explain why such a small number of immigrants from a single Italian region emerged as key protagonists in the modern history of American wine. Being from Piedmont did not automatically mean one had knowledge of the winemaking process, let alone the kind required by a modern wine industry. This was as much the case in the era of Italy's great migration as it is today. The narrative that described California as a Piedmont on the Pacific Ocean because of similarities in environment, climate, and landscape was just that, a narrative—one that brought together various ideas and images to form a convincing but largely deceptive overall picture. More important, the interpretive expedient of the Pavesian myth does little justice to the agency, work, and cultural imagination of the flesh-and-bone people who actually participated in the story. Those who would eventually become the leading Piedmontese producers of California wine relied far more on their entrepreneurial skills, tenacity, and business savvy than on their almost nonexistent technical expertise. Their lack of significant financial capital also meant that, at least in the beginning, the land they acquired was marginal and ill suited to be transformed into vineyards. The only reason their highly risky investment paid off at all was their access to and accumulation of another type of capital—social capital. The ability of Piedmontese wine entrepreneurs to procure intensive, low-paid work from rural Piedmont-born immigrants made all the difference in the development of their nascent enterprises. Not only did their ethnicity help them to recruit new employees from Piedmont and form professional chain migrations, but it also allowed them to organize their workforces and limit conflict to a degree that would have been impossible for winemakers of other ethnicities. Their social capital would in fact prove important in many different ways, often helping them transform the significant disadvantage of being a foreign entrepreneur in the United States into an advantage. A fine example of this is the role that the Italian Swiss Colony's Pietro Carlo Rossi played as a major point of reference in California for the Italian government and winemaking industry, not to mention the audience he secured with important European experts during his travels throughout the Continent.

The epic story of Piedmontese winemakers in the American West needs to be considered within its general historical context, which in turn it helps to illuminate. When the first Piedmontese immigrants arrived in California, they encountered a largely rural region with obvious, immense potential, in which European colonizers had been questioning and debating who would perform the labor required to exploit its resources. Black slaves, as occurred in the rest of the Southern United States (until 1865)? The Chinese, who were arriving to the United States in a semi-servile condition? Mexicans, who had been annexed through conquest? Or free European immigrants, as was taking place in the Northern states of the Union? By the late nineteenth century—when the first big Piedmontese wineries began to develop—the young state of California already hosted an extraordinarily composite population, and it was taken for granted that notions of racial difference would heavily influence economic development and the division of labor. The case of Piedmontese winemakers in California confirms not only how central race was in determining the socioeconomic success of various ethnic groups in the United States, but also how much it affected the formation of entrepreneurial and professional niches in which specific groups predominated.

The trajectories and fortunes of ethnic enterprises need to be deconstructed and examined from different perspectives, since differences of class and gender do not disappear within the boundaries of economic niches. From the point of view of Piedmontese immigrant workers, for example, coming to California around the turn of the century meant occupying an inbetween bracket of a rural labor market that was structured according to racial hierarchies. European farm laborers were in high demand in California after the legal ban on Chinese immigration and the abolishment of slavery in the United States before that. While being free white workers meant that Piedmontese laborers enjoyed the privilege of never having to occupy the lowest rung of the social ladder (something they quickly learned to appreciate), their status as late arrivals and their racial characterization as not quite white still relegated them to unskilled, poorly paid jobs. On the other hand, they had come to California with a purpose and were absorbed as members of a community immediately upon their arrival. Such a circumstance totally conflicts with the popular image of the wandering migrant searching the world over for work and freedom at the mercy of events, which migration history has shown is essentially a literary invention. Instead, these workers had been called to the United States to participate in the development of an ethnic wine industry by a group of entrepreneurs who shared their Piedmontese origins and had already made a name for themselves among the Italian American business community.

Piedmontese immigrant workers were not the only ones who lived in a sort of permanent state of tension. On the one hand, entre-preneurs like Rossi, Guasti, and the Gallos were fascinated by eco-nomic Americanism and aspired to be, perhaps more than anything else, accepted as great American businessmen, dazzling examples of entrepreneurial spirit and all that could be achieved in the "land of opportunity." Their ultimate dream was to create a mass wine market in the United States, and they devoted their best efforts to making this happen, especially when it came to being creative and innovative in the realm of marketing. On the other hand, their immigrant status could never be erased, and it weighed on them both negatively and positively.

Being rooted in the ethnic world certainly had its advantages for Piedmontese businessmen. In addition to their access to a vast reserve of low-cost, low-conflict labor from their homeland, they also enjoyed favorable credit conditions thanks to the success of Italian American finance in California. Further, the predominance of Pied-montese and other Italians among their supply and sales contacts gave them easy access to a wide market of fellow Italian immigrants with a favorable disposition toward their products. Yet, despite these benefits, Piedmontese entrepreneurs never fully overcame the signif-icant disadvantage of being "foreigners" who trafficked in a "foreign" product. Nor did they manage to achieve the total, unquestionable acceptance they sought as American businessmen. Even Ernest and

Julio Gallo, the men who eventually fulfilled the dream of first-generation Italian American winemakers and created a prodigious economic empire, continued to engender doubts among native-born Americans. Indeed, the general moral reproach contained within Ellen Hawkes's anti-biography of the Gallo family reverberates with nativist sentiment, suggesting from the title (*Blood and Wine*) onward that the Gallo brothers' actions were directly correlated to an indelible racial legacy.

Notions and practices of race in turn-of-the-twentieth-century California helped transform Italian regionalism into a specific form of social capital that Piedmontese immigrant winemakers used to their advantage. Immigrants from Monferrato, the Langhe, and the province of Turin began looking at themselves more precisely as Piedmontese, and they related to other Italians as such, even in antagonistic ways. At the same time, they also began viewing winemaking as a field that belonged to them and thus helped to build a strong affinity between Piedmontese identity and wine. The language of wine—that is, specialization in vineyard and winery work—functioned as a sort of lingua franca, a code through which to recognize one another and join forces. From this point of view, the stereotype of the Piedmontese winemaker, one of the cornerstones of the Pavesian paradigm, is more a product of life in California than an import from the Old World.

By the time the first Piedmontese wineries opened in the 1880s, the Hungarian winemaker Agoston Harastzky had already helped to form a well-defined image of the California wine industry as one dominated by immigrants. Starting as early as the mid-nineteenth century, wine in the United States was implicitly different by virtue of being produced by European immigrants whose ethnic origins differed from those of the Anglo-Saxon, Anglophone, and Protestant majority—that is, the Germans, the French, and, later, the Italians. While California wine was thus considered not quite American and prone to suspicion, its exotic nature was not only acceptable but even effective from a marketing standpoint owing to the prestige of the Americans who enjoyed European wines (the quality of which immigrant producers tried to match). But such privilege was not extended, for example, to Japanese winemakers, who were essentially prevented from developing their own presence in the industry by the severe racism they endured.

The inbetween, not-quite-American status of wine and its European American producers was complicated by the moral condemnation of alcohol that emerged in the late nineteenth century among a large and influential swath of American society. Going on to become one of the main topics of political debate at the beginning of the next century, this sea change would culminate in the 1920 enactment of Prohibition. Already by the turn of the twentieth century, wine producers were being subjected to bans, regulations, and widespread negative ethical judgment. Many American-born entrepreneurs and investors decided in turn to abandon the industry for safer, more profitable ones before everything came crashing down, as was already easy to predict by then. The themes of temperance and race thus became intertwined during and immediately after World War I, as did prohibitionist legislation toward alcohol and restrictions on immigration. Jeopardizing the production and sale of alcoholic beverages, including wine, meant jeopardizing the nonnative forces— papism, foreign cultures, radicalism, the Mafia—that some Anglo-Saxon Protestants believed were intent on destroying the United States and everything it represented. One of the main ways Prohibition finally managed to become a national law was in fact by mounting the horse of nativism.

Yet racial discrimination produced ambiguous results in this case as well. Prohibition generated an association between wine and illegality that drove many to flee the industry. This led to an especially significant loss when it came to the Germans, who had made important contributions to the development of California winemaking. The only ones to remain were those who were prepared and able to bear the added risks and burdens of a business whose legitimacy was fragile, to say the least. Among these were several Piedmontese who took what had become a stigma of difference and marginality and turned it into an opportunity to solidify their central position in the California wine industry. Like the educated Korean immigrants of the 1970s and 1980s whose inability to speak English fluently compelled them to open their own retail businesses, Piedmontese winemakers turned a disadvantage into an active impetus for change and adaptation. The immigrant, un-American product niche that wine had carved out for itself actually had a protective implication over the medium term, despite constant adversity. In fact, when selling grapes for domestic wine production became a supply source for illegal sales during Prohibition and the Great Depression, not only did wineries like the Italian Swiss Colony and the Italian Vineyard Company manage to survive, but—precisely because of the ban on wine's commercial production—they even made a decent profit. Further, the connections these wineries had already established with ethnic networks of brokers, wholesalers, retailers, restaurateurs, and consumers proved once again vital for their growth. Even later generations of Piedmontese winemakers, far removed from the partial alienation and total pioneering experience of their immigrant forefathers, would continue to lean on the old ethnic network when they set about modernizing, reorganizing, and redefining the limits of the industry during the postwar period. Most important, that network would serve as a crucial launching pad from which the E. & J. Gallo Winery would finally and truly conquer a national mass market.

The current burgeoning interest in American wine only emerged after a long post-Prohibition era ended in the late 1960s. The counterculture and identity politics that developed out of the civil rights, student, and feminist movements; the ethnic revival of third-generation descendants of turn-of-the-twentieth-century European immigrants; and the new appreciation for multiculturalism, which put a premium on cultural diversity as a social and even economic asset, were all instrumental in opening a new chapter in the history of wine in the United States. The popularity of distinctive, easily consumable expressions of cultural difference like ethnic food and drinks, food patterns, and cultures of commensality grew dramatically from the 1970s onward. Their demand was in turn supported by a restructuring of the food and wine industry that involved the development of diversified product lines for a variety of socio-demographic segments of consumers, thereby leading to the demise of the notion of an overall mass market. Wine now enjoys considerable success among middle-class consumers with cosmopolitan tastes bent on accumulating cultural capital by demonstrating their enological knowledge, and its reach extends far beyond the Catholic immigrant niche market that was once both the burden and the delight of first-generation Piedmontese winemakers.

Today, the many wineries run by descendants of turn-of-the-twentieth-century Piedmontese immigrants that dot the map of California occupy the most prestigious wine regions of the United States and follow state-of-the-art guidelines in the production, bottling, and labeling of the quality wine they make from grapes grown in choice vineyards. While these wines may be a far cry from the bulk version their ancestors shipped from California to the Little Italies of New York and Chicago well over a century ago, they form part of an invaluable legacy. Third-generation winemaker Pete Seghesio Jr. is at the helm of the Seghesio Family Vineyards in Healdsburg, Sonoma County, where the winery was originally established by ancestors Edoardo and Angela in 1895; Louis "Bob" and Evalyn Trinchero own Sutter Home Winery in St. Helena, in the heart of Napa Valley; Charles and Martha Barra manage Barra Winery in the Redwood Valley of Mendocino; Trudie Conrotto operates Anselmo Conrotto Winery in Gilroy; and George and Janice Guglielmo run the Guglielmo Winery of Morgan Hill in Santa Clara County. In addition to the regional origins of their immigrant founders, many of these wineries also share similar beginnings—sometimes as spin-offs of companies created and run by other Piedmontese immigrants—and enduring family management that suggests continuity between Old World knowledge and modern techniques. Even a brief visit to their websites, which are full of nostalgic, sepia-toned photographs, shows how today's Piedmontese American winemakers use their immigrant heritage as symbolic capital to generate greater market value for their products.

In the context of the postmodern interest in roots, traditions, and memory, the rich history of their founding fathers provides the work of third-millennium Piedmontese winemakers with a profoundly meaningful as well as highly marketable cultural dimension.

Notes

NOTES TO THE INTRODUCTION

1. The working notion of race that I have adopted in this book was drawn primarily from David R. Roediger, *The Wages of Whiteness: Race and the Making of the American Working Class* (New York: Verso, 2007); Matthew Frye Jacobson, *Whiteness of a Different Color: European Immigrants and the Alchemy of Race* (Cambridge: Harvard University Press, 1999); Michael Omi and Howard Winant, *Racial Formation in the United States: From the 1960s to the 1990s* (New York: Routledge, 1994).

2. Guido Rossati, *Relazione di un viaggio di istruzione negli Stati Uniti d'America fatto per incarico del Ministero* (Rome: Tip. Naz. G. Bertero, 1900), 188–196; Carlo Dondero, "Asti, Sonoma County: An Italian Swiss Agricultural Colony and What Is Has Grown To," *Out West* 42, no. 2 (1902): 252–265; Eliot Lord, *The Italian in America* (New York: B. F. Buck & Company, 1905), 135–142; Edmondo Mayor des Planches, *Attraverso gli Stati Uniti: Per l'emigrazione italiana* (Turin: Unione tipografico-editrice torinese, 1913), 30–37.

3. Lanier Bartlett, "An Immigrant in the Land of Opportunity," *World's Work* 17 (April 1909): 11375–11380; James Hofer, "Guasti and the Italian Vineyard Company," 1984, Wine and Wine Industry Collection, Special Collections and University Archives, University Library, Cal Poly Pomona; James Hofer, "Cucamonga Wines and Vines: A History of the Cucamonga Pioneer

Vineyard Association," master's thesis, Claremont Graduate School, 1983: the citation from the *Daily Report* (August 30, 1919) is on page 69.

4. Garrett Peck, *The Prohibition Hangover: Alcohol in America from Demon Rum to Cult Cabernet* (New Brunswick: Rutgers University Press, 2009).

5. Laurie Itow, "The Gallo Brothers' Secretive Empire," *San Francisco Examiner* (September 1, 1985): D8; Jacklyn Fierman, "How Gallo Crushes the Competition," *Fortune* (September 1, 1986): 24–31; Marvin R. Shanken, "Ernest Gallo at 90," *Wine Spectator* (June 30, 1999): 52–74; Jerry Hirsch, "At 75, Wine Giant Gallo Is Refining Its Palate," *Los Angeles Times* (April 4, 2008): C1.

6. Werner Sollors, "Introduction: The Invention of Ethnicity," in *The Invention of Ethnicity*, ed. Werner Sollors (New York: Oxford University Press, 1991), xvi. The quotation from the Chinese laundryman is from Hamilton Holt, ed., *The Life Stories of Undistinguished Americans as Told by Themselves* (New York: James Pott & Company, 1906), 289.

7. Kevin Starr, *Americans and the California Dream, 1850–1915* (New York: Oxford University Press, 1973); Kevin Starr, *Inventing the Dream: California Through the Progressive Era* (New York: Oxford University Press, 1998); Lawrence Culver, *The Frontier of Leisure: Southern California and the Shaping of Modern America* (New York: Oxford University Press, 2010). For the role of racial and ethnic minorities in shaping the West in American history and the national imagination, see Dan Moos, *Outside America: Race, Ethnicity, and the Role of the American West in National Belonging* (Lebanon: University Press of New England, 2005). On the literary construction, by Northern European writers and southbound travelers, of the Mediterranean as the paradigmatic place for the pleasures of the body and relaxed self-discipline from the sixteenth century onward, see, among others, Robert Aldrich, *The Seduction of the Mediterranean: Writing, Art, and Homosexual Fantasy* (New York: Routledge, 1993).

8. John Charles Frémont, *Narrative of the Exploring Expedition to the Rocky Mountains in the Year 1842 and to Oregon and North California in the Years 1843–44* (New York: Appleton and Company, 1856), 29.

9. Charles Victor Hall, *California: The Ideal Italy of the World: An Outline Mirror of the State for Health, Happiness, and Delightful Homes* (Philadelphia: Cooperative Printing Co., 1875).

10. Quoted in Dino Cinel, *From Italy to San Francisco: The Immigrant Experience* (Stanford: Stanford University Press, 1982), 15.

11. The geographer Gary Peters argues that wine regions and wine landscapes, and the sense of place they convey, are socially and culturally produced.

According to Peters, "America's viticultural landscapes, or winescapes, are human creations that have unfolded as the elements of the natural landscape—landforms, climates, vegetation, soils, and water supplies—have been brought together with the environmental needs of wine grapes. . . . We can understand more about viticultural landscapes by considering the three fundamental elements that shape them: (1) the grapes and their needs, (2) the natural environments that best meet those needs, and (3) the viticulturists and wine makers who determine everything from the varieties of grapes, spacing of the vines, and trellising systems to the final product that enters the bottle. Furthermore, all of these elements can come together to produce wine regions only within the broader context of cultural practices and economic viability." *American Winescapes: The Cultural Landscapes of America's Wine Country* (Boulder, CO: Westview Press, 1997), 7–8.

12. I mostly relied on two general histories of immigration and race in California: Tomás Almaguer, *Racial Fault Lines: The Historical Origins of White Supremacy in California* (Berkeley: University of California Press, 1994); and Mae Ngai, *Impossible Subjects: Illegal Aliens and the Making of Modern America* (Princeton: Princeton University Press, 2005). On the convergence of racism, rural labor, and social mobility in California since the mid-nineteenth century, see Alexander Saxton, *The Indispensable Enemy: Labor and the Anti-Chinese Movement in California* (Berkeley: University of California Press, 1971); Guerin-Camille González, *Mexican Workers and American Dreams: Immigration, Repatriation, and California Farm Labor, 1900–1939* (New Brunswick: Rutgers University Press, 1994); Madeline Hsu, *Dreaming of Gold, Dreaming of Home: Transnationalism and Migration Between the United States and South China, 1882–1943* (Stanford: Stanford University Press, 2000); Matt García, *A World of Its Own: Race, Labor and Citrus in the Making of Los Angeles, 1900–1970* (Chapel Hill: University of North Carolina Press, 2001); Stephen J. Pitti, *The Devil in Silicon Valley: Northern California, Race, and Mexican Americans* (Princeton: Princeton University Press, 2004); Eiichiro Azuma, *Between Two Empires: Race, History, and Transnationalism in Japanese America* (New York: Oxford University Press, 2005); José M. Alamillo, *Making Lemonade out of Lemons: Mexican American Labor and Leisure in a California Town, 1880–1960* (Urbana: University of Illinois Press, 2006). This scholarship, which documents the disproportionate suffering of non-European Californians, has somehow tended to obscure the diversity in the experiences of European immigrants and failed to account for the different ways each group has played the whiteness game. Elliot Robert Barkan reevaluated the role of European

immigrants in the history of California in light of whiteness studies in *From All Points: America's Immigrant West, 1870–1952* (Bloomington: Indiana University Press, 2007).

13. Works on Italian American whiteness include Robert A. Orsi, "In-Between People: Street Feste and the Problems of the Dark-Skinned Other in Italian Harlem, 1920–1990," *American Quarterly* 44, no. 3 (1992): 313–347; Peter D'Agostino, "Craniums, Criminals, and the 'Cursed Race': Italian Anthropology in American Racial Thought, 1861–1924," *Comparative Studies in Society and History* 44, no. 2 (2002): 319–343; Jennifer Guglielmo and Salvatore Salerno, eds., *Are Italians White? How Race Is Made in America* (New York: Routledge, 2003); Thomas Guglielmo, *White on Arrival: Italians, Race, Color, and Power in Chicago, 1890–1945* (New York: Oxford University Press, 2004).

14. Joseph Giovinco, "'Success in the Sun?' California's Italians During the Progressive Era," in *Struggle and Success: An Anthology of the Italian Immigrant Experience in California*, ed. Paola Sensi-Isolani and Phylis Cancilla Martinelli (New York: Center for Migration Studies, 1993), 20–39.

15. Thomas Kessner, *The Golden Door: Italian and Jewish Immigrant Mobility in New York City, 1880–1915* (New York: Oxford University Press, 1977).

16. James R. Barrett and David R. Roediger, "Inbetween Peoples: Race, Nationality, and the 'New Immigrant' Working Class," *Journal of American Ethnic History* 16, no. 3 (1997): 3–44.

17. United States Immigration Commission, "The Wine-Making Industry of California," in *Immigrants in Industries, Vol. 24: Japanese and Other Immigrant Races in the Pacific Coast and Rocky Mountain States* (Washington, DC: Government Printing Office, 1911), 275, 280.

18. For a thorough discussion of the multifarious ways in which race shaped Italian and other European immigrants' encounter with the United States, see David R. Roediger, *Working Toward Whiteness: How America's Immigrants Became White* (New York: Basic Books, 2005).

19. Analyzing the complex racialized terrain on which Piedmontese winemakers operated enhances our knowledge of the Italian immigrant entrepreneurial and mercantile middle class and its role in creating ethnic economic niches. In the historiography of Italian migration, by far the most widely studied economic figure (besides the proletarian) has been a distinctive type of labor entrepreneur, the ethnic broker called padrone. Small capitalists with a sufficient command of English and a knowledge of the larger society, padroni offered their services to construction, mining, and railroad companies to procure jobs, usually in labor gangs, for unskilled migrants. Early scholars

emphasized the exploitative, almost feudal nature of the padrone system, at its pinnacle between the last decades of the nineteenth century and World War I. They insisted on the semi-servile conditions faced by subcontracted migrants and the many schemes padroni contrived to exact money from their workers. By contrast, more recent works have identified a modern entrepreneurial dimension of the system, seeing padroni as intercultural middlemen who met companies' need for workers and immigrants' need for work, performing a vital role both for Italian migrants and the American economy, particularly in the West. For examples of the two perspectives, see Luciano J. Iorizzo, *Italian Immigration and the Impact of the Padrone System* (New York: Arno Press, 1980); and Gunther Peck, *Reinventing Free Labor: Padrones and Immigrant Workers in the North American West, 1880–1930* (New York: Cambridge University Press, 1990). Even though they exerted some of the same economic and cultural power over their vineyard workers that the padroni wielded on their construction gang laborers, Rossi, Guasti, and the Gallos were very different kinds of ethnic leaders. They pulled away from the image of the padroni as sellers of indentured workers to corporations craving disposable labor, instead promoting themselves as respectable American businessmen and proud employers of free white labor. Power relations in California vineyards were a long way off from the intermediation performed by padroni between employers and an unskilled immigrant workforce, established as they were between capitalists and workers who were both immigrants. Although Rossi, Guasti, and the Gallos insisted on present-ing themselves as role models for immigrant social mobility and for ethnic paternalism toward their Italian employees, they did not represent themselves primarily as ethnic middlemen but as savvy independent businessmen who invested their capital for profit.

20. The interest of the Italian government in the achievements of immigrant winemakers in California is discussed in Mark I. Choate, *Emigrant Nation: The Making of Italy Abroad* (Cambridge: Harvard University Press, 2008), 52, 88–89.

21. For a general treatment of turn-of-the-twentieth-century Italian migrants' long-standing attachment to their native communities, see Donna Gabac-cia, *Italy's Many Diasporas* (Seattle: University of Washington Press, 2000); and Samuel L. Baily, *Immigrants in the Lands of Promise: Italians in Buenos Aires and New York City, 1870–1914* (Ithaca: Cornell University Press, 2004). In the second half of the nineteenth century, the few political exiles and the immigrant mercantile elite who dominated Italian diasporic political life

in California tried to involve indifferent labor migrants, but their language was that of Italian nationalism—with no reference to regionalism. In San Francisco, Monarchists and Republicans argued just as much about the form of government the newly unified Italy should adopt as they did about the leadership of the local immigrant community, which they imagined as being part of a nation (albeit of different races). Originally, the conflict between Monarchists and Republicans might have had regionalist qualities: Liguria, a region with a long republican history, was forcibly handed to the Kingdom of Sardinia by the Congress of Vienna, and the many revolts against the Piedmontese rule that occurred in Genoa through the 1850s witnessed the unrelenting vitality of Ligurian republicanism. Some Ligurian immigrants to California were Republican refugees who continued their political activism in exile, especially by opposing the politics of the Piedmontese consuls in San Francisco. Whatever the relevance of such a confluence of localism and ideology may have been, however, it would not last long. As early as 1858, an Italian Mutual Benefit Society was created in San Francisco that accepted members from all regions—and whose leadership immediately became the object of desire of the opposing Monarchist and Republican factions. See Francesca Loverci, "Italiani in California negli anni del Risorgimento," *Clio* 15, no. 4 (1979): 469–547; Francesca Loverci, "Giuseppe Garibaldi e la comunità italiana in California," in *Garibaldi generale della libertà*, ed. Aldo Alessandro Mola (Rome: Ufficio storico dell'Esercito, 1984), 645–654; Francesca Loverci, "Le idee di Mazzini in California: Iniziative politiche e giornalistiche dei repubblicani italiani a San Francisco dagli anni del 'Gold Rush' al 1905," in *Il Mazzinianesimo nel mondo*, ed. Giuliana Limiti (Pisa: Istituto Domus Mazziniana, 1996), 83–151.

22. Cinel, *From Italy to San Francisco*, 196–227; Dino Cinel, "Between Change and Continuity: Regionalism Among Immigrants from the Italian Northwest," *Journal of Ethnic Studies* 9, no. 3 (1981): 19–36. Cinel's work on Italian immigration to California, commended and prized at the time of its publication, has been widely discredited by a combination of disturbing revelations about his personal life and criticism of his unsubstantiated argumentation and even alleged construction of nonexistent sources. See Sebastian Fichera, "The Disturbing Case of Dino Cinel," *History News Network* (April 28, 2003), http://hnn.us/articles/1420.html. However, I have found the part on the commercial dimension of Italian immigrant regionalism in the late nineteenth century, for which he relied on Italian newspapers published in San Francisco, sound and usable.

23. H. F. Raup, "The Italian Swiss in California," *California Historical Quarterly* (December 1951): 311.

24. Thomas Pinney, *A History of Wine in America: From the Beginnings to Prohibition* (Berkeley: University of California Press, 1989).

25. Thomas R. Pegram, *Battling Demon Rum: The Struggle for a Dry America, 1800–1933* (Chicago: Ivan R. Dee, 1998); Jack S. Blocker, *American Temperance Movements: Cycles of Reform* (Boston: Twayne, 1989); Ann-Marie E. Szymanski, *Pathways to Prohibition: Radicals, Moderates, and Social Movement Outcomes* (Durham: Duke University Press, 2003).

26. Donna R. Gabaccia, "As American as Budweiser and Pickles? Nation-Building in American Food Industries," in *Food Nations: Selling Taste in Consumer Societies*, ed. Warren Belasco and Philip Scranton (New York: Routledge, 2002), 175–193.

NOTES TO CHAPTER 1

1. Charles L. Sullivan, "Italian Swiss Colony: The First Half Century, 1881–1933," 1980, Sonoma County Public Library, Healdsburg, CA. See also Jack W. Florence, *The Legacy of a Village: The Italian Swiss Colony Winery and the People of Asti, California* (Phoenix: Raymond Court Press, 2004).

2. Edoardo Seghesio emigrated from Dogliani in 1886; Joe Vercelli was born in San Francisco in 1912 to immigrant parents from Valfernera, in the province of Asti. See Carol Hicke, *The Seghesio Family, Vineyards, and Winery: One Hundred Years in Alexander Valley: An Oral History with Rachel Ann and Eugene "Pete" Seghesio* (Healdsburg, CA: Alexander Valley Winegrowers Association, 1995); *Joe Vercelli: A Wineman for All Seasons: An Oral History by Joe Vercelli, with Remarks by Anne Vercelli* (Healdsburg, CA: Alexander Valley Winegrowers Association, 1999); "Joe Vercelli Interviewed," interview by Bob Mosher with Eric Davis, 1990, Sonoma County Public Library, Healdsburg, CA.

3. Edmund A. Rossi, "Italian Swiss Colony and the Wine Industry," interview by Ruth Teiser, 1971, Regional Oral History Office, University of California, Berkeley.

4. Edmund A. Rossi Jr., "Italian Swiss Colony, 1949–1989: Recollections of a Third-Generation California Winemaker," interview by Ruth Teiser and Lisa Jacobson, 1990, Regional Oral History Office, University of California, Berkeley.

5. *A History of California and an Extended History of Los Angeles and Environs, Vol. 2: Biographical* (Los Angeles: Historic Record Company, 1915), 202–207; Giuseppe Scaletta, *La chiesa cattolica di San Secondo d'Asti in Guasti, California*

(Asti, 2005), 17. According to Scaletta, Secondo Guasti's father-in-law, Giuseppe Amillo, had arrived in San Francisco around 1860 and in 1868 had married Caterina Bernero, who was "almost surely born in the province of Cuneo in 1852."

6. These investors included Giovanni De Matteis of Viale d'Asti, Giovanni Gai of Isola d'Asti, Ferdinando and Angelo Bessolo, Leopoldo Schiappapietre, A. Ferrario, J. Pagliano, A. Vignolo (Spirito) Bodrero, A. Dell'Acqua, and Giacomo Barlotti. See Cleto Baroni with Guido Brogelli and G. M. Tuoni, *Gente italiana in California* (Los Angeles: L'italo americano [192?]), 68.

7. Italian Vineyard Company, *Souvenir 1915 and Some Choice Recipes* (Los Angeles: Young & McAllister, 1915).

8. G. M. Tuoni and Guido Brogelli, *Attività italiane in California* (San Francisco: Mercury Press, 1929), 143–144, 281.

9. Hofer, "Guasti and the Italian Vineyard Company."

10. Ernest Gallo and Julio Gallo, *Ernest and Julio: Our Story* (New York: Random House, 1994); Ellen Hawkes, *Blood and Wine: The Unauthorized Story of the Gallo Wine Empire* (New York: Simon & Schuster, 1993).

11. Valerio Castronovo, *Il Piemonte* (Turin: Einaudi, 1977).

12. Paola Corti, "L'emigrazione piemontese: Un modello regionale?" *Giornale di storia contemporanea* 3, no. 2 (2000): 22–41; Dionigi Albera, "Dalla mobilità all'emigrazione: Il caso del Piemonte sud-occidentale," *Recherches régionales* 3 (1995): 25–64.

13. Gianfausto Rosoli, *Un secolo di emigrazione italiana: 1876–1976* (Rome: Cser, 1978), 356–358, 365–366.

14. Paola Corti, "L'emigrazione italiana in Francia: Un fenomeno di lunga durata," *Altreitalie* 26 (January–June 2003): 4–25; Matteo Sanfilippo, "L'emigrazione italiana nelle Americhe in età preunitaria," *Annali della Fondazione Luigi Einaudi* 42 (2008): 65–79; *C'era una volta la Merica: Immigrati piemontesi in Argentina* (Cuneo: L'Arciere, 1990); Paola Corti, "Women Were Labor Migrants Too: Tracing Late-Nineteenth-Century Female Migration from Northern Italy to France," in *Women, Gender, and Transnational Lives: Italian Workers of the World*, ed. Donna Gabaccia and Franca Iacovetta (Toronto: University of Toronto Press, 2002), 133–159.

15. Patrizia Audenino, "Biellesi a New York: Una comunità di passaggio?" in *L'emigrazione biellese nel Novecento*, ed. Valerio Castronovo (Milan: Electa, 1988), 115–166.

16. Simone Cinotto, "I Won't Be Satisfied Until I've Traveled the Entire World: The Transnational Imagination of an Italian Immigrant in the United States,

1905–1942," in *The Place of Europe in American History*, ed. Maurizio Vaudagna and Elisabetta Vezzosi (Turin: Otto, 2006), 371–403; Caroline Waldron Merithew, "Domesticating the Diaspora: Remembering the Life of Katie DeRorre," in *Intimacy and Italian Migration: Gender and Domestic Lives in a Mobile World*, ed. Loretta Baldassar and Donna Gabaccia (New York: Fordham University Press, 2011), 69–82.

17. Cesare Pavese, *The Moon and the Bonfires*, trans. R. W. Flint (New York: New York Review Books, 2002), 13.

18. Ibid., 6.

19. Maurizio Rosso, *Piemontesi nel Far West: Studi e testimonianze sull'emigrazione piemontese in California* (Cavallermaggiore: Gribaudo, 1990); Giancarlo Libert, "Contributi astigiani e piemontesi alla vitivinicoltura californiana," *Il Platano* 28 (2003): 171–184; Cesare Pitto, "Un segno della memoria: La coltivazione della vite e le comunità piemontesi nell'America del Nord," in *Dai feudi monferrini e dal Piemonte ai nuovi mondi oltre gli oceani*, ed. Laura Balletto (Alessandria: Società di storia, arte e archeologia, 1993), 669–682.

20. Vincent P. Carosso, *The California Wine Industry, 1830–1895: The Formative Years* (Berkeley: University of California Press, 1951); Leon D. Adams, *The Wines of America* (New York: McGraw-Hill, 1985); Pinney, *A History of Wine in America: From the Beginnings to Prohibition*; Thomas Pinney, *A History of Wine in America: From Prohibition to the Present* (Berkeley: University of California Press, 2005); Charles L. Sullivan, *A Companion to California Wine: An Encyclopedia of Wine and Winemaking from the Mission Period to the Present* (Berkeley: University of California Press, 1998); Ruth Teiser and Catherine Harroun, *Winemaking in California: The Account in Words and Pictures of the Golden State's Two-Century-Long Adventure with Wine* (New York: McGraw-Hill, 1983). A partial exception is John Melville's *Guide to California Wines* (New York: E. P. Dutton & Co., 1955), which includes several brief biographies in which the regional origin of each winegrower is meticulously identified.

21. United States Immigration Commission, *Immigrants in Industries, Vol. 21: Recent Immigrants in Agriculture* (Washington, DC: Government Printing Office, 1911), 36–37.

22. The most important study to document the role of Italian immigrants in the agriculture of California is an unpublished dissertation: Hans Christian Palmer, "Italian Immigration and the Development of California Agriculture," PhD diss., University of California, Berkeley, 1965.

23. Andrew Rolle, *The Immigrant Upraised: Italian Adventurers and Colonists in an Expanding America* (Norman: University of Oklahoma Press, 1968). Studies on

Italian immigration to California have largely concentrated on the community surrounding San Francisco. See Sebastian Fichera, *Italy on the Pacific: San Francisco's Italian Americans* (New York: Palgrave Macmillan, 2011); Cinel, *From Italy to San Francisco*; Deanna Paoli Gumina, *The Italians of San Francisco, 1850–1930* (New York: Center for Migration Studies, 1978); Rose Scherini, *The Italian American Community of San Francisco: A Descriptive Study* (New York: Arno Press, 1980); Paul Radin, *Italians of San Francisco: Their Adjustment and Acculturation* (New York: Arno Press, 1975). The main texts on the Italian American community of Los Angeles are Gloria Ricci Lothrop, *Italians of Los Angeles* (Los Angeles: Historical Society of Southern California, 2003); Gloria Ricci Lothrop, "California's Italians: A Promise Fulfilled," in *Fulfilling the Promise of California: An Anthology of Essays on the Italian American Experience in California*, ed. Gloria Ricci Lothrop and Andrew Rolle (Spokane, WA: Arthur H. Clark Company, 2000), 233–245; Rosalind Giardina Crosby, "The Italians of Los Angeles, 1900," in *Struggle and Success: An Anthology of the Italian Immigrant Experience in California*, ed. Paola Sensi-Isolani and Phylis Cancilla Martinelli (New York: Center for Migration Studies, 1993), 38–57. For an article specifically devoted to Pietro Carlo Rossi's Italian Swiss Colony, see Deanna Paoli Gumina, "Andrea Sbarboro, Founder of the Italian Swiss Colony Wine Company: Reminiscences of an Italian American Pioneer," *Italian Americana* 2, no. 1 (1975): 1–17.

24. Sebastian Fichera, "California's Italian-American Wine Makers: A Business Trajectory," *Studi Emigrazione* 37, no. 138 (2000): 329–350. See also Sebastian Fichera, "Entrepreneurial Behavior in an Immigrant Colony: The Economic Experience of San Francisco's Italian Americans, 1850–1940," *Studi Emigrazione* 32, no. 118 (1995): 321–345.

25. Donna Gabaccia, "Ethnicity in the Business World: Italians in American Food Industries," *Italian American Review* 6, no. 2 (1997/1998): 1–19.

26. Moos, *Outside America*.

27. On the formation and dynamics of village-based diasporas among mobile Italians in the age of mass migration, see Baily, *Immigrants in the Lands of Promise*.

28. Almaguer, *Racial Fault Lines*.

NOTES TO CHAPTER 2

1. Doreen Massey, *Space, Place, and Gender* (Minneapolis: University of Minnesota Press, 1994); Edward W. Soja, *Postmodern Geographies: The Reassertion of Space in Critical Social Theory* (New York: Verso, 1989); Henri Lefebvre, *The Production of Space* (New York: Blackwell, 1991).

2. Quoted in Starr, *Americans and the California Dream*, 366.

3. Mike Davis devotes a few pages to the late nineteenth-century mythology of California as a place of good health, pleasure, and rest in his masterful *City of Quartz: Excavating the Future in Los Angeles* (New York: Verso, 2006).

4. Massimo Carloni, "Nazionalismo, eurocentrismo, razzismo e misoginia nel 'Ciclo del Far West' di Emilio Salgari," *Problemi* 97 (1993): 170–181; Ilaria Crotti, "Salgari: l'America in eccesso," in *L'impatto della scoperta dell'America nella cultura veneziana*, ed. Angela Caracciolo (Rome: Bulzoni, 1990), 45–55; Emy Beseghi, ed., *La Valle della Luna: Avventura, esotismo, orientalismo nell'opera di Emilio Salgari* (Florence: La Nuova Italia, 1992); Ann Lawson Lucas, "Fascism and Literature: 'Il Caso Salgari,'" *Italian Studies* 45 (1990): 32–47; Ann Lawson Lucas, "Salgari, the Atlas, and the Microscope," in *Literature and Travel*, ed. Michael Hanne (Amsterdam: Rodopi, 1993), 79–92.

5. For an example of the arguments in favor of Italian peasant immigration, most prominently the resemblance of California's climate and soil to those of Italy, see "Supplanting the Chinese: Importing Italian Fruit Growers to Take Their Places," *Daily Alta California* (February 26, 1886): 1.

6. *L'Italia* (June 9, 1903): 1, quoted in Giovinco, "Success in the Sun?" 24.

7. *L'Italia e l'Opera degl'Italiani sul Pacifico, Part 2: Magazine Section of L'Italia* (October 24, 1927).

8. Lord, *Italian in America*, 143.

9. Rolle, *Immigrant Upraised*, 15–16.

10. Marco Armiero, *Elsewhere: Italians in the Frontiers (United States, 19th–20th Centuries)*, http://www.yale.edu/agrarianstudies/colloqpapers/25elsewherel.pdf.

11. Patrizia Audenino, "Storie di pietra: Gli scalpellini di Barre e l'Aldrich Public Library," *Movimento operaio e socialista* 9, no. 3 (1986): 425–432; Patrizia Audenino, "The Paths of the Trade: A Group of Stonemasons in America," *International Migration Review* 20 (Winter l986): 779–798.

12. Rossati, *Relazione di un viaggio di istruzione negli Stati Uniti*, 188.

13. Andrea Sbarboro, "Life of Andrea Sbarboro: Reminiscences of an Italian American Pioneer," 1911, Butler Library, University of California, Berkeley. Sbarboro's memoirs were reprinted in "Andrea Sbarboro: An Early American Success Story: Memoir of an Italian-American Entrepreneur and Pioneer," *Argonaut* 7, no. 2 (1996–1997): 16–101. The citations in the following chapters are drawn from this latter edition.

14. Antonio Perelli-Minetti, "A Life in Wine Making," interview by Ruth Teiser, 1969, Regional Oral History Office, University of California, Berkeley, 114.

15. "The Italian Swiss Colony of Asti, California: The History of Its Organization and Progress," 1914, Butler Library, University of California, Berkeley.

16. Quoted in Bartlett, "Immigrant in the Land of Opportunity," 11376.

17. Ibid. Perelli-Minetti painstakingly describes the apparent uselessness of the land and the disasters provoked by wind and sand in the vineyards of Cucamonga in "A Life in Wine Making," 120–121.

18. "Oral History Interview with David and Marie Correggia," January 24, 1977, Wine and Wine Industry Collection, Special Collections and University Archives, University Library, Cal Poly Pomona.

19. Hawkes, *Blood and Wine*, 23–25.

20. United States Immigration Commission, "North Italian Farmers of Sonoma County," *Immigrants in Industries, Vol. 24: Japanese and Other Immigrant Races in the Pacific Coast and Rocky Mountains States* (Washington, DC: Government Printing Office), 459–464.

21. Gallo and Gallo, *Ernest and Julio*, 13–25.

22. Ernest Gallo, "The E. & J. Gallo Winery," interview by Ruth Teiser, 1969, Regional Oral History Office, University of California, Berkeley.

23. Gallo and Gallo, *Ernest and Julio*, 104.

24. Pavese, *The Moon and the Bonfires*, 13.

NOTES TO CHAPTER 3

1. Leo Loubere, *The Red and the White: The History of Wine in France and Italy in the Nineteenth Century* (Albany: State University of New York Press, 1978), 89–92.

2. Ibid., 93–108.

3. Castronovo, *Il Piemonte*, 14–22.

4. Francesco Meardi, *Atti della Giunta per l'inchiesta agraria e sulle condizioni delle classi agricole*, tomo 1. fasc. 1 (Rome, 1883), 219, cited in Castronovo, *Il Piemonte*, 27. On the expansion of the small property that accompanied the hill region's reconversion to grape cultivation, see Vittorio Rapetti, *Uomini, collina e vigneto in Piemonte da metà Ottocento agli anni Trenta* (Alessandria: Dell'Orso, 1984), 44–56.

5. Rapetti, *Uomini, collina e vigneto*, 124–137.

6. Loubere, *The Red and the White*, 46–57.

7. Quoted in ibid., 93.

8. "Joe Vercelli Interviewed," 1–2, 5.

9. Castronovo, *Il Piemonte*, 237–238.

10. Ibid., 236.

11. Rossi, "Italian Swiss Colony and the Wine Industry," 10–14.

12. *History of California and an Extended History of Los Angeles and Environs*, 202–207.

13. Scaletta, *La chiesa cattolica di San Secondo*, 17.

14. Gallo and Gallo, *Ernest and Julio*, 56.

15. Ibid., 8.

16. Ibid., 14–15.

17. Hawkes, *Blood and Wine*, 121.

18. Ibid., 193–194.

19. "Gallo of Sonoma," *Wine Spectator* (June 30, 1999): 67–73.

20. Pinney, *History of Wine in America: From the Beginnings to Prohibition*, 237–243.

21. Starr, *Inventing the Dream*, 128–147.

22. Pinney, *History of Wine in America: From the Beginnings to Prohibition*, 243–268.

23. Julius L. Jacobs, "California's Pioneer Wine Families," *California Historical Quarterly* 54, no. 2 (1975): 139–174.

24. Pinney, *History of Wine in America: From the Beginnings to Prohibition*, 341–355.

25. W. J. Rorabaugh, *The Alcoholic Republic: An American Tradition* (New York: Oxford University Press, 1979); Ian R. Tyrrell, *Sobering Up: From Temperance to Prohibition in Antebellum America, 1800–1860* (Westport, CT: Greenwood Press, 1979); John J. Rumbarger, *Profits, Power, and Prohibition: Alcohol Reform and the Industrializing of America, 1800–1930* (Albany: State University of New York Press, 1989); Pegram, *Battling Demon Rum*.

26. Andrea Sbarboro, "Wine as a Remedy for the Evil of Intemperance" (Hanford? 1906?); Andrea Sbarboro, *The Fight for True Temperance: Practical Thoughts from a Practical Man* (San Francisco, 1908).

27. James H. Timberlake, *Prohibition and the Progressive Crusade* (Cambridge: Harvard University Press, 1967); Joseph R. Gusfield, *Symbolic Crusade: Status Politics and the American Temperance Movement* (Urbana: University of Illinois Press, 1986); Michael A. Lerner, *Dry Manhattan: Prohibition in New York City* (Cambridge: Harvard University Press, 2007).

28. Lynn Dumenil, *The Modern Temper: American Culture and Society in the 1920s* (New York: Hill and Wang, 1995).

29. Gabaccia, "As American as Budweiser and Pickles?"

30. Castronovo, *Il Piemonte*, 50–53.

31. Pinney, *History of Wine in America: From the Beginnings to Prohibition*, 331–336. The Icarian experiment's possible influence on Sbarboro's communitarian

ideas, which are explored in the next chapter, is discussed in "Joe Vercelli Interviewed," 15–16.

NOTES TO CHAPTER 4

1. Fichera, "Entrepreneurial Behavior in an Immigrant Colony."
2. Alexis de Tocqueville, *Democracy in America, Part 2* (London: Saunders and Otley, 1840), 219–228.
3. Sbarboro, "Andrea Sbarboro: An Early American Success Story," 42–43.
4. Ibid., 47.
5. Ibid., 48.
6. See Micaela di Leonardo, *The Varieties of Ethnic Experience: Kinship, Class, and Gender Among California Italian Americans* (Ithaca: Cornell University Press, 1984), 49–52, 58–59.
7. Sbarboro, "Andrea Sbarboro: An Early American Success Story," 49.
8. Rossi, "Italian Swiss Colony and the Wine Industry," 21–22.
9. "Italian Swiss Colony, Producers of Fine California Wines and Brandies," 1911, Butler Library, University of California, Berkeley.
10. Pinney, *History of Wine in America: From the Beginnings to Prohibition*, 359.
11. Palmer, "Italian Immigration and the Development of California Agriculture," 272–275.
12. Sbarboro, "Andrea Sbarboro: An Early American Success Story," 47.
13. Sebastian Fichera, "The Meaning of Community: A History of the Italians of San Francisco," PhD diss., University of California, Los Angeles, 1981, 129.
14. Fichera, "Entrepreneurial Behavior in an Immigrant Colony," 338–339.
15. Ronald Takaki, *A Different Mirror: A History of Multicultural America* (Boston: Little, Brown, 1993), 268–270.
16. Gallo and Gallo, *Ernest and Julio*, 49, 62–63, 67–68.
17. Ibid., 163.

NOTES TO CHAPTER 5

1. Min Zhou, "Revisiting Ethnic Entrepreneurship: Convergences, Controversies, and Conceptual Advancements," *International Migration Review* 38, no. 3 (2004): 1039–1046.
2. Alejandro Portes, "Economic Sociology and the Sociology of Immigration: A Conceptual Overview," in *The Economic Sociology of Immigration: Essays on Networks, Ethnicity, and Entrepreneurship*, ed. Alejandro Portes (New York: Russell Sage Foundation, 1998), 3–6.

3. The concept of social capital is also commonly used in a parallel sense that refers to the overall value (immaterial but quantifiable in economic terms) of the willingness to do things for others, civic culture, and responsibility toward the res publica of a specific society. According to the theorist Robert Putnam, social capital understood as such is an essential element of democracy because its deficit is expressed in low levels of civil participation and trust in institutions. Robert Putnam, *Bowling Alone: The Collapse and Revival of American Community* (New York: Simon & Schuster, 2000).

4. Donna Gabaccia, *We Are What We Eat: Ethnic Food and the Making of Americans* (Cambridge: Harvard University Press, 1998).

5. The classic definition of cultural capital as a sociological category belongs to Pierre Bourdieu, who introduced it in his discussion of the differences between social classes (specifically in 1970s France) and various types of capital that in a system of exchange constitute the resources of different classes and the individuals therein. For Bourdieu, each individual is "marked" from birth, through primary socialization, by an imprint of his or her class— the *habitus*. This profoundly conditions one's tastes, ways of doing things, bodily expressions, and gestures, and is independent of relative and variable quantities of economic capital (wealth), social capital (resources based on relationships and group memberships), and cultural capital (the combination of knowledge, skills, abilities, attitudes, and expectations that give individuals a higher status in society). Unlike the sense implied by Portes, who alludes to a symbolic collective universe, Bourdieu's definition refers mainly to the "high culture" of academic education; knowledge; owning, understanding, and appreciating works of art; or having a command of foreign languages, all of which can easily be converted into economic capital. See Pierre Bourdieu, *Distinction: A Social Critique of the Judgement of Taste* (Cambridge: Harvard University Press, 1984).

6. Portes, "Economic Sociology and the Sociology of Immigration," 6–16.

7. Alejandro Portes and Rubén G. Rumbaut, *Immigrant America: A Portrait* (Berkeley: University of California Press, 2006).

8. Ivan Light and Edna Bonacich, *Immigrant Entrepreneurs: Koreans in Los Angeles, 1965–1982* (Berkeley: University of California Press, 1988).

NOTES TO CHAPTER 6

1. Giovanni Levi, *Italiani: Racconto etnografico* (Rome: Meltemi, 2001), 138.

2. Hicke, *Seghesio Family, Vineyards, and Winery*, 1–3.

3. Perelli-Minetti, "A Life in Wine Making," 116.

4. This is one of the circumstances that the Gallos would always deny to support the argument that they had started the E. & J. Gallo Winery completely from scratch in 1933, without any technical know-how. See Hawkes, *Blood and Wine*, 25–39.

5. Gallo, "E. & J. Gallo Winery," 6–7, 13–14.

6. See, for example, the case of the transnational family originally from Biella described in Franco Ramella and Samuel L. Baily, *One Family, Two Worlds: An Italian Family's Correspondence Across the Atlantic, 1901–1922* (New Brunswick: Rutgers University Press, 1988).

7. The post-Prohibition history of the Italian Swiss Colony is summarized in Palmer, "Italian Immigration and the Development of California Agriculture," 273–278.

8. Giuseppe Scaletta and Giulii Zobelein, "La famiglia Giuseppe Amillo di Los Angeles in California," [2000?], Wine and Wine Industry Collection, Special Collections and University Archives, University Library, Cal Poly Pomona.

9. Ibid., 17, 49–50.

10. The history of the Italian Vineyard Company from the introduction of Prohibition onward is reconstructed in Hofer, "Guasti and the Italian Vineyard Company"; Horace O. Lanza and Harry Baccigaluppi, "California Grape Products and Other Wine Enterprises," interview by Ruth Teiser, 1971, Regional Oral History Office, University of California, Berkeley; Philo Biane, "Wine Making in Southern California and Recollections of Fruit Industries Ltd.," interview by Ruth Teiser, 1972, Regional Oral History Office, University of California, Berkeley.

11. Gallo and Gallo, *Ernest and Julio*, 4–5.

12. Hawkes, *Blood and Wine*, 195.

13. Peter H. King, "Trial Pops Lid off Gallo Family Feud," *Press Democrat* (December 25, 1988).

14. Gallo and Gallo, *Ernest and Julio*, 51–52.

15. Fierman, "How Gallo Crushes the Competition," 31.

16. Karen Southwick, "Gallos Yank Time Ads After Rare Interview by *Fortune*," *San Francisco Examiner* (September 10, 1986); Linda Di Pietro, "Gallo Blasts 'Fortune' Story as 'Vicious,' Pulls Ads in Retaliation," *San Francisco Examiner* (September 11, 1986): C3.

NOTES TO CHAPTER 7

1. Hawkes, *Blood and Wine*, 52, 118.

2. The Ellis Island Foundation online database (http://www.ellisisland.org/) shows that upon their arrival in the United States, many immigrants from Rocca d'Arazzo indicated Asti, California, as their next destination.

3. United States Department of Commerce, Bureau of the Census, *Fourteenth Census of the United States, 1920: Population*, Guasti Village, San Bernardino County, California, Supervisor District no. 9. Enumeration District no. 152, National Archives and Record Administration, Washington, DC; Rosso, *Piemontesi nel Far West*, 77–80, 139–154. A collection of family stories of Piedmontese immigrants in Guasti can be found in Marcia Stumpf, *Grapevines and Peppertrees: Family Stories from Guasti* (Phoenix, 2002).

4. "Joe Vercelli Interviewed," 14; Biane, "Wine Making in Southern California," 21; Shirley Swierstra, "Oral History Monologue: Guasti," Wine and Wine Industry Collection, Special Collections and University Archives, University Library, Cal Poly Pomona; Rita Antonelli D'Amico, "La comunità italiana di Guasti esempio di una felice integrazione nella società americana," master's thesis, University of California, Los Angeles, 1986, 16–17.

5. Ngai, *Impossible Subjects*; Jacobson, *Whiteness of a Different Color.*

6. United States Immigration Commission, "Wine-Making Industry of California," 274–275, 280.

7. Sbarboro, "Andrea Sbarboro: An Early American Success Story," 48.

8. D'Amico, "La comunità italiana di Guasti," 33.

9. United States Immigration Commission, "Wine-Making Industry of California," 276.

10. Ibid.

11. Perelli-Minetti, "A Life in Wine Making," 20.

12. United States Immigration Commission, "Wine-Making Industry of California," 277.

13. Barrett and Roediger, "Inbetween Peoples."

14. Lorenzo Feraud, *Da Biella a San Francisco di California: Ossia storia di tre valligiani andornini in America* (Turin: Paravia, 1882), 119–120.

15. Saxton, *Indispensable Enemy*, 3–18, 258–284; Paul S. Taylor, "Foundations of California Rural Society," *California Historical Society Quarterly* 24, no. 3 (1945): 193–228. For the most recent general account of anti-Chinese discrimination in California, see Jean Pfaelzer, *Driven Out: The Forgotten War Against Chinese Americans* (New York: Random House, 2007).

16. United States Immigration Commission, "Wine-Making Industry of California," 276.

17. Ibid., 278, 281.

18. Sbarboro, "Andrea Sbarboro: An Early American Success Story," 87.

19. *Il Proletario* (May 6, 1916), cited in Nunzio Pernicone, *Carlo Tresca: Portrait of a Rebel* (New York: Palgrave Macmillan, 2005), 88.

20. Bartlett, "Immigrant in the Land of Opportunity," 11379.

21. Swierstra, "Oral History Monologue: Guasti," 3.

22. Roediger, *Wages of Whiteness*; W. E. B. Du Bois, *Black Reconstruction in America: An Essay Toward a History of the Part Which Black Folk Played in the Attempt to Reconstruct Democracy in America, 1860–1880* (New York: Free Press, 1965), 700.

23. "New Church Dedicated at Guasti: San Secondo D'Asti Is Patron," *Tidings* (October 8, 1926): 4.

24. Cited in R. Bruce Harley, "Two Italian Families, Their Wineries, and Their Churches," *Heritage Tales: City of San Bernardino Historical and Pioneer Society* (1996): 41.

25. Bartlett, "Immigrant in the Land of Opportunity," 11380.

26. "Italian Swiss Colony, Producers of Fine California Wines and Brandies," 20.

27. "Fine Modern Improvement at Asti," *Pacific Wine and Spirit Review* 54, no. 2 (1911): 13–14.

28. Marcia Stumpf, "Growing up in Guasti," 1999, Wine and Wine Industry Collection, Special Collections and University Archives, University Library, Cal Poly Pomona.

29. D'Amico, "La comunità italiana di Guasti," 23. For analogous, contemporary observations on the Italian Swiss Colony, see Frank Norris, "Italy in California," *The Wave* (October 24, 1896).

30. Hofer, "Guasti and the Italian Vineyard Company," 4.

31. "The Story of Villa Pompeii," Italian Swiss Colony Archives, Beringer Vineyards Inc., St. Helena, CA; Amelia Giampaoli, "Asti Oral History: Life at Villa Pompeii," Italian Swiss Colony Archives, Beringer Vineyards Inc., St. Helena, CA.

32. Stumpf, "Growing up in Guasti," 12. For more information on the Guasti villa, see Kevin Smith, "Guasti Mansion Returns to Its Former Beauty," *Inland Valley Daily Bulletin* (May 2, 2003): 9; Pam Noles, "Saffron Adds Spice to Guasti Mansion," *Los Angeles Times, Inland Valley Voice* (March 26, 2003): A1–A2; Mark Petix, "Guasti Villa Stands as a Remnant of an Empire," *Inland Valley Daily Bulletin* (June 2, 2006): A6.

33. "The Story of the Italian Swiss Colony," [1910?], Sonoma County Public Library, Healdsburg, CA; Joann Lumsden, "New Life for an Historic Chapel," *Journal of the Sonoma County Historical Society* (August 1989): 6–7.

34. Harley, "Two Italian Families, Their Wineries, and Their Churches."

35. "Un appello alla popolazione italiana e svizzera degli Stati Uniti," 1910, Fondazione Einaudi, Turin.

36. Bartlett, "Immigrant in the Land of Opportunity," 11380.

NOTES TO CHAPTER 8

1. Sullivan, "Italian Swiss Colony," 18.

2. Sbarboro, "Andrea Sbarboro: An Early American Success Story," 55–58; "Italian Swiss Colony of Asti, California," 28–29.

3. Sullivan, "Italian Swiss Colony," 43.

4. Ibid., 32; W. Blake Gray, "A New Wine Country Rose from the Ruins," *San Francisco Chronicle* (April 13, 2006): F1.

5. Sullivan, "Italian Swiss Colony," 43.

6. Ibid.

7. Hofer, "Guasti and the Italian Vineyard Company," 5–6.

8. Fierman, "How Gallo Crushes the Competition," 24.

9. Charles Crawford, "Recollections of a Career with the Gallo Winery and the Development of California Wine Industry, 1942–1989," interview by Ruth Teiser, 1990, Regional Oral History Office, University of California, Berkeley, 53. Other oral histories on the enological research of the E. & J. Gallo Winery include William Bonetti, "A Life of Winemaking at Wineries of Gallo, Schenley, Charles Krug, Chateau Souverain, and Sonoma-Cutrer," interview by Carole Hicke, 1998, Regional Oral History Office, University of California, Berkeley; R. Bradford Webb, "Brad Webb, Innovator," interview by William Heintz, 1988, Wine Library Associates of Sonoma County Oral Histories, Sonoma County Public Library, Healdsburg, CA.

10. Gallo and Gallo, *Ernest and Julio*, 158–159; Richard Paul Hinkle, "The Gallo Graduates," *Friends of Wine* (March–April 1979).

11. Hawkes, *Blood and Wine*, 281.

12. Becky McClure, "Hills Moved to Make Room for Wine Grapes," *Modesto Bee* (September 7, 1986); Tim Tesconi, "Gallo Reshapes Hillside for Prime Vineyards," *Press Democrat* (September 8, 1986): 8B.

13. Gallo and Gallo, *Ernest and Julio*, 198.

14. Sullivan, "Italian Swiss Colony," 18, 25, 39.

15. Ibid., 14, 20–23.

16. "Italian Swiss Colony's New Bottling Plant," *Pacific Wine and Spirits Review* 53, no. 9 (1911): 40.

17. Mitchell Okun, *Fair Play in the Marketplace: The First Battle for Pure Food and Drugs* (DeKalb: Northern Illinois University Press, 1986); James Harvey

Young, *Pure Food: Securing the Federal Food and Drugs Act of 1906* (Princeton: Princeton University Press, 1989); Lorinne Swainston Goodwin, *The Pure Food, Drink, and Drug Crusaders, 1879–1914* (Jefferson, NC: McFarland & Co., 1999).

18. "Italian Swiss Colony's New Sparkling Wine," *Pacific Wine and Spirits Review* 53, no. 5 (1911): 18.

19. Sullivan, "Italian Swiss Colony," 19, 27, 37.

20. "California Wines Win Highest Honors," *Pacific Wine and Spirits Review* 53, no. 12 (1911): 28.

21. Sullivan, "Italian Swiss Colony," 30.

22. "A Handsome Souvenir of California," *Pacific Wine and Spirits Review* 52, no. 9 (1910): 26.

23. Marylin Halter, *Shopping for Identity: The Marketing of Ethnicity* (New York: Schocken Books, 2000).

24. "Italian Swiss Colony, Producers of Fine California Wines and Brandies," 12.

25. Norris, "Italy in California"; Dondero, "Asti, Sonoma County"; Arthur Inkersley, "The Vintage in California and Italy," *Overland Monthly* 41, no. 10 (1909): 406–411.

26. *Pacific Wine and Spirits Review* (May 31, 1898), cited in Sullivan, "Italian Swiss Colony," 29; "Hundred Couples Dance in a Big Wine Vault: Unique Social Event at the Italian Swiss Colony in Sonoma County," *The Call* (May 15, 1898).

27. Hofer, "Guasti and the Italian Vineyard Company," 5–7.

28. Gallo and Gallo, *Ernest and Julio*, 89.

29. Legh F. Knowles Jr., "Beaulieu Vineyards from Family to Corporate Ownership," interview by Ruth Teiser, 1990, Regional Oral History Office, University of California, Berkeley, 25–26.

30. Gallo and Gallo, *Ernest and Julio*, 268–271.

31. Ibid., 102.

32. Ibid., 103.

33. Ibid., 96–97; "Gallo Buys Cribari Winery, Inventory," *Wines and Vines* 35 (May 1954): 8.

34. Gallo and Gallo, *Ernest and Julio*, 96–97, 183–195; Fierman, "How Gallo Crushes the Competition," 29.

35. Gallo and Gallo, *Ernest and Julio*, 169–170, 212–214, 215–217.

36. Ibid., 261.

37. Ibid., 176.

38. Hawkes, *Blood and Wine*, 186, 189–192, 198–201, 356–358.

39. Gallo and Gallo, *Ernest and Julio*, 99.

40. Hawkes, *Blood and Wine*, 191–192.

41. Sullivan, "Italian Swiss Colony," 45.

42. "Governor Gillett at Asti, California," *Pacific Wine and Spirits Review* 52, no. 4 (1910): 48.

43. Ibid.

44. Sbarboro, "Andrea Sbarboro: An Early American Success Story," 86–91.

45. Ibid., 79–85.

46. Ibid., 70–74.

47. Stumpf, "Growing up in Guasti," 12; Terry Carter, "Tracking Down the Mussolini Who Came to Dinner," *Inland Valley Times* (April 4, 2001): 8.

48. Gallo and Gallo, *Ernest and Julio*, 175–176; Pinney, *History of Wine in America: From Prohibition to the Present*, 201–202.

49. Gallo and Gallo, *Ernest and Julio*, 215; Pinney, *History of Wine in America: From Prohibition to the Present*, 202.

50. Gallo and Gallo, *Ernest and Julio*, 253.

51. Hawkes, *Blood and Wine*, 388–389.

52. Ibid., 281–283.

53. Brooks Jackson and Jeffrey H. Birnbaum, "'Gallo Amendment' Backed by Wine Family Opens Multimillion-Dollar Estate-Tax Loophole," *Wall Street Journal* (October 31, 1985): 56; David Gourevitch, "'Gallo Amendment' May Reap Millions for Winemakers' Heirs," *San Francisco Chronicle* (November 1, 1985): 41; Patrice Duggan, "Before the Loophole Closes," *Forbes* (October 2, 1989): 239; Jeffrey H. Birnbaum and Viveca Novak, "The Corporate Dole," *Time* (September 23, 1996): 34; Glenn F. Bunting, "Politics and Money: Dole Lent Clout to Gallo Winery; Vintner, Other Firms Gave Generously After Help; Aide Says He Backs What He Believes In," *Los Angeles Times* (October 16, 1996): 1.

NOTES TO CHAPTER 9

1. Carlo A. Corsini and Mauro Reginato, "L'emigrazione piemontese nel contesto italiano: Una sintesi storico-demografica dei flussi," in *Emigrazione piemontese all'estero: Rassegna bibliografica*, ed. Mauro Reginato, Patrizia Audenino, Carlo A. Corsini, and Paola Corti (Turin: Regione Piemonte, 1999), 31–48.

2. Valerio Castronovo, *Economia e società in Piemonte dall'Unità al 1914* (Milan: Banca commerciale italiana, 1969), 101–102, 249–256; Castronovo, *Il Piemonte*, 102–108, 151, 219–223.

3. Corti, "L'emigrazione piemontese."

4. Fernand Braudel, *La Méditerranee et le monde méditerranéen a l'époque de Philippe II* (Paris: Colin, 1966), 46.

5. Corti, "L'emigrazione piemontese," 28.

6. See the study *Biellesi nel mondo* (Biella Natives Around the World), whose research was supported by the Fondazione Sella in Biella, coordinated by Valerio Castronovo, and published as a multivolume work under the same title (Milan: Electa, 1986–2001).

7. Corti, "L'emigrazione piemontese," 34.

8. Ibid., 35.

9. Ibid., 38.

10. Nelson Moe, *The View from Vesuvius: Italian Culture and the Southern Question* (Berkeley: University of California Press, 2002), 156–186.

11. The enormously successful *Cuore* by Edmondo De Amicis (1st ed., Turin, 1886) is the most representative example.

12. Antonio Gramsci, "Some Aspects of the Southern Question," in *The Antonio Gramsci Reader: Selected Writings, 1916–1935*, ed. David Forgacs (New York: NYU Press, 2000), 173.

13. The most complete survey of the studies on race and nation by Italian positivist anthropologists is Vito Teti, *La razza maledetta: Origini del pregiudizio antimeridionale* (Rome: Manifestolibri, 1993).

14. For an illustration of how Italian scientific thought was imported into American debates over race, see D'Agostino, "Craniums, Criminals, and the 'Cursed Race'"; and Donna R. Gabaccia, "Race, Nation, Hyphen: Italian Americans and American Multiculturalism in Comparative Perspective," in *Are Italians White? How Race Is Made in America*, ed. Jennifer Guglielmo and Salvatore Salerno (New York: Routledge, 2003), 44–59. The complexity of "orientalist" and "racialist" narratives of the Mezzogiorno in the context of Italian nation building is examined in John Dickie, *Darkest Italy: The Nation and Stereotypes of the Mezzogiorno, 1860–1900* (New York: St. Martin's Press, 1999); Moe, *View from Vesuvius*; Pasquale Verdicchio, *Bound by Distance: Rethinking Nationalism Through the Italian Diaspora* (Madison: Fairleigh Dickinson University Press, 1997); Aliza S. Wong, *Race and the Nation in Liberal Italy, 1861–1911: Meridionalism, Empire, and Diaspora* (New York: Palgrave Macmillan, 2006). For a general historical perspective on scientific and political interpretations of Italian racism, see the essay collection edited by Alberto Burgio, *Nel nome della razza: Il razzismo nella storia d'Italia, 1870–1945* (Bologna: Il Mulino, 1999).

15. Giovanni Giacomo Ruatta, "L'America dei cow-boy," in *Il mondo dei vinti: Testimonianze di vita contadina*, ed. Nuto Revelli (Turin: Einaudi, 1977), 149.

16. Fichera, "Meaning of Community," 69.

17. Palmer, "Italian Immigration and the Development of California Agriculture," 365.

18. Cited in Rolle, *Immigrant Upraised*, 259.

19. Cited in Saxton, *Indispensable Enemy*, 278.

20. "A Home for Assassins: That Is What Our Immigration Laws Are Making This Country," *San Francisco Chronicle* (March 16, 1909): 6.

21. Bartlett, "Immigrant in the Land of Opportunity," 11380.

22. As Sbarboro and other immigrant entrepreneurs recommended to Italian Commissioner Adolfo Rossi during his visit to San Francisco. Adolfo Rossi, "Per la tutela degli italiani negli Stati Uniti: Dal Texas alla California," *Bollettino dell'Emigrazione* 16 (1904): 113–117, cited in Cinel, *From Italy to San Francisco*, 224.

23. *L'Italia* (September 21, 1911): 3, cited in Giovinco, "Success in the Sun?" 35.

24. Interview with Dorothy Calvetti Bryant quoted in Rosso, *Piemontesi nel Far West*, 247. For other similar testimony, see Leonardo, *Varieties of Ethnic Experience*, 162–168.

25. Cinel, *From Italy to San Francisco*, 216.

26. *La Voce del Popolo* (October 29, 1869); *L'Italia* (December 3, 1903), cited in Cinel, *From Italy to San Francisco*, 214.

27. Cinel, *From Italy to San Francisco*, 212–218, 222–233.

28. Henry Fisk, "The Fishermen of the San Francisco Bay," *Proceedings of the National Conference of Charities and Corrections*, 1906, cited in Cinel, *From Italy to San Francisco*, 219.

29. *San Francisco Chronicle* (September 8, 1907), cited in Cinel, *From Italy to San Francisco*, 219.

30. *La Voce del Popolo* (September 12, 1898), cited in Cinel, *From Italy to San Francisco*, 220.

31. Cinel, *From Italy to San Francisco*, 218–221.

32. "Pier Carlo Rossi, San Francisco, California," in *Gli italiani negli Stati Uniti d'America* (New York: Italian American Directory Co., 1906), 415.

33. Leonardo, *Varieties of Ethnic Experience*, 162.

34. Palmer, "Italian Immigration and the Development of California Agriculture," 301–302.

NOTES TO CHAPTER 10

1. Dumenil, *Modern Temper*, 226.
2. *General Baptist Convention of California and Auxiliary Organizations, San Francisco, 1894*, 30, cited in Gilman M. Ostrander, *The Prohibition Movement in California, 1848–1933* (Berkeley: University of California Press, 1957), 66.
3. Ostrander, *Prohibition Movement in California*, 65, 72.
4. *California Voice* (October 31, 1889) and (May 8, 1890), cited in ibid., 66.
5. Ostrander, *Prohibition Movement in California*, 66.
6. Cited in ibid., 15.
7. Ostrander, *Prohibition Movement in California*, 36–37, 99–100, 135–141.
8. Pinney, *History of Wine in America: From Prohibition to the Present*, 14; Gabaccia, *We Are What We Eat*, 134–135.
9. *New York Times* (April 28, 1929), cited in Ostrander, *Prohibition Movement in California*, 179.
10. John R. Meers, "The California Wine and Grape Industry and Prohibition," *California Historical Society Quarterly* 46 (March 1967): 19–32, cited in Rolle, *Immigrant Upraised*, 271.
11. Rossi, "Italian Swiss Colony and the Wine Industry," 39.
12. Pinney, *History of Wine in America: From Prohibition to the Present*, 19.
13. Baroni, *Gente italiana in California*, 49–52.
14. Rossi, "Italian Swiss Colony and the Wine Industry," 41–43.
15. Cited in Vivienne Sosnowski, *When the Rivers Ran Red: An Amazing Story of Courage and Triumph in America's Wine Country* (New York: Palgrave Macmillan, 2009), 96–98.
16. Ibid., 97.
17. Ibid., 99–100.
18. Pinney, *History of Wine in America: From Prohibition to the Present*, 16–17.
19. Ibid., 10.
20. Gallo, "The E. & J. Gallo Winery," 20–21.

Index

168; Pink Chablis, 168; political
lobbying, 175–181; Ripple, 168, 177;
technical innovation and mecha-
nization of production, 154–156;
Thunderbird, 168–170, 176
German Americans, 1, 22, 71, 81, 84, 133,
145, 194, 209, 211–212, 215, 218, 231.
See also European immigrants
Giannini, Amadeo P., 104, 174–175
Gillett, James N., 172–173
Giulì, Aurelia Amillo, 121
Giulì, Nicola, 121, 204
Gold Rush, The, 13, 68, 73, 199
Gompers, Samuel, 194
Grape varieties: Alicante Bouschet, 58;
Barbera, 11; Cabernet Sauvignon,
78; Carignane, 78; Gewürztraminer,
78; Grignolino, 154; Mission, 72,
80; Moscato, 64; Nebbiolo, 10–11,
64, 77; Pinot Noir, 78; Riesling, 78;
Sauvignon Blanc, 78; Semillon, 78;
Sylvaner, 78; Zinfandel, 58, 78. *See
also* Wines
Guasti, Louisa Amillo, 29, 117, 121–122,
143–144
Guasti, Secondo Jr., 6, 30, 121–122
Guasti, Secondo, 5–7; early life in Italy,
68; marriage and family relation-
ships, 121; and the origins of the
Italian Vineyard Company, 28–30,
55–57, 80–81; racial identity, 145, 195;
trips to Europe, 121
Guglielmo, George, 235
Guglielmo, Janice, 235

Hall, Charles V., 9
Haraszthy, Agoston, 75–80, 119, 231
Haraszthy, Arpad, 82

Harris, Thomas L., 91
Hawkes, Ellen, 124–125, 178–179, 231

Immigration Act (1924), 22, 130, 132,
189–190, 208
Immigration Commission (Dillingham
Commission) (1907–1910), 14, 16,
132, 134–135, 137–138, 145, 189–190,
211
Inchiesta Jacini (1881–1886), 63–64
Indian Americans, 138
Irish Americans, 73, 84, 87, 133, 145,
209, 211–212. *See also* European immigrants
Italian Swiss Colony, 4; ban on nonwhite labor, 14, 139; church, 147–
148; community events, 162–164;
corporate acquisition of, 121; during
Prohibition, 217–224; exports, 5,
158–159; Golden State Champagne,
154, 160, 162, 171; housing for workers, 145–147; labor, 53–55, 95–98,
133–135, 139–140, 163; marketing
and advertising, 149, 154, 159–164;
origins, 26–27, 53–55, 91, 95–98; political lobbying, 170–174; technical
innovation and mechanization of
production, 151–154; Tipo Chianti,
160–161, 171; underground wine
tank, 100, 152, 163–164
Italian Vineyard Company, 5; church,
143–144, 148–149; community
events, 146–147; corporate acquisition of, 121–122; discrimination
against non-white labor, 141–143;
exports, 164; housing for workers,
146–147; labor, 56–57, 141; marketing and advertising, 164–165;

About the Author

Simone Cinotto is Assistant Professor of Twentieth-Century History at the University of Gastronomic Sciences, Pollenzo (Italy). He was previously Tiro a Segno Visiting Professor of Italian American Studies at the Department of Italian Studies at NYU. He is the author of *Una famiglia che mangia insieme: Cibo ed etnicità nella comunità italo-americana di New York, 1920–1940* (A Family That Eats Together: Food and Ethnicity in the Italian American Community of New York City, 1920–1940) (2001), which is now available in a new English edition.

NATION OF NEWCOMERS: IMMIGRANT
HISTORY AS AMERICAN HISTORY

General Editors: Matthew Jacobson and Werner Sollors

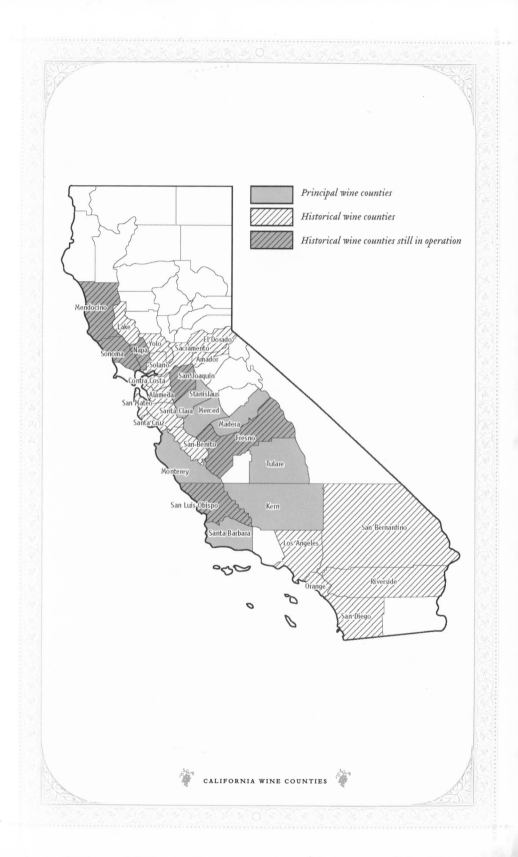

Mendocino
Lake
Yolo
Sonoma
Napa
Solano
Contra Costa
Alameda
San Mateo
Santa Clara
Santa Cruz
El Dorado
Sacramento
Amador
San Joaquin
Stanislaus
Merced
Madera
Fresno
San Benito
Monterey
Tulare
San Luis Obispo
Kern
Santa Barbara
Los Angeles
San Bernardino
Orange
Riverside
San Diego

CALIFORNIA WINE COUNTIES